SPANISH

This book hopes to make the task of learning Spanish pleasant as well as profitable. It provides a good grounding in the essentials of the language and tells the reader something about Spain. Anyone who has worked carefully through the lessons should be able to make himself understood in Spanish-speaking countries and tackle a book or newspaper in Spanish.

TEACH YOURSELF BOOKS

Anyone who works through this volume intelligently should be able to read and speak Spanish. No adult student of Spanish should fail to obtain this excellent course of instruction.

Journal of the Incorporated Association of Assistant Masters

SPANISH

N. Scarlyn Wilson
M.A.

TEACH YOURSELF BOOKS
Hodder and Stoughton

First printed 1939
Ninth impression 1974
Tenth impression 1976

This volume is published in the U.S.A. by David McKay Company Inc., 750 Third Avenue, New York, N.Y. 10017

ISBN 0 340 05819 6

Printed in Great Britain
for Teach Yourself Books,
Hodder and Stoughton, London,
by Richard Clay (The Chaucer Press), Ltd., Bungay, Suffolk

PREFACE

SPANISH, whether for cultural or commercial reasons, is well worth studying. It is spoken not only in Spain, but throughout Latin America, with the exception of Brazil, and even there, where the official language is Portuguese, you could make yourself understood. That is, of course, if you can also make yourself understood to a Spaniard. It is the purpose of this book to enable you to do so.

When you have worked through it, you should be in a position to read any Spanish novel or newspaper, to speak enough of the language to be able to converse and to write it comprehensibly, though your rendering will not be faultless.

This book follows in the main the model of *Teach Yourself French*, published in the same series. There are several reasons for this. In the first place, I hope that some who studied that volume may be encouraged to tackle this one, and, knowing the ways of the first, they will find it the more easy to embark upon its companion. Secondly, what proved successful in one case, may reasonably be considered likely to prove acceptable in another, so that people coming fresh to this book should be able to make as good use of it as those who studied *Teach Yourself French*.

At first sight it would seem that, by following the methods of another volume, I lay myself open to a charge of plagiarism. This accusation leaves my withers (whatever they may be) unwrung. For, as I was responsible for modernising Sir John Adams' admirable *Teach Yourself French*, I see no reason why I should not be allowed to borrow from myself. After all, as the lunatic very luminously observed : " If I can't bang my head against my own mantelpiece, whose mantelpiece can I bang it against ? "

This book, then, follows the same lines as *Teach Yourself French*—so far, that is, as the different natures of the two languages will permit. It aims at steering a middle course between dreary sentences about Grandmother's thimble and phrases of idiomatic slang. For those, by the way, who do want to acquire racy up-to-date idiom, I would recommend the perusal of *Brighter Spanish*, by Sr. L. de Baeza (Bles), and of *Brush Up Your Spanish*, by the same author (Dent).

Obviously, however, one must first have something to brush. It is the modest aim of this book to provide that foundation, to give any student of it a knowledge of the essentials of Spanish, to tell him something about Spain, and to fit him to learn a good deal more about both. If this purpose is in any way achieved, it will be largely due to the help given me by Srta. Miren de Albizuri of Bilbao, especially in the preparation of the Spanish passages for translation.

I am also obliged to Mr. Gil Nevaz, whose suggestions have led to some corrections and improvements in this edition of the book.

N. SCARLYN WILSON.

P.S.—There are certain differences between the Spanish of Spain and the tongue of S. America. Still, the structure and essentials are the same, though the pronunciation and the use of certain words are not identical. But anyone who has gone from Somerset to Lancashire will be aware that such divergencies are not confined to Spanish. *Guapo*, for instance, means handsome to one man and brave to another. With us, to greet does not mean the same thing to the Scot as it does to the Englishman. But we contrive to understand one another. So does it matter?

INTRODUCTION

HOW TO USE THE BOOK

THE purpose of this book is to enable the student to learn Spanish, and that without any help other than that which this book provides. It is not a formal grammar. Nevertheless each fact is presented as it is required in the process of preparing the student, in the smallest possible number of lessons, for the task of reading Spanish.

The two parts of the book are complementary. Part I contains most of the actual instruction, together with a series of exercises in turning Spanish into English and *vice versa*. The Spanish–English exercises, up to Lesson XV, are distinguished by the letter *a*, the English–Spanish by the letter *b*. Part II contains a Key to all the exercises in Part I. In addition, it supplies by means of Notes a good deal of information to cover any points of difficulty arising in the various exercises. Part I contains sufficient information to enable the student to tackle the exercises. Part II throws light upon difficulties which can only be fully realised after an attempt has been made to do them.

Both Parts should be carried on abreast, since any given, exercise in Part I implies a knowledge of everything in Part II prior to the Key to the actual exercise concerned.

The book should be worked through systematically. Thus, for instance, Exercise 5*a* in Part I should be written out and corrected by means of the Key to it in Part II, before 5*b* is attempted. A careful comparison of his version with the correct one will help greatly to increase the student's understanding of the points explained in the lesson. When uncertain how to turn an English sentence into Spanish, the best course is to refer to the preceding set of Spanish–English sentences, which will nearly always provide a model on which to work.

It may be advisable to halt and revise after every five lessons. A good way of doing this is to study each lesson in Part I, as at the first reading, but for exercises to turn to the corresponding section in Part II, and then use Part I as the key to correct these. This gives entirely fresh practice, since what was formerly English–Spanish now becomes Spanish–English.

Students who find the exercises difficult might work in this way : After studying each lesson carefully, translate the Spanish into English and check by reference to Part II. Then, instead of turning back to Part I, stay at Part II, and do the Spanish–English there, using Part I as the key. Thus the student would write the English for 5*a* in Part I and correct it by 5*b* in Part II. Then he could write the English for 5*b* in Part II and correct it by 5*b* in Part I. By this means he could go through the whole book doing nothing but Spanish–English, afterwards working through a second time, but in the regular way.

Students who find little difficulty in going through the book in the normal manner might revise the whole by doing all the exercises in the form of Spanish–English exercises.

This book, then, can be used in many ways, in each of which the student will find within it all that he needs to test his work.

The Vocabulary at the end is Spanish–English only. From a choice of two or three English equivalents for a Spanish word it is easy enough to choose the one that suits the English translation. But to choose the right Spanish word out of two or three to fit into a Spanish version of an English sentence is much more difficult. The proper place in which to look for the Spanish equivalent of an English word is one's memory rather than a dictionary, for the reason that the words in our memory are there because we have actually used them. Experience tells us what they mean. But a word borrowed from a Spanish–English dictionary may be quite wrong. The word " office," for example, may be rendered, as a dictionary will show, by *oficio*. But to use it for a man going into his office is quite wrong. The word we want is *oficina* or, possibly, *despacho*. By using this book and storing the word in our minds when we come across it, this mistake and others, inevitable if a dictionary is our sole means of information, can be avoided.

The Vocabulary has been made as short as possible, consistent, that is, with the satisfactory working of the exercises. This has been done by the omission of those words which occur very frequently and which the student cannot fail to have mastered after doing a very few of the opening lessons. A short table of definitely irregular verbs is provided immediately prior to the Vocabulary. But these are few in Spanish. There are, however, a large number of verbs which deviate slightly from the normal. The rules governing these are explained in some of the later lessons. But, as it is impossible to tell from the look of these verbs whether they do indulge in little eccentricities, not amounting to irregularities, the 1st Person of the Present Tense is shown in brackets in the case of the verbs which are slightly abnormal in this respect. With the explanation given in the lessons these verbs will then present no difficulty.

Another reason for the shortness of the Vocabulary is that, since there is a worked out version for every exercise in the book, an elaborate word-list is not needed. Nevertheless it cannot be too strongly emphasised that the Key should not be used as a short cut. The exercises are so arranged that, in almost every case, you can find the translation of every Spanish and English word used in them, either in the Vocabulary or in some previous exercise. In any case, before the Key is referred to, the student should at least make an attempt at producing a version of every sentence. He has a right to depend ultimately on the Key for help; but if he is to obtain any lasting profit from using this book, he must not resort to consulting the Key whenever he finds himself in a momentary difficulty. The mere fact of facing a problem helps one to appreciate the ultimate solution, whereas if every difficulty is removed by immediate reference to Part II, little impression is made on the mind, and no lasting benefit can result. A dictionary, too, should the student have one, should be used with caution. It is an excellent idea in translation to guess at the meaning of a word and then check the accuracy of the translation by reference to the dictionary. It lends a certain sporting element to the pursuit of knowledge. Observation of these various points should enable the student to make the best use of the information obtainable from this little book.

NOTE

When this book was first published the rate of exchange was about 29 pesetas to the pound sterling. It is now about 167. In this edition, therefore, alterations have been made here and there to take this into account, but the reader should remember that rates of exchange are liable to fluctuate.

CONTENTS

xiii

CONTENTS

PART II

PART I

SPANISH PRONUNCIATION

No one can learn to pronounce Spanish properly from a book. Yet, if you learn a language at all, you want your accent to be reasonably correct. This book can, at least, set your feet on the right path. Of course, if your object in learning a foreign tongue is only to read and write it, you might pronounce the words according to the rules of English. To do so, however, would surely be an unworthy shirking of difficulties, and would certainly halve the value of your studies. This book cannot give you a *good* Spanish accent, but it can offer hints which will enable you to produce sounds recognisable to a Spaniard. It will help you to know the difficult sounds—those that are tricky for an Englishman to master. Then, experience of hearing a Spaniard speak will make it easy for you, once the foundation is laid, to correct by your own ear the short-comings in your pronunciation.

For this reason you should try to hear as much Spanish spoken as you can, even though you may not, at first, understand a great deal of what is said. Still, you will get the " feel ", so to speak, of the language, and that is half the battle. Thanks to the radio, almost every student nowadays has the opportunity of hearing Spanish spoken. You should make a point of listening as often as possible to broadcast plays, speeches or news bulletins. Gramophone records, too, are useful, if you can get hold, either by purchase, cajolery or violence, of the admirable set issued by the Linguaphone Company. In any case, there is a supplementary method of improving your accent which is simple and very useful. Practise reading aloud (prefer- ably by yourself to avoid domestic squalls) from a Spanish novel or from one of the newspapers, such as *El Sol*, which can be readily obtained from the Librairie Hachette

15

(127 Regent Street, London, W.1) or through any reasonably enterprising newsagent. One word of warning, however. Many people (chain-smokers, for example !) can or, at least, do speak English with a cigarette in their mouths. An Englishman cannot hope to do his Spanish accent justice if he tries to speak with a Woodbine (or even a Balkan Sobranie) adhering to his upper lip. There is no need to gesticulate wildly in talking a foreign tongue, but the Spanish sounds cannot be properly uttered unless free play be given to the muscles of the jaw. So don't light that cigarette until you have finished your reading aloud !

Accent.—Most people know at all events a little French, and are therefore aware that, in that language, the pronunciation of words is often affected by the presence or absence of an accent. This piece of knowledge must not, however, be applied indiscriminately to Spanish. In Spanish only the acute accent (') is employed. Its uses are as follows :—

(1) To indicate that the emphasis or stress is to be laid on the vowel over which it is placed.

(2) In such words as *cuando* (when) and *donde* (where) to make them interrogative. *¿ Cuándo ?* = When ? *¿ Dónde ?* = Where ?

Note that in Spanish the signs of interrogation (also of exclamation) are placed both before and after the phrase, the first one being inverted.

(3) To distinguish between words spelt alike but of different meaning : *el* = the, *él* = he.

Note that, as opposed to the French practice, the acute accent in Spanish does not alter the actual pronunciation of the word (save in indicating the syllable to be stressed).

Unless you are in exceptionally good form, you will not be able to master the following remarks on Spanish pronunciation at one sitting. But try to get the general drift, and then refer back constantly for guidance in the pronunciation of words you encounter when you have started the exercises.

Pronunciation of the Vowels.—The Spanish *vowels* are *a,
e, i, o, u,* and *y. a* sounds like *ah,* the vowel-sound in *far*;
e sounds like *ay,* the vowel-sound in *late*; *i* or *y* sounds
like *ee,* the vowel-sound in *feet*; *o* sounds like *o,* the vowel-
sound in *rope*; *u* sounds like *oo,* the vowel-sound in *hoot.*

Note. (1) The vowels are clearly pronounced in Spanish,
whereas consonants are frequently suppressed. Even when
the syllable is not stressed, the vowel in it retains its sound,
though perhaps more faintly.

(2) *y* is a vowel only when standing alone, as in *y* = and,
or at the end of a word, e.g., *rey* = king.

Stress in Pronunciation.—The principal rule is so important that it deserves to be printed in capitals.

IN WORDS ENDING IN A CONSONANT THE LAST SYLLABLE
IS STRESSED.

IN WORDS ENDING IN A VOWEL THE LAST SYLLABLE BUT
ONE IS STRESSED.

IN WORDS CONFORMING TO THESE RULES THE PRINTED
ACCENT MARK IS NOT NEEDED AS A GUIDE TO PRONUNCIA-
TION AND IS THEREFORE DISPENSED WITH.

Note that the consonants *n* and *s*, often added to form
the plural of a word, do not affect the stress. It would be
unreasonable if they did. The stress, therefore, is always
on the same syllable in the plural as it is in the singular.

It follows from this that those words whose pronunciation is NOT according to the general rule take an acute
accent on the stressed syllable to show where the emphasis
does fall. Hence a word ending in a vowel, but pronounced
with the stress on the last syllable, requires the accent
mark on the last syllable, as this is a breach of the main
rule.

Thus : *yo hablo* = I speak, but *él habló* = he spoke.

In the past tense the stress comes on the last syllable,
and this, being contrary to the general rule for the pronunciation of words ending in vowels, needs the accent
mark to indicate it.

Again, if a word ending in a consonant (other than *n* or
s) is stressed elsewhere than on the last syllable, this, being
contrary to the rule for the pronunciation of words ending
in a consonant, must be indicated by the insertion of the
accent mark over the syllable where the stress does fall.

Thus : *dificil* = difficult ; *lápiz* = pencil.

Finally, it follows that *all* words accented on a syllable previous to the last but one require an accent mark, because such pronunciation is a breach of the rule whether the word ends in a vowel or a consonant.

Thus : *médico* = doctor ; according to rule the stress should come on the second syllable ; as it does not, the accent syllable must be indicated. Again : *régimen* = diet.

All this sounds somewhat complicated. Actually, it is quite simple. You have only to bear constantly in mind the general rule and put the accent mark on the stressed syllable of any word that does not conform with it.

Pronunciation of Two or More Vowels.—Two strong vowels coming together are pronounced separately and form distinct syllables.

deseo = desire ; *real* = real (pron. day-say-o, ray-ahl).

a, o, e are called strong vowels, *i* and *u* weak vowels.

If one of the pair of vowels in a word is *i* or *u*, the other vowel takes the emphasis, the *i* or *u* being only lightly pronounced, so that the two vowels count as one syllable.

E.g., *viaje* = voyage (pron. ve-áh-hay).

If *i* and *u* occur together, the stress is on the one which comes last, the two again counting as one syllable, the first vowel being passed rapidly over.

E.g., *ruido* = noise (pron. rooéetho) ; *viuda* = widow (pron. veeóotha).

Note that in these diphthongs the unstressed *i* or *u* almost loses its vowel force, the letters becoming equivalent to *y* and *w*. Thus, for instance, the pronunciation of *muy* = very, could more fairly be represented by *mwee* than by *moo-ee*.

In some words the accented vowel is the weak not the strong one. In this case the accent mark must be inserted, and since the vowels now each have their force, the word is not a diphthong.

E.g., *tío* = uncle (pron. tée-o).

Remember that a diphthong (*i.e.*, a combination of two weak vowels, or of one strong and one weak, but *not* of two *strong* vowels) counts as one syllable. Words ending in a vowel are normally accented, as we have seen, on the last syllable but one. In *iglesia* = church, the stress falls on the *e*, but no accent mark is required, because *sia* is only one syllable, the two vowels forming a diphthong.

Pronunciation of Consonants.—The letters *k* and *w* occur in Spanish only in words of foreign origin.

The consonants *f*, *k*, *l*, *m*, *n*, *p* and *x* are pronounced as in English; the letter *w* is pronounced according to the rules of the foreign language of the word's origin.

b is not as forcibly sounded as in English. The student should aim at producing a *b* slightly less downright and emphatic than the English sound.

> Examples : *bueno* = good; *blanco* = white; *bastante* = enough.

c has two sounds. Followed by *e* or *i* it is pronounced like *th* in *thin*. In other cases it has the hard sound of *k*.

> Examples :   *centro* = centre;   *vecino* = neighbour; *contar* = to relate.

ch is pronounced like *ch* in *charm*.

> Examples : *muchacho* = boy; *mucho* = much.

d is pronounced in very much the same way as in English. This is particularly so when it is the first letter of a word or is immediately preceded by an *n* or an *l*. It is, sometimes, however, more lightly pronounced than in English as, for instance, in such endings as *-ado* or *-ido*.

> Examples : *diente* = tooth; *donde* = where; *marido* = husband; *entregado* = delivered.

g has two sounds. Followed by *e* or *i* it has a guttural sound like the *ch* of the Scottish word *loch*. In other cases it has the hard sound of *g* in *gate*.

> Examples : *gigante* = giant; *general* (hehnehrahl) = general; *gato* = cat.

h, for all practical purposes, is not pronounced.

> Examples : *hablar* = to speak; *ahora* = now.

j has the same explosive sound that the Spanish *g* has when followed by *e* or *i*.

Examples : *jugar* = to play; *bajo* = low.

ll has the sound of *lli* in the English *million*.

Examples : *caballo* = horse; *calle* = street.

In many parts of Spain *ll* is pronounced like a double *y*, but the student should avoid this.

ñ (with the *tilde* to distinguish it from the ordinary *n*) has very much the sound of *ni* in the English words *onion* and *companion*.

Examples : *niño* = child; *mañana* = to-morrow.

q, always followed, as in English, by *u*, has the sound of *k*.

Examples : *quince* = fifteen; *siquiera* = at least.

r is rolled more than in English, especially at the beginning and end of words.

Examples : *tomar* = to take; *río* = river; *geografía* = geography.

s has the hissing sound of *s* in *taste* and NEVER the sound of *s* in *pleasure*.

Examples : *seso* = brain; *sábado* = Saturday; *visitar* = to visit.

t is pronounced more sharply and vigorously than in most English words.

Examples : *traer* = to bring; *trabajo* = work.

v is pronounced very much as in English, though less so in some areas of Spain or Latin America.

Example : *viejo* = old.

y is only a consonant at the beginning of a word or syllable; it is then more vigorously pronounced than in English.

Examples : *ya* = already; *yo* = I; *yegua* = mare.

z sounds like *th* in *thin*.

Examples : *zapato* = shoe; *juez* = judge; *brazo* = arm.

Note.—In Spanish America and some parts of Spain this lisping pronunciation of *z* and of *c* (before *e* or *i*) is not followed. But it is the practice in Castille, generally supposed to be the place in which the best Spanish is spoken, so the student would do well to observe it.

Pronunciación.—A useful way of practising the pronunciation of single Spanish words is to learn off the numerals from one up to twenty. The pronunciation given is according to the rules of English. But remember that the unstressed vowels are passed rapidly over.

1.	uno (masc.), una (fem.), pronounced oóno, oóna.		
2.	dos	„	dose.
3.	tres	„	trace.
4.	cuatro	„	koóahtro.
5.	cinco	„	thínko.
6.	seis	„	sáyiss.
7.	siete	„	seáytay.
8.	ocho	„	ócho.
9.	nueve	„	noo'áyvay
10.	diez	„	deéth.
11.	once	„	ónthay.
12.	doce	„	dóthay.
13.	trece	„	tráythay.
14.	catorce	„	kahtórthay.
15.	quince	„	kínthay.
16.	diez y seis		—
17.	diez y siete		—
18.	diez y ocho		—
19.	diez y nueve		—
20.	veinte	„	váyintay.

Liaison.—In speaking English we do not always pronounce each word in a sentence separately. We are apt to run some of them together. Sometimes this is due to slovenliness. But in Spanish, in certain instances, it is perfectly correct. The word *naranja* means an orange. When the name of this fruit first passed into English, it might possibly have been spelt " a norange ". Ultimately the *n* was transferred from the noun to the article. But when we say the words quickly, it is almost impossible to tell where the letter belongs. This running together of words to produce a pleasant, smooth sound is called *liaison*. It is very widely used in French. In Spanish, in speaking, though *not* in writing, if a word ends in a vowel (as so many do) and is followed by a word beginning with a vowel, the two are pronounced as though both formed part of the same word. This does not mean that you should slur all your words together; far from it. But when you come across a vowel at the end and beginning of adjoining words, don't be afraid of running them together. At all events, don't keep them rigidly apart. E.g., *mi abuelo* = my grandfather, would sound *mia-bue-lo*; *una iglesia* = a church, would sound *u-nai-gle-sia*.

To round off this section, here is a passage from a Spanish book printed in ordinary type and underneath, in italics, the equivalent English sounds. It will be worth your while to study this extract carefully, and to read it aloud to yourself, preferably more than once. The sign (⁻) over an *a* or *o* indicates the long sound as in *far* or *tow*.

Siguiendo el curso del arroyo, y sobre todo en
Seeghee-enthoel koorso del ahrroyio, ee sobray totho en
las hondonadas, hay muchos álamos y otros
lās onthonahthas, aee moochōss áhlahmōss ee otrōss
árboles altos, que, con las matas y hierbas,
áhrboles ahltoss, kay, kon lās mahtas ee yerbas
crean un intrincado laberinto y una sombría
krayan oon eentreenkatho lahbayréento ee-oona sombréea
espesura. Mil plantas silvestres y olorosas
esspaysoora. Meel plahntas seelvestres ee ōlōrohsas
crecen allí de un modo espontáneo, y por
kraythen al-lyee day oon motho espontáhnayo, ee, por
cierto que es difícil imaginar nada más
theeáirto kay ess deeféethil eemahinar nahtha mās
esquivo, agreste y verdaderamente solitario,
eskéevo, ahgrestay ee vairthathairaméntay soleetareeo
apacible y silencioso que aquellos lugares.
ahpahtheeblay ee seelentheeoso kay ahkellyos loogares.

LESSON I
VERBS AND PRONOUNS

One great difference between English and Spanish (French, too, for that matter, which, like Spanish, is largely derived from Latin) is that Spanish, far more than English, indicates changes of meaning by changes in the ending of words. For instance, let us choose the English word *to take*, of which the Spanish equivalent is *tomar*. Like the *to* before the English verb, the *ar* at the end of the Spanish verb tells the Spaniard that only the general idea of *taking* is concerned without reference to who is doing it or at what time or by what means. This part of any verb which tells the idea of the verb and nothing more is called the infinitive. So *to take* and *tomar* are both infinitives.

When a verb makes a plain statement, it is said to be in the indicative mood, and if the action is now going on, we have what is called the

Present Indicative

I take	yo tomo.
thou takest	tú tomas.
he (she) takes	él (ella) toma.
we take	nosotros tomamos.
you take	vosotros tomáis.
they take	ellos (ellas) toman.

In English the pronoun *I* is always written with a capital. In Spanish *yo* is written with a small *y*, except when it begins a sentence.

If we call the part of the verb that does not change, the *stem*, and the part that does, the *termination*, then *tak-* and *tom-* are the stems. In English we have three terminations : *-e*, *-est* and *-es*; in Spanish we have six : *-o*, *-as*, *-a*, *-amos*, *-áis* and *-an*.

It follows that the Spanish terminations are more informative than the English. It is true that *takest* must be used with *thou*, and *takes* with *he* (*she* or *it*). But *take* might go with *I* or *we*, or *you* or *they*. In Spanish there is no such uncertainty. The termination *o* of necessity goes with *yo*, *as* with *tú*, *a* with *él* (*ella*), *amos* with *nosotros*, *áis* with *vosotros* and *an* with *ellos* (*ellas*). This means that where two words are needed in English to make the meaning clear, one would suffice in Spanish. In fact, though during the early exercises the pronouns should be inserted for practice, later on we shall find that we can often omit them without making the meaning less clear. This difference between the two languages is illustrated again in the

FUTURE INDICATIVE

I shall take	yo tomaré.
thou wilt take	tú tomarás.
he (she, it) will take	él (ella) tomará.
we shall take	nosotros tomaremos.
you will take	vosotros tomaréis.
they will take	ellos (ellas) tomarán.

Here again the Spanish terminations are all different, so that the pronouns are not indispensable, as they are in English. (*Note*, incidentally, the accent marks and their effect on the pronunciation as compared with the Present Indicative.)

The difference caused by the different pronouns is known in grammar as *person*. The person speaking is always *first* person : so *yo* and *nosotros*, meaning *I* and *we*, are first person. The person spoken to is always *second* person : so *tú* and *vosotros*, meaning *thou* and *you*, are second person. The person or thing spoken about is always *third* person : so *él* (*ella*) and *ellos* (*ellas*), meaning *he* (*she*) and *they*, are third person.

We have seen that all the terminations of the Spanish verb in the Present Indicative are different : no two are alike. These endings are well worth noting, firstly because, when we know them, we can find out the *person*, whether the pronouns are there or not, and, secondly, because a very large number of other Spanish verbs besides *tomar* have these same endings. The Future Indicative terminations are even better worth studying, because the Future tense of *every* Spanish verb has the same terminations as *tomar*.

Exercise I

(*a*) Put the proper pronouns before the following verbs :
(1) compramos; (2) hablas; (3) trabajan; (4) andáis; (5) tocaré; (6) jugaremos; (7) pasarán; (8) dejará; (9) viviréis; (10) comprarás.

(*b*) Put the proper terminations to the following verbs, using the present tense for the first five sentences and the future indicative for the last five : (1) tú toc-; (2) ellos trabaj-; (3) nosotros habl-; (4) vosotros and-; (5) él pas-; (6) nosotros dejar-; (7) tú trabajar-; (8) yo vivir-; (9) ellos hablar-; (10) vosotros comprar-.

(*c*) The verb *comprar* (to buy) exactly resembles our model verb *tomar*. Its stem is *compr-*. Write out in Spanish, referring to the model if necessary, the three persons of the singular and of the plural of both the Present Indicative and of the Future Indicative of *comprar*.

We now come to a point of great importance. The English *thou* is practically never used. We use *you* whether we are addressing one person or a crowd. In Spanish, *tú* is only used in Biblical or poetical style, and in addressing close relations, small children and animals. One would expect, therefore, that *vosotros* would be used in all other cases, like the English *you*. But this is not so. *Vosotros* is only used in speaking to two or more of the beings in addressing whom the familiar *tú* would be used, were there but one of them. How, then, are we to translate *you*, because, even if we have Spanish acquaintances, we are unlikely to be on sufficiently intimate terms with them to be justified in using the familiar *tú* or *vosotros*? And to do so without having the right would be unpardonably rude.

Spanish politeness is proverbial. The word *you* is rendered by *usted* (singular) and *ustedes* (plural). *Usted* is a contraction of *Vuestra Merced*, meaning Your Honour or Your Grace. This is the *only* form of *you* that the student is ever likely to use in addressing adults or to hear addressed to himself. For purposes of reference the parts of tenses preceded by *tú* and *vosotros* will be given, but the translation of *you* which we shall invariably use (except occasionally for practice in exercises) is *usted* (Plural *ustedes*). But, having made up our minds to translate *you* (singular) by *usted*, and *you* (plural) by *ustedes*, we have got to be careful about using the right *person* of the verb with these pronouns. Remember that, though we regard *usted* as meaning *you*, strictly speaking it means Your Grace. In other words, it is really *third*, not *second* person. Therefore despite its meaning *you*, the verb with *usted* will always be, whatever the tense, in the *third*, and not the *second*, person. In the light of this new piece of knowledge let us look once more at the Present Indicative of *tomar*. It will now be :—

yo tomo	I take.
(tú tomas)	(thou takest).
usted toma	you take.
él (ella) toma	he (she) takes.
nosotros tomamos	we take.
(vosotros tomáis)	(you take).
ustedes toman	you take.
ellos (ellas) toman	they take.

Notes. (1) The two forms bracketed will practically never be used.

(2) Instead of writing *usted* in full, it is shortened to *Vd.* As it really stands for Your Honour, it is written with a capital letter, whereas the other pronouns have a small one. Similarly in the plural *Vds.*

(3) *Nosotras, vosotras* and *ellas* are the feminine forms of *nosotros, vosotros* and *ellos*, as is *ella* of *él.*

Henceforward, unless the use of *tú* or *vosotros* is specially indicated (by the word " familiar " in brackets), *you* will be translated always by *Vd.* or *Vds.* and the verb will be in the THIRD person.

LESSON II

GENDER

There is in grammar a thing called gender which presents no difficulty to English people. For us gender corresponds to sex. The name of a male creature is *masculine*, of a female *feminine*, of an inanimate object, a thing, neither masculine nor feminine, but what we call *neuter*. A soldier is masculine, a cow is feminine, a book is neuter, and that is the last word to be said in the matter. Spanish is not so accommodating. A table = *mesa*, for instance, is feminine; a ship = *buque*, is masculine, and, as far as nouns are concerned, there is no neuter at all. A Spanish noun must, that is to say, be either masculine or feminine. It is not so much a matter of sex, as of the termination or derivation of the word.

Unfortunately no very satisfactory rules for knowing the gender of a Spanish noun at sight can be given.

But here are some :—

(1) Nouns ending in *a, d, ion* or *z* are feminine.
(2) Nouns ending in *o, or, al* or *ador* are masculine.
(3) Male beings (men, well-known animals, etc.) are masculine, even though the noun may end in *a*.
(4) Female beings (women, well-known animals, etc.) are feminine.

These rules are not infallible, but they will be decidedly helpful.

Corresponding to this difference in gender of nouns there is a difference in the form of the words (articles and adjectives) that go with them.

The definite article *the* has the following singular forms in Spanish :—

el (masculine).   *la* (feminine).

The indefinite article *a* or *an* has the following forms in Spanish :—

un (masculine).   *una* (feminine).

Masculine nouns require a masculine, feminine nouns a feminine article.

El hombre, the man.	*La mujer*, the woman.
El muchacho, the boy.	*La casa*, the house.
El amigo, the (male) friend.	*La puerta*, the door.
El libro, the book.	*La mesa*, the table.
Un soldado, a soldier.	*Una manzana*, an apple.

Just as the article must " agree " in gender with the noun following it, so also must the adjective that qualifies or " goes with " the noun.   This point, however, will be dealt with in a subsequent lesson.

The Verb *to have* in Spanish is *tener*.

Here is the Present Indicative :—

yo tengo	I have.
(tú tienes)	(thou hast).
Vd. tiene	you have (singular).
él (ella) tiene	he (she) has.
nosotros tenemos	we have.
(vosotros tenéis)	(you have).
Vds. tienen	you have.
ellos (ellas) tienen	they have.

Have I? Has he? etc., are rendered by reversing the order of the words—e.g., *¿ tengo yo ? ¿ tiene él ?*, etc.   Has the man ? = *¿ tiene el hombre ?*

Not is translated by *no*, which is placed *before the Verb*— e.g., *yo no tengo* = I have not.   *¿ no tiene él ?* = has he not ? *¿ no tienen los hombres ?* = have not the men.

The word *got* in such expressions as *I have got a dog* is not translated = *Tengo un perro.*

Exercise 2(a)

1. El muchacho tiene un libro. 2. La casa tiene una puerta. 3. El amigo comprará una manzana. 4. ¿ No tiene Vd. una mesa ? 5. Ellos no tienen un libro. 6. ¿ Tomarán Vds. la manzana ? 7. Yo no tengo un caballo. 8. ¿ Compraremos nosotros la mesa ? 9. La mujer no tiene una casa. 10. ¿ Cuándo comprará él el libro ?

Exercise 2(b)

1. We have a house. 2. Haven't you (singular) a book ? 3. The boy will take the apple.   4. The woman buys the house. 5. Have you (familiar plural) a horse? 6. The house hasn't a door. 7. They have a house. 8. Will you (plural) not take the book? 9. Have we a table? 10. The man has not a house.

There is one further point about the use of the singular article. The Spanish for *water* is *agua*. This is feminine. One would therefore expect *the water* to be *la agua*. But this is very awkward to say clearly, particularly as, according to the general rule, the stress falls on the first *a* of the noun. So, to avoid the combination of two distinctly pronounced *a*'s, the masculine form *el* of the article is substituted for *la*. This is merely for ease of pronunciation. It does not alter the gender of the word : *agua* is still feminine, so that an adjective agreeing with it would be in the feminine gender. As the letter *h* is not pronounced in Spanish, the same alteration is made with nouns beginning with that letter. So we can express it in this way :—

Feminine nouns beginning with *accented a* or *ha* require the form *el* (not *la*) when the article comes immediately before the noun. If an adjective comes between the two this change is not made.

Thus we should say : *el agua* = the water ; *el hacha* = the axe ; *el ala* = the wing, although these words are all feminine. But we should say : *la araña* = the spider ; *la hazaña* = the exploit ; and *la alfombra* = the carpet, because in these words the stress does not fall on the first syllable.

(It is worth noting, in passing, that this rule applies to nouns, not to adjectives : you do, for instance, write *la alta dignidad* = the lofty rank. There is no need to bother about this. The point is only made in case you should encounter in your reading a phrase that seems to break the rule previously given to you.)

Exercise 2(c)

1. Has she not the carpet ? 2. You will take the axe. 3. Where shall I buy the water ? 4. The man and woman have not a horse. 5. Shall we take an axe ? 6. Haven't you a carpet ?

LESSON III

NUMBER—POSSESSIVES

In Spanish, as in English, the singular of a noun is generally made into the plural by adding *s* : *soldado* = a soldier ; *soldados* = soldiers.

If a noun is plural, the article accompanying it must likewise be plural.

The definite article has the following plural forms :—

Los (masculine) = the plural of *el*.
Las (feminine) = the plural of *la*.

Similarly *un* has the plural form *unos*, and *una* the plural *unas*. The plural meaning of both is *some (any)*. Actually *some (any)* is generally omitted in Spanish. I have some money = *Tengo dinero*.

Nouns ending in a vowel form their plural by adding *s* to the singular :—

El palacio = the palace.   *Los palacios* = the palaces.

Una iglesia = a church.   *(Unas) iglesias* = some churches.

El agua (fem.) = the water.   *Las aguas* = the waters.

Nouns ending in a consonant or in *y* add *es* to the singular :—

La ciudad = the city.   *Las ciudades* = the cities.
El tren = the train.   *Los trenes* = the trains.
El rey = the king.   *Los reyes* = the kings.

If, however, a word ends in the singular in *z*, the plural is formed by changing *z* into *ces*.

El lápiz (pencil), plural *los lápices*.
La voz (the voice), plural *las voces*.

We shall see later that adjectives form their plurals in the same way as nouns.

Possessives

The following table shows some very important possessive adjectives. THESE WORDS CAN ONLY BE USED BEFORE
NOUNS.

	Masculine.		*Feminine.*	
	Sing.	*Plural.*	*Sing.*	*Plural.*
My	mi	mis	mi	mis
Thy	tu	tus	tu	tus
His (her, its) .	su	sus	su	sus
Our	nuestro	nuestros	nuestra	nuestras
Your . . .	vuestro	vuestros	vuestra	vuestras
Their . . .	su	sus	su	sus

We have seen that the Spanish article must " agree " in
gender and number with the noun it precedes. There is a
difference between the English and Spanish (or French)
attitudes towards possessives. If a man owns a book, we
talk about HIS book. If two men own a house, they will
speak of OUR house. But in Spanish we have got to
remember that the gender of the possessive word is determined not by the sex of the owner, but by the gender of
the thing possessed. The word *casa* (house) is feminine.
Therefore, just as the article used with it must be feminine,
so must the possessive adjective, whatever the sex of the
owner. So, if a house is owned by two males, they must
not say *nuestro casa*, but *nuestra casa*, because the Spanish
noun is feminine.

Similarly, two girls, referring to their motor-car, must
speak of it as *nuestro automóvil*, because the noun is
masculine. This rule presents no difficulty in the case of
mi, *tu* and *su*, in which the masculine and feminine forms
are identical; but with *nuestro* and *vuestro* you must be
continually on the look-out.

There is another thing to remember. It was pointed
out in the previous lesson that YOU will, for all ordinary
purposes, always be rendered by *Vd.* or *Vds.* and never by
tú or *vosotros*. Now, *Vd.* (meaning literally Your Honour)
is third person. The corresponding possessive, therefore,
cannot possibly be *tu* or *vuestro*, which are second person.
In other words, since we have excluded *tú* and *vosotros* as

normal renderings of YOU, so also we must rule out *tu* and *vuestro*, in all their forms, as translations of YOUR. In writing a formal refusal in the third person to a wedding reception, it would be wrong to address the hostess as follows : " Mr. X regrets that he cannot accept the kind invitation of Lady Duckweed on the occasion of the marriage of your daughter ". Since the reply is couched in the third person, the writer must put "her daughter". In the same way, since we are to translate YOU by the third person expression *Vd.* (*Vds.*), so we must render YOUR by the third person possessive. Consequently, in addition to HIS, HER, ITS and THEIR, *su*, a very hard-worked word, is used also for YOUR. Thus : *su sombrero* may mean HIS hat, HER hat, possibly ITS hat, and certainly YOUR hat. One might expect this to result in confusion. Actually the pronoun or noun used with the verb will nearly always put the exact meaning of *su* in any particular sentence beyond doubt. Thus : *él tiene su sombrero* would obviously mean "he has his hat". But if the man has appropriated another's property, you could make the meaning clear by writing *él tiene el sombrero de* (of) *Vd.—i.e.*, "he has your hat". But this construction is only necessary in ambiguous cases. Normally *su* will do for YOUR, as well as for HIS, HER or ITS.

VOCABULARY

luego = shortly, immediately.	*llegar* = to arrive.
botella = bottle.	*con* = with.
habitación = room.	*de* = of, from.
vino = wine.	*a* = to, at.
taza = cup.	*en* = in.
café (m.) = coffee.	*plaza* = square.
estación = station.	*hay* = there is, there are.

NOTE.—*In this and all the lists of words that follow, the gender is not indicated unless the word is an exception to the rules given in Lesson II.*

Exercise 3(a)

1. En el centro de la ciudad hay una plaza. 2. El tren llegará luego a la estación. 3. El hombre toma una taza

de café con sus amigos. 4. Nuestro rey tiene un palacio en la ciudad. 5. Tenemos quince libros. 6. El general llega en el tren con su mujer. 7. ¿Tiene Vd. su botella de vino? 8. Yo hablaré a mis amigos. 9. ¿No tiene Vd. mi sombrero? 10. En la estación de nuestra ciudad hay diez trenes. 11. La mujer y su marido llegarán luego en su automóvil. 12. En la plaza de nuestra ciudad hay una iglesia. 13. Tenemos en nuestra casa diez habitaciones. 14. ¿Cuando llegaremos a Madrid? 15. ¿Tiene Vd. los libros de mi amigo? 16. El comprará la casa de Vd. 17. No hay agua en mi botella. 18. Mi amigo y su mujer tienen una casa en la plaza de la ciudad.

Exercise 3(b)

1. My grandfather takes a cup of coffee with his wife. 2. The soldier hasn't his bottle of wine. 3. My friend and his wife will take the train immediately. 4. Your friend has a house with eight rooms. 5. We shall arrive at Madrid in our car. 6. There are twelve houses in the street. 7. She will buy some apples. 8. Have you wine in your bottle? 9. We shall buy a house in the centre of the town where there is a square. 10. They have two motor-cars, the doctor has six horses. 11. Will you not buy my house? 12. When will you take your hat? 13. The women and their husbands will take the train. 14. Kings have their palaces, we have our houses. 15. I will speak to my husband and (to) his friends. 16. Will you not buy some pencils? 17. Where is there a church? 18. I will buy your house : it has seven rooms.

LESSON IV

CONTRACTIONS OF WORDS—THE VERB *HABER*

We have seen that *of* or *from* is translated by *de* and *to* or *at* by *a*. Thus, *of the house* and *to the church* are rendered by *de la casa* and *a la iglesia* respectively. One would therefore expect *of the palace* and *to the king* to be translated as *de el palacio* and *a el rey*. But this would sound ugly. Consequently *de el* is contracted to *del* and *a el* to *al*, and we write *del palacio* and *al rey*. No such contraction, however, takes place with any other form of the article but *el*, because in other cases the ugly sound does not occur. Thus : *to the men = a los hombres* and *of a father* (*mother*) = *de un*(*a*) *padre* (*madre*).

In English we use the apostrophe *s* to denote possession —e.g., *John's letter* or *my brother's* (*sister's*) *house*. In Spanish, as in French, there is no such usage, and we must alter the phrases to *the letter of John* and *the house of my brother* (*sister*), and say *la carta de Juan* and *la casa de mi hermano* (*hermana*).

The verb *haber*. In Spanish there are two verbs " to have ", *tener* and *haber*. Of these *tener* is used as a principal verb and means to hold, to possess.

Haber is used as an auxiliary verb. It cannot stand alone, but is used to form the compound tenses, as they are called, of other verbs. It is generally, therefore, followed by a past participle—*i.e.*, that part of a verb which we generally use in English after " I have "—taken, seen, written, etc.

Thus, I have a watch = *tengo un reloj*, but I have bought (sold, lost) my watch = *yo he comprado* (*vendido*, *perdido*) *mi reloj*. In the first sentence it is the fact of possessing the watch that is important, in the second the buying, selling, or losing of it, the " have " merely indicating that the action took place recently.

PRESENT TENSE OF *Haber*

I have	yo he.
(Thou hast)	(tú has).
He (she) has	él (ella) ha.
You have	Vd. ha.
We (m.) have	nosotros hemos.
We (f.) have	nosotras hemos.
(You have)	(vosotros habéis).
You have	Vds. han.
They (m.) have	ellos han.
They (f.) have	ellas han.

In compound tenses (*i.e.*, those formed by a tense of

haber + some past participle) the negative *no* comes *before* the auxiliary :—

> (*Yo*) *no he visto el cuchillo* = I have not seen the knife.
> *Vd. no ha escrito la carta* = you have not written the letter.

When the present tense of *haber* is used in an interrogative sentence, the subject is generally placed AFTER the past participle.

> *¿Han llegado los hombres?* = have the men arrived?
> *¿Han gastado Vds. su dinero?* = have you spent your money?
> *¿No ha hallado él sus libros* = hasn't he found his books?
> *¿Ha comprado ella café?* = has she bought any coffee?

It will be noticed from this last sentence that *any* is usually untranslated in Spanish before a noun.

> *¿Tiene Vd. dinero?* = have you any money?

But, of course : *¿Ha perdido Vd. el dinero?* = have you lost the money?

There remains one final point to complete this lesson. It can be best illustrated by example. Look at these two sentences, involving the word *buscar*, to look for or seek :—

> *Busco mi sombrero* = I look for my hat.
> *Busco a mi hija* = I look for my daughter.
> *Busco a Carlos* = I look for Charles.

In English the three sentences are almost identical. In Spanish the preposition *a* has been introduced before the object in the second and third sentences. Yet what is the difference between the three? In the first the object is a hat, in the second a girl, in the third the proper name of a person. On the face of it there seems no reason to make a distinction between them. But the Spanish do. The first object is a *thing*, the second and third are people. From this we get this important rule. If the direct object of an active verb is a definite person (or personified animal or thing, as in a fable, for instance), the preposition *a*, untranslated in English, is inserted before it.

Vocabulary

llamar = to call.	*periódico* = newspaper.
mandar = to send.	*bolsillo* = pocket, purse.
que = who, which, that.	*hoy* = to-day.
ayer = yesterday.	*bastante* = enough.
para = in order to.	*peseta* = peseta.
Vd(s). quiere(n) = you wish, want, like.	

Exercise 4(a)

1. No tengo el reloj que Vd. quiere comprar. 2. Hemos vendido ayer el libro de Carlos. 3. He escrito hoy cinco cartas. 4. No tengo bastante dinero para comprar vino. 5. Mi hermano no ha llegado a Madrid. 6. ¿No quiere Vd. comprar el automóvil del médico? 7. ¿Ha visto Vd. al rey? 8. Hemos gastado las cuatro pesetas que he hallado hoy. 9. Buscaremos a la hija del general. 10. ¿No ha visto Vd. el cuchillo que he perdido en una de las habitaciones de su casa? 11. Yo llamaré al muchacho que habla en la calle con el tío de Juan. 12. ¿Quiere Vd. comprar (unos) periódicos? Tengo una peseta en mi bolsillo. 13. Los generales han perdido el tren. 14. ¿Ha visto Vd. a los soldados que han llegado de Madrid? 15. He vendido mis libros y tengo bastante dinero para comprar dos botellas de vino. 16. ¿Cuándo ha escrito él a su hermano? 17. La mujer ha mandado una carta a su hijo que tiene una casa en Bilbao. 18. Busco el periódico que ha perdido Juan.

Exercise 4(b)

1. Have you any newspapers? 2. Have you bought the watches? 3. Have they not sold their cars? 4. The man wishes to call his wife. 5. Have you seen the doctor's uncle? 6. Have you enough money in your pocket (in order) to buy any apples? 7. Have you seen John to-day? 8. Are you looking for your brother? 9. Will you send the letter to-day? 10. Will you (do you wish to) take a cup of coffee? 11. I will look for the newspaper which you have lost. 12. When did you see the soldiers? 13.

---

[1] Strictly, the compound tense is used when the period of the action is not completely over (e.g. to-day), the past definite when it is (e.g. yesterday). But at this stage the inaccuracy may be forgiven.

John's uncle, who will arrive to-day from Madrid, has lost his money. 14. I have in my house ten books which you wish to buy. 15. I will take the ten pesetas which you have in your pocket. 16. I have not taken your newspaper. 17. Won't you (not the future) call Charles? 18. Haven't you seen the girl? 19. To where have you sent the woman?

LESSON V

ADJECTIVES—THE VERB 'TO BE'

Spanish adjectives agree with their nouns in Gender and Number. If the noun is feminine plural the adjective must be also. We have learned how to form the plural of nouns. In so doing we have also learned how to form the plural of adjectives. The rules (Praise be !) are the same.

Thus :   *blanco* (white)   plural   *blancos*.
          azul (blue)   ,,   *azules*.
          feliz (happy)   ,,   *felices*.

As to the formation of the feminine, the following remarks will help.

Adjectives ending in *o* change *o* into *a* : *hermoso* (beautiful), fem. *hermosa*. So, for example, with *barato* (cheap), *pequeño* (small), *rico* (rich), *largo* (long), *bonito* (pretty), *casado* (married), *cansado* (tired), *ruso* (Russian), *caro* (dear), *melodioso* (tuneful), *contento* (pleased), etc.

Most adjectives not ending in *o* make no difference in form between masculine and feminine singular. For instance : *hábil* (clever), *célebre* (famous), *valiente* (brave), *cortés* (polite), *pobre* (poor).

Those ending in *án* or *ón* add *a* in the feminine : *holgazán* (lazy), *holgazana*. So do those in *or* : *hablador*(a) (talkative), provided that they are not comparatives like *mejor* (better), *peor* (worse), *superior, exterior, inferior*, etc., which remain unchanged in the feminine singular.

Adjectives of nationality ending in a *consonant* add an *a*. Thus : *inglés* (English), *inglesa* ; *español* (Spanish), *española* ; *francés* (French), *francesa* ; *alemán* (German), *alemana*.

These adjectives, which are also used as nouns, to mean the language of the country concerned, are written with a small letter. Meaning a native of the country, they are generally written with a capital letter :—

Un labrador español = a Spanish farmer.
La Inglesa ha aprendido francés = the Englishwoman has learnt French.

THE POSITION OF ADJECTIVES

In English, adjectives generally come before the noun. In Spanish they generally come AFTER. This applies, for instance, to adjectives of colour, size, nationality and to adjectives much longer than their nouns : *café negro* (black coffee), *amigos franceses* (French friends), *obreros aplicados* (industrious workmen). On the other hand, if an adjective is very short, if it is little more than an ornament, if it is a mere general epithet applying to a whole class rather than distinctively to the one instance, or if it is used in a figurative sense, it will come BEFORE the noun. For instance : *una estrecha amistad* = a close (literally narrow) friendship. Friendship is not measurable in inches or yards. The adjective is used figuratively, and therefore precedes the noun. Similarly you would translate " the learned professor " as *el docto profesor*, because the adjective is a mere ornament. If he were not learned, the man would not be (or oughtn't to be) a professor. But one would certainly write : *el soldado docto*, because this is distinctive (not to say unusual). *Bueno* (good) and *malo* (bad) come before the noun. By a peculiarity of their own, they are shortened to *buen* and *mal*, but only when immediately preceding a masculine singular noun. Similarly *grande* (great) drops the *de* BEFORE a singular noun of either gender, but only when it indicates *importance*, not *size*. When referring to size, it usually FOLLOWS its noun:—

Un gran general = a great general.
Un general grande = a tall general.
Un gran día = a great day.

There are many adjectives over whose position you will hesitate. But don't worry. One Spaniard will not invariably put the adjective in the same position as another might. If in doubt, put the adjective after the noun. You will be far more often right than wrong.

Spanish has two verbs meaning " to be " : *ser* and *estar*. Here are the present tenses.

Ser.	*Estar.*	
yo soy	yo estoy	= I am.
(tú eres)	(tú estás)	= (thou art).
Vd. es	Vd. está	= you are.
él es	él está	= he is.
nosotros somos	nosotros estamos	= we are.
(vosotros sois)	(vosotros estáis)	= (you are).
Vds. son	Vds. están	= you are.
ellos son	ellos están	= they are.

These verbs are not interchangeable. *Estar* is used of a temporary condition, *ser* of a permanent one.

Estoy cansado = I am tired (but I shall be better after a rest).

Soy médico = I am a doctor (a virtually permanent state or occupation).

Ella es bonita = she is pretty (good looks don't last for ever, but they are not purely accidental or temporary).

Ser expresses an inherent or essential quality; *estar* an accidental or external state or quality.

El alumno es atento = the student is attentive (by nature).

El alumno está atento = the student is attentive (for the moment).

La botella está vacía = the bottle is empty (accidental).

La botella es de vidrio = the bottle is of glass (inherent).

Ser is used to express the ownership of anything, the material of which it is made, for trades, professions, hours of the day, origin of a person or thing—in short, in most cases where the action or condition is not temporary by its very nature. On the other hand, *estar*, derived from the Latin word meaning " to stand ", is always used to indicate the position of a person or thing, even when it is permanent. *Ser* is used to form the passive. *Estar* is used with the present participle to express what anyone is doing *at the time only*.

Examples of the foregoing :—

Este caballo es mío = this horse is mine.
El reloj es de oro = the watch is of gold.
Es panadero = he is a baker.

NOTE that the indefinite article (*un, una*) is not used before a noun used like an adjective to express profession or some other quality of the subject.

¿ Qué hora es ? = What time is it ?
La criada es de Málaga = the servant is (comes) from Malaga.
Está en el palacio = he is in the palace.
El hombre ha sido muerto = the man has been killed.
Compra un periódico = he buys a paper.
Está leyendo un periódico = he is reading a paper (at this moment).

VOCABULARY

escuela = school.	*más* = more.
pájaro = bird.	*que* = than.
cantar = to sing.	*lleno* = full.
escuchar = to listen (to).	*viajar* = to travel.
pero = but.	*mucho* = much.
tendero = shopkeeper.	*cocinera* = cook.
campo = field.	*trabajar* = to work.
recibido = received.	*siempre* = always.
visitar = to visit.	*aquí* = here.

Exercise 5(a)

1. El hombre que ha visto Vd. es tendero. 2. La botella azul que he comprado está llena de agua. 3. Mis hermanos son más ricos que el médico. 4. Nuestra cocinera es holgazana : no trabaja mucho. 5. Las mujeres españolas son siempre habladoras. 6. He recibido hoy una carta de mi hija : está en Barcelona. 7. ¿ Es casada la pobre mujer ? Es viuda. 8. Los alumnos están en la escuela, escuchando al docto profesor. 9. Los obreros que trabajan en los campos no son muy aplicados. 10. Las calles de muchas ciudades españolas son muy estrechas. 11. Escucharé hoy los pequeños pájaros que cantan en los

campos. 12. ¿Dónde está la hija del valiente general X?
13. Está en Inglaterra con su madre que quiere siempre
viajar. 14. El tendero no tiene relojes baratos, son todos
de oro. 15. La hija de mi buen amigo Carlos es muy
bonita. 16. Un gran general francés ha llegado aquí para
visitar al rey. 17. ¿No quiere Vd. visitar el palacio de
los reyes españoles? 18. Mi tío es labrador. No es rico,
pero es siempre feliz. 19. Los obreros no son corteses, pero
son muy hábiles. 20. El célebre palacio que buscan Vds.
está en la calle del Rey.

Exercise 5(b)

1. The streets of the city are long. 2. To-day I have
worked much, but I am not tired. 3. The workman's white
horse is small. 4. I have not seen your brother. Where
is he? 5. He is in England with his great friend. He
travels a lot (much), when he has enough money. 6. The
birds which sing in the fields are very beautiful. 7. My
uncle is a learned man, but he is lazy. 8. Our cook is not
here : she is in the church which you have visited to-day.
9. White wine is better than black coffee. 10. Her
daughter is not married. 11. The men who are in the fields
are always happy. 12. The church is small but very
beautiful. 13. The bottles which you have bought are full
of water. 14. I am listening to the birds : their voices
are very tuneful. 15. Where is the farmer's pretty
daughter? 16. Good books are cheap here. 17. German
soldiers are in the city. 18. French workmen are very
industrious. 19. We are doctors; my brother is from
Madrid, but I come from Bilbao. 20. The beautiful English
woman does not speak Spanish, but she has learned French.

LESSON VI

DEMONSTRATIVES AND POSSESSIVES

In English, this (these) and that (those) are used to
indicate to which of two or more persons or things we
refer. The Spanish have three words for this purpose :
este, *ese* and *aquel*. The last two each mean " that ", but
with this distinction : *ese* denotes something near to or

associated with the person addressed, whilst *aquel* refers to something remote both from the speaker and the person spoken to.

The forms of the three are as follows :

	Masc.	*Fem.*	*Neut.*	*Meaning.*
	este	esta	esto	this
Sing.	ese	esa	eso	that (near you)
	aquel	aquella	aquello	that (yonder)
	estos	estas	—	these
Plur.	esos	esas	—	those (near you)
	aquellos	aquellas	—	those (yonder)

Look at these examples of their use :—

Este libro que he leído = this book which I have read.
Ese libro que Vd. tiene = that book which you have.
Aquel libro que mi primo tiene = that book which my cousin has.
Esta mañana = this morning.
En aquellos días (lugares) = in those days (places).

The neuter forms *esto*, *eso* and *aquello* never refer to definite nouns, but to an idea, a whole phrase or a statement.

¿ Ha oído Vd. eso ? = did you hear that? (*i.e.*, what was said, for instance).
Esto no es posible = this is not possible.

There is a further use of demonstratives. We do not say " This hat and that hat ", but " This hat and that (one) ". When a Spanish demonstrative is used in this way, to avoid the repetition of a noun, it takes the written accent to distinguish it.

This book and that one (yonder) = *este libro y aquél.*
Do you want those books (over there) or those (nearer)?
= *¿ quiere Vd. aquellos libros ó ésos ?*

In English we talk about the former and the latter to distinguish between two. In Spanish the former = *aquél*, the latter = *éste*. This is not what one would expect. The Spanish argument is that, on encountering " the latter " on a page, you cast your eye back, and the latter of two things referred to will meet your eye, as you look back, before the former of the pair. In other words, " the latter " is the nearer. So the Spanish call the latter *éste* and the former *aquél*. The French reason in the same way.

In English we often use " the one " or " the ones ". Frequently " that " or " those " could be replaced by " the one(s) ". We are not making a distinction between two contrasted things, but merely drawing attention. For instance, the proverb : " People (those) who live in glass houses shouldn't throw stones ", is a case in point. For this use of the pronoun the Spanish *el* is employed. In fact, the various forms of the definite article are borrowed and do duty (with the meanings of that, those, the one, the ones, etc.) instead of the other demonstratives, to avoid the repetition of a noun already referred to or understood by implication.

My house and the one you are buying = *mi casa y la que Vd. compra*.

The black ink and the blue (one) = *la tinta negra y la azul*.

The roof of my house and that of the one you are buying
= *el tejado de mi casa y el de la que Vd. compra*.

In the above example, you see, the same usage occurs twice, *el* referring to the roof, and *la* to the house.

In contrasting, of course, the ordinary demonstrative is used.

My house and that (yonder) = *mi casa y aquélla*.

That brings us to another point. We should translate " my house and yours " as " my house and the one of you ", and say : *mi casa y la de Vd*. But how should we say " Your house and mine " ?

We know that my house is *mi casa*. But now we want the possessive " mine " used, to avoid the repetition of a noun. This is *mío*. And there are others. Just as we avoid *tú* and *vosotros*, so, as foreigners not on intimate terms with Spaniards, we shall avoid *tuyo* (thine) and *vuestro* (yours). There remain *suyo* (*suya*), his, her, its, yours and theirs; *nuestro* (*nuestra*), ours; and, of course, *mío* (*mía*), mine—all of which form their plurals by the addition of an *s*. We are now in a position to translate " your house and mine ". It will be : *su casa* (or, better, *la casa de Vd.*) *y la mía.* Similarly, " my horses and theirs " = *mis caballos y los suyos.* But *suyo* has various meanings. Therefore, here again we use *el* with its meaning, already noted, of " the one ", and write : *mis caballos y los de ellos.* In most cases, in fact, it is preferable, for the sake of clearness, to avoid *suyo* and put the appropriate personal pronoun with *de* in front of it.

Sometimes *mío,* etc., is used without the article. For instance, " the house is mine " = *la casa es mía* (and not *la mía*). We can make a simple rule out of this. When the possessive has before it some part of the verb *ser,* used with the idea of ownership, the article must be left out. "This car is ours" = *este auto(móvil) es nuestro.* "The money is mine " = *el dinero es mío.* For " the money is his " we should say : *el dinero es de él* (avoiding *suyo*).

There are two other instances when *mío* is used. Firstly, in emphasis or contrast. " He is my friend " might be : *es mi amigo.* But, stressing the word to imply that the person is my friend, not someone else's, you would use *mío,* putting it AFTER the noun, and say : *es amigo mío.* Secondly, such phrases as " of mine ", " of his ", etc., are generally translated without the " of " being rendered. For instance, "a friend of mine (his)" would be : *un amigo mío* (*suyo*). Even " one of his friends " is better translated by : *un amigo suyo* than by : *uno de sus amigos.* One last word. Remember that the article is omitted with *ser,* but not with *estar.* " This handkerchief is mine " = *este pañuelo es mío.* " Here is my handkerchief. Where is yours? " = *Aquí está mi pañuelo. ¿ Dónde está el suyo* (or, *el de Vd.*) *?*

VOCABULARY

sobre = on.	*vecino(a)* = neighbour.
cama = bed.	*todo* = all, every.
pariente = relation.	*dado* = given.
cuadra = stable.	*o* = or.
no = no, not.	*sí* = yes.

Exercise 6(a)

1. Las manzanas que están sobre la mesa son mías. 2. Este libro es mío, aquél es de mi hermano. 3. Estos

lápices son mejores que los de Vd. 4. Hay muchos libro en mi habitación : los que he comprado esta mañana están sobre la cama. 5. ¿Quiere Vd. este periódico o aquél? 6. Un pariente mío está en Madrid. 7. ¿Ha visto Vd. a Carlos? Dos amigos suyos llegarán hoy de Barcelona. 8. Ese auto no es mío, es de Juan. 9. Aquel tendero es más rico que éste. 10. ¿Dónde está mi caballo? El nuestro está aquí, el de Vd. está en la cuadra. 11. Hoy estamos muy contentos : dos primos nuestros han llegado aquí de Inglaterra. 12. ¿Es mía esta botella? No, es de ella. 13. Mi padre y el suyo han trabajado todo el día en los campos. 14. Mi casa y la de nuestros vecinos son pequeñas. 15. ¿Ha perdido Vd. su pañuelo? No, éste es mío. 16. Aquí hay dos relojes : éste es mío, ése es de Vd. 17. He dado el dinero a Luis y a un amigo suyo. 18. Mi perro y el de ella están en la calle. 19. ¿Es este auto nuestro o de Vds.? 20. Su caballo de Vd. y el de su criado están en la cuadra.

Exercise 6(b)

1. These apples are mine, those are yours. 2. Her voice is more tuneful than her sister's (the one of her sister). 3. A neighbour of ours has a white house with a blue roof. 4. I have read my letters, I have not read yours. 5. The gold watch (which) you have found is mine. 6. The money I have spent is John's. 7. Charles will arrive here with two friends of his. 8. The servant (fem.) has lost my handkerchiefs but not yours. 9. I have not enough money to buy this car : that one is cheaper (more cheap). 10. Is this newspaper yours? (turn to : yours this newspaper). 11. Have you seen the farmer and his son? They are friends of ours. 12. These apples are better than the ones (which) I (have) bought this morning. 13. Two relations of his have bought that house (yonder). 14. Our cook and our neighbour's do not wish to work this morning. 15. My hat and yours are on the table. 16. This is not my book, it is hers. 17. We have seen our mother but not hers. 18. One of my neighbours has sold his house : he wants to buy mine. 19. He does not wish to buy books : the ones he has are good. 20. Is yours the horse which is in the stable?

LESSON VII

INTERROGATIVES—REGULAR VERBS

So far we can ask a question in Spanish only by reversing the subject and verb. *¿ Tiene Vd. su sombrero ?* = have you (got) your hat ? *¿ Ha olvidado Vd. la palabra ?* = have you forgotten the word ? Remember that the pronoun comes AFTER the past participle " forgotten ". Sometimes we must be ready to allow another word to intervene between the verb and the subject. For instance, for " Is your friend a shopkeeper ? " we shall not write : *¿ es el amigo suyo tendero ?* but : *¿ es tendero el amigo suyo ?* This is because we cannot logically separate the two. We are not concerned merely with whether the person *is*, but with whether he is a shopkeeper, so the two words must stay together while the subject beats a retreat to the end.

Many questions, however, are introduced in English by such words as who?, which? or what?, and it is now our business to cope with their Spanish equivalents. The commonest translation of what ? is *¿ qué ?* Thus : What do you want ? = *¿ qué quiere Vd. ?* What is that ? = *¿ qué es éso ?* What dog? = *¿ qué perro ?* It is also used in exclamations, meaning : " What a ——" but the *a* is NOT translated. *¡ Qué perro !* = what a dog ! What a pity ! = *¡ qué lástima !* If an adjective goes with a noun in such expressions, the word *tan* (so) is usually put in for emphasis. What an ugly picture ! = *¡ qué cuadro tan feo !* We can also use *qué* with a preposition before it. Of what are you talking? (what are you talking about?) = *¿ de qué habla Vd. ?* or, if the action is going on at that very moment, *¿ de qué está Vd. hablando ?*

Cuál (pl. *cuáles*) is used of persons or things and means which (one(s)). It is seldom used just before a noun, so which car ? implying one of several would be *¿ cuál de los autos?* But what general is that ? = *¿ qué general es ese ?* because identity, not selection, is involved. *Cuál*, meaning What ? is used with reference to things before a tense of *ser*. What is the date of his arrival? = *Cuál es la fecha de su llegada?*

Who? or Whom? are translated by *quién* (sing.) and *quiénes* (plural). Any preposition may be used before them. *¿ Quién es Vd. ?* = who are you? *¿ Con quiénes habla Vd. ?* = with whom do you speak? *¿ A quien ha visto Vd. ?* = whom have you seen? (*Note:* the preposition *a* used when the object of the verb is a person). Whose? is best translated by : *¿ de quién (quiénes) ?* Whose house is this? = *¿ de quién es esta casa ?* (lit. of whom is this house?). There is a word *cuyo* meaning "whose?", but, though common, as we shall see later, as a relative pronoun, it is rarely used as an interrogative, and *de quién(es)* is much safer to use.

We have already met the relative pronoun *que* (who, that, etc.). It will be found later that relatives are mostly identical in form with interrogatives, save that they do not have the accent mark. This applies also to the words "why" and "because". Why = *¿ por qué ?* (compare the French *pourquoi ?*), and because = *porque.* Another useful interrogative is *¿ Cuánto(a) ?* = how much? The plural is *¿ cuántos (cuántas) ?* = how many? *¿ Cuánto dinero ?* = how much money. *¿ Cuántas vacas ?* = how many cows?

The majority of Spanish verbs end in *ar* in the infinitive. We have dealt already with such verbs as *hablar*, whose present tense may be formed by adding to the stem *habl-* the terminations *-o, -as, -a, -amos, -áis, -an.*

There are two other classes of Spanish verbs : those whose infinitives end in *er* or *ir.* Typical of these are *comer* = to eat, and *vivir* = to live, with stems *com-* and *viv-* respectively. Here are their present tenses :—

yo como (I eat).	yo vivo (I live).
(tú comes).	(tú vives).
Vd., él, ella come.	Vd., él, ella vive.
nosotros comemos.	nosotros vivimos.
(vosotros coméis).	(vosotros vivís).
Vds., ellas, ellos comen.	Vds., ellos, ellas, viven.

With the exception of some 300 irregular verbs—*ser* and *estar* are examples—all Spanish verbs are conjugated like one of these model verbs *hablar, comer* or *vivir*, according to whether their infinitive ends in *ar, er* or *ir.*

In English we turn " he speaks " into a question by saying : " Does he speak ? " In Spanish you write the equivalent of " speaks he ? " = ¿ *habla él* ? In other words, do, does, did, etc., are not translated. This applies to negatives also. He does not speak = *él no habla* (lit. he speaks not).

We have seen that when the object of a verb is a person, not a thing, the preposition *a* is inserted before this object. You will find, incidentally, that an intelligent animal, such as a horse or a dog, is sometimes regarded, for the purposes of this rule, as a person. Two important verbs, however, are exceptions. They are *tener* and *querer*.

" I have a sister " is *tengo una hermana* (*tengo a mi hermana* would mean " I hold my sister ").

Similarly *querer* means to want, *querer a* means to love. So that *querer una cocinera* and *querer a una cocinera* are not the same thing. Far from it ! But these two verbs are the only exceptions to the rule that *a* must be put before the object when it is a person.

In English the present tense of " to speak " means I speak, I do speak, I am speaking. In Spanish it is the same. But, I am speaking, as has already been touched upon, should be expressed by *estoy hablando*, if the action is unfinished and actually continuing at the moment. Since the action is purely temporary, *estar*, and NEVER *ser*, is employed in this connection.

Hablando is equivalent to the English " speaking ". This is the present participle (gerund). There is also the past participle " spoken ". The present and past participles of *ar* verbs are formed by adding *-ando* and *-ado* respectively to the stem :—

> *viajar* (to travel) ; *viaj-ando* (travelling) ; *viajado* (travelled).

Of *er* and *ir* verbs by adding *-iendo* and *-ido* to the stem :—

> *beber* (to drink) ; *bebiendo* (drinking) ; *bebido* (drunk).
> *recibir* (to receive) ; *recibiendo* (receiving) ; *recibido* (received).
> *visto* (seen) and *escrito* (written) are irregular.

Vocabulary

ver = to see.
dicho = said.
salir = to start, depart, leave.
comprender = to understand.
posada = inn.
abogado = lawyer.

acabar = to finish.
asunto = matter, affair.
siempre = always.
ahora = now.
oficial = officer.
allí = there.

Exercise 7(a)

1. ¿Cuál de mis libros ha leído Vd.? El que está sobre la mesa en su habitación. 2. ¿Qué ha dicho Vd. al abogado? 3. ¿Cuántas calles hay en esta ciudad? 4. ¿Cuál es el número de la habitación de Vd.? 5. ¿Cuáles de los lápices son míos? ¿Estos ó aquéllos? 6. Hemos perdido el tren. ¡Qué lástima! 7. ¡Qué muchacha tan bonita! ¿Quién es (ella)? 8. Es la hija de un amigo mío. 9. ¿Por qué no ha acabado Vd. su trabajo? 10. ¿De qué está Vd. hablando? De asuntos que Vd. no comprende. 11. ¿De quién son las vacas que están en aquel campo? Son de Carlos. 12. ¿De dónde es Vd.? Soy madrileño (adjective of Madrid), pero vivo ahora en Burgos. 13. ¿Quién vive en la casa del primo de Vd.? (de su primo). Mi tío vive allí, pero mi tía está en Inglaterra. 14. Este oficial francés bebe siempre vino blanco. 15. ¿Cuánto dinero tiene Vd. en su bolsillo? 16. ¿A quién está Vd. escribiendo? Al hijo del médico. 17. Los que están bebiendo en la posada no son amigos míos. 18. El tren ha salido de la estación. 19. Quiero ver al rey. ¿Dónde está su palacio? 20. Este soldado quiere mucho a la cocinera, pero es casada.

Exercise 7(b)

1. To which officer did you speak this morning? To that one (yonder). 2. Which of these cars is yours? This one. 3. Whose are those horses? They are not mine. 4. Which of his sons have you seen? 5. Why are you not working? I do not work because I am tired. 6. I want to see the lawyer. Where is he? He is not here. 7. The bird is singing in the garden. What a tuneful voice! 8. To what man do you wish to speak? 9. Which cow have you bought? The white (one). 10. I have given five

pesetas to that farmer who is drinking in the inn with his son. 11. We are natives of Madrid, but we live in Santander. 12. She is writing to her cousin. 13. What a man! He has drunk five bottles of wine. 14. I have two sisters and a brother. 15. How many churches are there in this city? 16. She has two sons. The one who writes to your friend is a doctor. 17. Where is the general? He is working in his garden. 18. There are many trains which leave this station. 19. Those men (yonder) do not live here. They come from Valencia. 20. How many workmen did you see in the fields?

LESSON VIII

COMPARISON OF ADJECTIVES—FUTURE OF VERBS

It frequently happens that we want to compare one thing or person with another to establish their relative merits or qualities. In so doing we use what is called the comparative of an adjective. In English if an adjective ends in a consonant we add *er* to it to make it comparative: *e.g.*, long—longer. If it ends in an *e* we merely add *r*: *e.g.*, ripe—riper. One or two adjectives, such as " good " and " bad ", change their form altogether and become " better " and " worse " respectively. With adjectives of a fair length we put " more " or " less " in front of them and make no change in the word itself: *e.g.*, more important, less difficult.

In Spanish this last is the method generally employed, and we have already encountered it casually during previous exercises. The Spanish for " more " = *más*, for " less " = *menos*. (The word *mas* without the accent sign means " but ". To avoid confusion, however, it is preferable to use *pero*.) In using a comparative we generally require the word "than", which, as we already know, is *que*. Perhaps it would be as well to recall that, whereas English adjectives are invariable in form, Spanish adjectives must agree in gender and number with the noun to which they refer, whether they are separated from it by a verb or not. For instance, Our house is older than yours = *nuestra casa es más vieja que la de Vd*. Is your sister bigger than mine? = *¿ es más grande su hermana que la mía ?* (*note* the Spanish order).

There are one or two irregular comparisons in Spanish:—

> *bueno*, good ; *mejor*, better.
> *malo*, bad ; *peor*, worse.
> *grande*, great ; *mayor*, greater.
> *pequeño*, small ; *menor*, smaller.

The last two, however, can be compared regularly (*más grande*, *más pequeño*), the irregular forms generally meaning older and younger, respectively, or occasionally referring to eminence rather than size. *El hermano mayor* = the elder brother. *La calle mayor* = the main street.

" Than " in comparisons is normally *que*. But "than" before a NUMBER is *de* (as in French). Thus :—

More than I = *Más que yo.* More than ten = *más de diez.*

To digress, but with a purpose, for a moment. We have seen in dealing with the demonstratives that " he who ", " the one who ", etc., are translated by *el que* and *los que*. In the same way, " what ", when it really means " that which ", referring to a whole clause rather than to some definite noun, is rendered by *lo que* (the French *ce qui*).

I do not listen to what he says = *no escucho lo que dice.*

This same usage is turned to account when " than " comes before a verb, *de* being put before it.

This boy is cleverer than (what) he says = *este muchacho es más hábil de* (not *que*) *lo que dice.*

But, of course, if we have " the one(s) " referring to some definite noun, then the ordinary *el que* (*los que*) may be used.

These apples are better than the ones you have bought = *estas manzanas son mejores que las que Vd. ha comprado.*

THE FUTURE OF VERBS

In an early lesson it was pointed out that the future of *tomar* (to take) was *tomaré* (I shall take). This tense can

be formed by adding the endings *-é, ás, á, -emos, -éis, -án*
to the infinitive.   It was also mentioned that ALL Spanish
verbs have these same endings in the Future Tense.   We
already know the Present Tense of *comer* (to eat) and *vivir*
(to live).   By adding the above endings to their infinitives
we shall get the Future without any difficulty.

> *comer-é -ás -á -emos -éis -án* = I shall eat, etc.
> *vivir-é   -ás -á -emos -éis -án* = I shall live, etc.

The other verbs we have encountered so far are *tener*,
ser, *estar* and *haber*.   These are irregular verbs in certain
tenses, but, even so, they have the normal future endings.

> *Tendr-é -ás -á -emos -éis -án* = I shall have, etc.
> *Ser-é   -ás -á -emos -éis -án* = I shall be, etc.
> *Estar-é -ás -á -emos -éis -án* = I shall be, etc.
> *Habr-é -ás -á -emos -éis -án* = I shall have, etc.

VOCABULARY

frío = cold.	*caliente* = warm, hot.
fuerte = strong.	*cerveza* = beer.
otro = other, another.	*dependiente* = clerk.
quedar = to remain.	*también* = also.
mañana (adv.) = to-morrow.	*mañana* (noun) = morning.
vender = to sell.	*si* (no accent) = if.
Vd(s). dice(n) = you say.	*oficina* = office.

Exercise 8(a)

1. Estos hombres son más fuertes que Vd.   2. ¿No es
más vieja esta mujer que aquélla?   3. Esta cerveza es
buena, es mejor que el vino blanco de Vd.   4. Hemos
recibido menos de cinco pesetas.   5. Gasta más dinero de
lo que dice.   6. ¿Es más barato el auto de Vd. que el
nuestro?   7. Venderemos nuestra casa, es muy pequeña.
8. Estos obreros son más holgazanes que los que trabajan
en el jardín de Vd.   9. Mi hermano está en Madrid.
Mañana yo estaré allí también.   10. Si Vd.[1] vende esos
libros, tendrá (Vd.) bastante dinero para comprar los que

[1] Although in theory *Vd.*, being really a noun, cannot be left out,
in practice it is omitted after being used once, if the meaning is
quite clear.

(Vd.) quiere. 11. Mi amigo quedará aquí más de ocho días. 12. Uno de mis dependientes está en mi oficina : no he visto esta mañana a los otros. 13. Tenemos en esta ciudad iglesias más grandes que las de Madrid. 14. Aquel abogado es más rico que el médico. Su casa tiene más de doce habitaciones. 15. Mañana estaré muy cansado, por que trabajaré todo el día en los campos. 16. El general dice que sus soldados no quedarán aquí más de dos días. 17. Estas manzanas no son buenas, son peores que las de Vd. 18. ¿Cuándo escribirá Vd. a su primo? 19. Los ricos no son siempre más felices que los pobres. 20. Mis vecinos son menos ricos de lo que dicen.

Exercise 8(b)

1. Your daughter is prettier than that girl. 2. Is not her house larger than ours? 3. Are not these clerks more idle than the ones who work in your cousin's office? 4. Those shopkeepers are richer than they say. 5. To-morrow we shall be in Bilbao with a relation of ours. 6. Will you not remain here more than three days? 7. The streets of this city are narrower than those of Madrid. 8. Have you lost your handkerchief? Yes, but I have another in my pocket. 9. He writes longer letters than I. (Remember that if an adjective is one that normally follows its noun, it will also do so in the comparative degree.) 10. The horses in my stable are better than the ones in his. 11. Charles is bigger than his younger brother. 12. Her house is in the main street, but it is smaller than ours. 13. When will the train leave (*saldrá*) the station? 14. The people who (those who) live here are relations of mine. 15. These officers are less brave than the general says. 16. I will look for your aunt. Will she not be in the garden? 17. This Englishwoman has more money than she spends. 18. We shall receive to-morrow the letter which he has written to-day. 19. Isn't that girl (yonder) more hardworking than your cook? 20. We shall miss this train, but there are many others[1] which leave this station for (*para*) Valencia.

[1] Others many.

LESSON IX

SUPERLATIVES—IMPERFECT TENSE

Many English superlatives are formed by putting " the most " before the adjective : *e.g.*, " the most important ". Short or common adjectives form their superlative by adding *st* or *est* : *e.g.*, largest, longest. One or two, such as " best " and " worst ", make a change in the body of the word itself.

In Spanish the method is to put the definite article before the comparative form : the biggest = *el más grande*, the best (worst) = *el mejor* (*peor*). Both article and adjective, of course, agree in gender and number with the noun to which they refer :—

These workmen are the most skilful = *estos obreros son los más hábiles*.

If the adjective is one that follows the noun, the definite article remains in front :—

The narrowest streets = *las calles más estrechas*.

In theory this might mean " the narrower streets ", but in practice there is seldom any doubt of the meaning. The English word " in " must be turned into " of " following a superlative for purposes of translation :—

The largest city in the world = *la ciudad más grande del mundo*.

In Spanish (as in French) a possessive pronoun placed before the comparative of an adjective also has the effect of making it superlative. In this case, naturally, the definite article is not used as well :—

Este libro es su mejor obra = this book is his best work.
Mi hermano mayor = my eldest (possibly, elder) brother.

Often the word " most " is used with no idea of comparing some person or thing with another, but merely with the meaning of " very " or " extremely " : *e.g.*, it is most (very, extremely) important. The Spanish for very is *muy*, so we can say : *es muy importante*. Actually, a more vivid way of conveying the idea is to add *ísimo* (*-ma, -mos, -mas*) to the adjective, first dropping the final vowel of the adjective if it ends in one :—

This city is very beautiful = *esta ciudad es muy hermosa ;* but, more colourfully : *esta ciudad es hermosísima*.

Still, the *muy* form is never grammatically wrong, and you will perhaps find it safer to stick to it.

By the way, remember that though an adjective may ordinarily come before the noun, if used with *muy* it must follow it—e.g., *es un buen hombre*, but *es un hombre muy bueno*.

NOTE, in passing, that *bueno* and *malo*, used with *estar* (not *ser*), refer to health, not goodness :—

Estoy bueno = I am well.

In the last lesson we were making unequal comparisons. But there is also a comparison of equality when, for instance, something is not better or worse than another, but as good as it. This will involve the use of the expressions " as —— as " : *e.g.*, my car is as good as yours. The first " as " in Spanish is *tan*, the second *como*. These words are invariable, and are used with adjectives and adverbs. We should therefore write : *mi auto es tan bueno como el de Vd.* If the sentence were negative, the first " as " would probably be changed into " so ". But in Spanish there is no change.

These children are not as (so) intelligent as those = *estos niños no son tan inteligentes como aquéllos*.

In sentences of this kind we shall also want to be able to say : " as much —— as ", or " so much —— as ". In such sentences " as much " will be followed by a noun. *Tan* can only be used with adjectives or adverbs, so here we want *tanto —— como*.

In dealing with interrogatives we have already met *¿cuánto?* = how much? The plural means " how many? " In the same way *tantos* (*tantas*) means " as (so) many ",

and agrees in gender and number with the noun. Sometimes it will agree with a noun previously mentioned, but
not actually repeated :—

> We have as many cows as you = *tenemos tantas vacas
> como Vd.*
> How much beer have you? I haven't as much as you
> = *¿ Cuánta cerveza tiene Vd.? No tengo tanta como
> Vd.*

The Imperfect of Regular Verbs

The imperfect indicative of *ar* verbs is formed by adding
to the stem the following endings : *-aba, -abas, -aba,
-ábamos, -abais, -aban.* In the case of both *er* and *ir* verbs
it is formed by adding to the stem *-ia, -ias, -ia, -iamos,
-iais, -ian.* Thus :—

hablaba	comía	vivía
(hablabas)	(comías)	(vivías)
hablaba	comía	vivía
hablábamos	comíamos	vivíamos
(hablabais)	(comíais)	(vivíais)
hablaban	comían	vivían

The imperfect tenses of *tener, haber* and *estar* are all
regular : *tenía, había, estaba,* etc. *Ser* has the following
forms : *era, (eras), era, éramos, (erais), eran.* Almost all
other Spanish verbs, even when irregular in other tenses,
form their imperfect on the regular model.

The present tense of *hablar,* a common verb, means I
speak, I do speak, or I am speaking. For the last meaning
estoy hablando may be substituted for *hablo,* when the point
is emphasised that the action is actually proceeding at the
moment in question.

The imperfect *hablaba* means I spoke, I used to speak,
or I was speaking. Here again *estaba hablando* may be
used when the action was in progress at the moment in
question. But this use is limited, and the student will
not find himself using it frequently. For instance : " I
was speaking to my cousin the other day " would probably
be : *hablaba el otro día con mi primo.* The imperfect is
the tense of habitual or repeated action in the past. For

example : he always missed the train = *perdía siempre el tren*. It was habitual with him. The tense is likewise used for general descriptions of the countryside or of people. Look at this extract from the first page of *Don Quijote* (Don Quixote).

Tenía en su casa una ama que pasaba de los cuarenta, y un mozo de campo, que así ensillaba el rocín como tomaba la podadera. Frisaba la edad de nuestro hidalgo con los cincuenta años : era de complexión recia, seco de carnes y amigo de la caza. (He had in his house a housekeeper a little over forty, and a farm lad who both saddled the nag and handled the pruning hook. The age of our gentleman was close upon fifty : he was of a robust constitution, lean of flesh and a keen sportsman.)

The imperfect, then, is NOT the tense of single complete actions in the past, but of description and habitual or repeated action. There is no doubt that " was speaking " or " used to speak " involves the use of the imperfect. Very often " he spoke " means " he used to speak ", and then the imperfect tense must be used. In using the imperfect, since the first and the third persons singular are alike, it may be necessary for the sake of clearness not to omit the pronoun.

For instance : *no sabía que vivía aquí* might mean either " I did not know that he (you) lived here ", or " you (he) did not know that I lived here ". So, while observing the general custom of omitting pronouns when possible, we must be careful about doing so with the imperfect tense.

VOCABULARY

joven = young.
delicioso = delicious, delightful.
tiempo = time.
autor = author.
naranja = orange.
aldea = village.

habitante = inhabitant.
a menudo = often.
jamás = ever.
todos los días = every [day.
feo = ugly.
soberbio = proud.

Exercise 9(a)

1. Barcelona es una de las ciudades más grandes de España, pero no es tan grande como Londres. 2. Estas naranjas no son tan buenas como las que yo compraba

cuando vivía en Sevilla. 3. ¿No tenía Vd. un auto muy excelente? 4. Yo viajaba mucho cuando era joven. 5. Mi mejor amigo es uno de los autores más célebres del mundo. 6. Cuando estábamos en Inglaterra escribíamos muchas cartas. 7. No tenemos tantos parientes como Vd. 8. Esta mujer, que es ahora tan fea, era en aquellos días la muchacha más hermosa de la aldea. 9. Cuando vivíamos en Aranjuez mi padre tomaba el tren para Madrid todos los días. 10. En aquellos días la ciudad tenía muchos habitantes. 11. La habitación en donde estábamos era de mi hermano. 12. ¿No son tan importantes estos asuntos como los de que Vd. hablaba? 13. Cuando yo aprendía español olvidaba a menudo las palabras más ordinarias. 14. Éste es el vino más delicioso que he bebido jamás. 15. Ella no es tan aplicada como su hermana menor. 16. Él bebía mucha cerveza, pero no comía tanto pan como yo. 17. Yo hablaba todos los días con el médico : era un hombre muy inteligente. 18. Cuando éramos jovenes no teníamos bastante dinero para viajar. 19. No he leído las mejores obras de los grandes autores rusos. 20. ¿Cuántos libros tiene Vd.? No tengo tantos como él.

Exercise 9(b)

1. Why is that girl so haughty? Because her father used to be one of the richest men in the city. 2. Which train used you to take? 3. Did you see that woman? She used to be very handsome. 4. Her husband came from Málaga : he had a house in the main square. 5. How many bottles of wine used he to drink every day? More than six. 6. When we lived in Seville we used to have a car. 7. These clerks are not as idle as yours. 8. I have seen the lawyer to-day : he was in your cousin's office. 9. Our cook used not to be as talkative as hers. 10. This is the finest house I have ever seen. 11. This servant (girl) was not as hardworking as the other. 12. My friend's elder brother was very rich, but he has lost all his money. 13. I was looking this morning for my brother. 14. Where was he? He was writing letters. 15. This is the longest street in the city. 16. He used to be the most skilful of my workmen. 17. He was a shopkeeper when he lived in London. 18. Every day I used not to receive

less than ten pesetas. 19. The richest man in the village was (the) son of a poor farmer. 20. In those days he had less money than he spent.

LESSON X

THE PAST DEFINITE TENSE—COMMON PREPOSITIONS

The last lesson showed that such an expression as " he spent money " would be translated by *él gastaba dinero*, if the meaning is that he used to spend money or constantly did so. But what if the spending only took place once? Here clearly the imperfect, the tense of habitual or repeated action, cannot be used. We need another. It is generally called the Past Definite (occasionally the Preterite), and can be formed, as shown below, by the addition of certain endings to the stem.

Past Definite Tense

habl-é	vend-í	viv-í
(habl-aste)	(vend-iste)	(viv-iste)
habl-ó	vend-ió	viv-ió
habl-amos	vend-imos	viv-imos
(habl-asteis)	(vend-isteis)	(viv-isteis)
habl-aron	vend-ieron	viv-ieron

It will be noticed that the Past Definite of *er* and *ir* verbs are alike throughout, as in the case of their imperfect tense. Also that the first person plural of verbs in -*ar* and -*ir* is the same as the corresponding person in the present indicative.

Tener, haber, estar and *ser* are irregular verbs and make an alteration to their stems, which become *tuv-, hub-, estuv-* and *fu-* respectively.

Their past definite is as follows :—

tuv-e	hub-e	estuv-e	fu-í
(tuv-iste)	(hub-iste)	(estuv-iste)	(fu-iste)
tuv-o	hub-o	estuv-o	fu-é
tuv-imos	hub-imos	estuv-imos	fu-imos
(tuv-isteis)	(hub-isteis)	(estuv-isteis)	fu-isteis
tuv-ieron	hub-ieron	estuv-ieron	fu-eron

For *future* reference it may be helpful to point out that when the actual stem of the verb is irregular, the singular terminations (except in the familiar second person) are nearly always those of *ar* verbs, the plural those of *er* or *ir* verbs.

The first persons of the past definite of these seven verbs shown mean respectively : I spoke, I sold, I lived, I had, I was.[1] But their imperfects may also have these same meanings. How, then, are we to know which tense to use ? By way of arriving at a solution, consider this short extract from a Spanish novel. The verbs in the past definite are italicised to distinguish them from those in the imperfect.

Sobre la llanura del mar, el cielo aparecía estriado de nubes matizadas de violeta y rosa. A las diez de la mañana el sol *rompió* su envoltura, *disipáronse* las nubes, y *comenzó* a ventar fresco. A partir de esta hora, *fué* aumentando por momentos la fuerza del vendaval. *Comenzó* a sentirse en el pueblo la agitación del miedo. Las mujeres dejaban las ocupaciones de la casa y salían a las puertas y se miraban asustadas.

(Over the flat expanse of the sea, the sky appeared streaked with clouds blended of violet and pink. At ten o'clock the sun broke through its veil, the clouds were scattered and a fresh wind sprang up. From that moment the violence of the sea wind went on increasing. In the town confused alarm began to make itself felt. The women were soon leaving their work about the house and standing at the doors looking at one another in alarm.)

Obviously all expressions involving " used to " or " was-ing ", together with expressions that can be turned without loss of sense into " used to " or " was-ing ", will be in the imperfect. Those do not worry us. It is that over-lapping of " I spoke ", for instance, which might be either imperfect or past definite, from the look of it, that is the difficulty. But from the passage above we see that the first two lines or so are descriptive, and the imperfect is used. Then something happens—once. " The sun broke through." That is a single complete action in the past.

[1] *Fui*, etc., is also the past definite of *ir* (to go) and therefore means either *I was* or *I went*.

It is not descriptive. It carries the narrative forward. It is, as it were, an answer to the question : what happened then ?

So when a past tense is not merely descriptive of a scene or a person, when it shows a complete single action, wholly over, the past definite, not the imperfect, must be used. For such sentences, therefore, as " he killed the dog ", " Napoleon died in 1821 ", or " he missed the train " the past definite is required.

" Napoleon was a great man " is descriptive, and the imperfect would be used. " Napoleon marched to Moscow " is a single action, and the past definite must be employed.

If one action is proceeding when another breaks in on it, the first is in the imperfect, the second in the past definite. *E.g.*, while I was writing, he came into the room = *mientras yo escribía, entró en el cuarto*.

One more point in this connection. " I spoke " might be expressed also in the perfect tense. The past definite is used if the action is regarded as wholly over. But if the period in which it was performed is not yet finished, then the perfect should be used. " I have spoken " would, of course, be *he hablado*, but " I spoke this morning " would also be *he hablado esta mañana*, because to-day is not yet over. Remember that a past participle cannot be used as a finite verb without some part of *haber*. " I seen " or " I spoken " is meaningless in English, so that if you decide to translate " I spoke " by the perfect, the auxiliary *he* must be inserted before the past participle.

To sum up. " I have spoken " is *he hablado*. So is " I spoke ", if the period is not yet over. " I spoke " will be *yo hablaba* when referring to repeated or habitual actions, or to descriptions *which do not help the narrative forward*. Single complete actions in the past require the past definite.

Rompía siempre las ventanas = he always broke the windows (habit).

Rompió las ventanas = he broke the windows (single past action).

Ha roto hoy las ventanas = he broke the windows to-day (period not yet wholly over).

The interrogative of " I spoke " is " did I speak ? ", the

negative " he didn't speak ". When the word " did " occurs, therefore, we shall also have to consider carefully which of the three tenses to use.

COMMON PREPOSITIONS

We know that *a* means " to " and that *en* means " in ". But *a* implies motion and *en* rest, so that " to arrive in Madrid " is *llegar a* (not *en*) *Madrid*. *En*, besides meaning " in," may sometimes mean " on," particularly in such expressions as " to be sitting (seated) on a chair (bench) " = *estar sentado en una silla* (*un banco*). In other cases " on " is generally *sobre*, which also means " concerning " or " about ". *Hasta* means " until " (of time), and " up to ", " as far as " (of place). *Hacia* means " towards ", *entre* " among " or " between ", *según* " according to ", and *sin* " without ".

There are certain common prepositions which require the insertion of *de* before the following noun. In English we say " far from the church ". The Spanish is *lejos de la iglesia*. *Cerca* means " near ". The palace is near = *el palacio está cerca*. But : he lives near the palace = *vive cerca del palacio*, because a noun follows; in other words, " near " is a preposition, not an adverb. Similarly *delante* (*de*), in front of, *debajo* (*de*), underneath, *encima* (*de*), over, on top of, *después* (*de*), after.

VOCABULARY

pronunciar = to deliver, utter.
discurso = speech.
andar = to walk.
sábado = Saturday.
río = river.
zapatero = shoemaker.
pasar = to spend (of time).

hacer = to make, do.
nacer = to be born.
duda = doubt.
vida = life, living.
ganar = to earn.
tienda = shop.
hora = hour.

Exercise 10(a)

1. El docto profesor pronunció un discurso sobre las obras de Lope de Vega. 2. Aquel célebre autor nació en Madrid. 3. Mi primo estaba sentado en un banco delante

de su casa cuando entraron los soldados en [1] su jardín.
4. ¿Cuánto dinero ha gastado Vd. esta mañana? No he
gastado más de dos pesetas. 5. Todos los días yo andaba
hasta el río. 6. El sábado fuí a la aldea para hacer una
visita a un amigo mío. 7. Hemos andado hoy hasta la
iglesia. 8. Según lo que (that which—what) dice el
médico, ella está buena. 9. Mientras yo llamaba a la
muchacha, su hermana entró con una amiga suya. 10.
Cuando llegamos a la estación, estábamos muy cansados.
11. Sin duda aquel abogado no tuvo dinero. 12. No
tenían mucho dinero cuando llegaron aquí. 13. Mis amigos
nacieron en una casa cerca de la plaza. 14. Después de
dos días llegamos al río que buscábamos. 15. Este zapatero
trabajaba mucho para ganar su vida. 16. Todos los días
pasaba muchas horas en su tienda. 17. Después de la llegada
de nuestros parientes fuimos con ellos a la iglesia. 18.
Vivimos cinco años en la ciudad más deliciosa de España.
19. ¿No viajó mucho en Francia el hermano de Vd.? 20.
Sí. Pasó dos años en París, pero está ahora en Sevilla.

Exercise 10(b)

1. When did you (plural) arrive in London? 2. We
arrived on (put " the ") Saturday, but my brother arrived
here this morning. 3. I was talking to the shoemaker
when your cousin entered the shop. 4. Have you seen
Charles? Yes. When I went to the (market) Square he
was sitting on a bench in his garden. 5. After the arrival
of the train we left the station. 6. I was born in Málaga,
but I spent many years in Tarragona. 7. Our house was
not far from the river. 8. In those days this clerk was
very idle: he used to spend many hours in the inn near
the square. 9. While she was in the street the boy broke
the windows of her house. 10. The professor is very
intelligent, and on Saturday he delivered a very excellent
speech. 11. According to what (*lo que*) this officer says the
soldiers will be here to-morrow. 12. Every day he walked
as far as the church. 13. On Saturday I went towards
the river. 14. They found the money which we were look-

---

[1] *En* generally denotes a state of rest, but it has sometimes the
idea of direction, differing from *a* in that it also conveys the notion
of penetration; *i.e.*, entering, falling into, etc.

ing for. 15. Those men who used to be as rich as your uncle lost all their money. 16. Haven't you written to your relations? 17. I wrote to my aunt on Saturday. 18. Without doubt they worked to earn their living. 19. He broke the bottle which was on the table. 20. How many years did you spend in France?

LESSON XI

PRONOUNS

In the previous lesson we dealt with certain prepositions. They were followed, in the sentences given, by nouns. Prepositions, however, are frequently followed by personal pronouns. In English we say: " I spoke of him (her) ", and the Spanish would be *hablé de él* (*ella*). Similarly we could write: *hablé de ellos* (*ellas*) or *hablé de Vd.* (*Vds.*). Likewise " of us " is *de nosotros* (*nosotras*) and " of you ", using the familiar plural, would be *de vosotros* (*vosotras*). All these are identical in form with the pronouns already familiar to us as the subjects of verbs. But with " of me " and " of thee " (should we ever have occasion to use the latter) there is a difference. " Of me " is *de mí* (*mi* meaning " my " has no accent sign), and " of thee " is *de tí*. Of course, the same rules apply to the use of the pronouns with other prepositions besides *de*. In fact, we employ these forms with every preposition except *con* (with). " With him (her) " is *con él* (*ella*), but for " with me " and " with thee " we write, by exception, *conmigo* and *contigo* in one word. But this is purely exceptional, and applies only to *con*. One further point. *Con él* means " with him ", but cannot refer to the subject of the sentence. For this we want *consigo*.

I was speaking with him = *yo hablaba con él*.
He was speaking with himself = *él hablaba consigo*.

From the writing of any tense of a Spanish verb we know the various forms of the pronouns as subject of a sentence. We have just dealt with the forms of the pronoun when governed by a preposition. There remain to be considered the forms of the pronouns as direct (accusative) and indirect (dative) objects of a verb : *i.e.*, in such sentences as "he sees me (direct)" and "he gives me (indirect object) a letter (direct object)".

Here are the various words in tabular form. You will see that many are similar to one another.

Nominative.	Dative.	Accusative.	Prepositional.
yo	me	me	mí
tú	te	te	tí
él	le	le, lo	él
ella	le	la	ella
(ello)	(none)	(lo)	(ello)
nosotros	nos	nos	nosotros
nosotras	nos	nos	nosotras
vosotros	os	os	vosotros
vosotras	os	os	vosotras
ellos	les	los	ellos
ellas	les	las	ellas

The first and fourth columns have already been dealt with. They are only included for purposes of comparison with the middle two, which now concern us. It will be noticed that there is no difference except in the third person between the dative and accusative forms, so examples will mostly be given in the third person, to make the distinction clear. We rarely use *tú*, or *vosotros*, translating "you" by Vd. This, grammatically, is third person, so that *le*, in addition to being the dative of *él* and meaning "to him", is also the dative of *Vd.*, and may therefore mean also "to you".

You probably know a little French. If so, what now follows will not greatly surprise you. In English the object pronoun (direct or indirect) comes after the verb. In Spanish (as in French) it comes BEFORE it. The only occasions on which the object pronoun follows the verb in Spanish are when we use, not an ordinary tense, but the infinitive, the gerund and, sometimes, the imperative. But this can more comfortably be dealt with in a later lesson. If we want to put "I found her" into Spanish, the order of the words will be : "I her found". Reference to the table will show that the accusative of *ella* (she) is *la* (her). We shall therefore put *yo la hallé*. The ending of the verb, however, indicates quite clearly that it was I who found her, so we can quite well omit the subject pronoun and put simply : *La hallé*. A pronoun means a word that stands for or instead of a noun. It follows that the pronoun must take the gender and number of the noun for which it stands. Suppose we were referring to a table, and not to a woman, we should say in English " I found it ". But in Spanish every noun must be either masculine or feminine. *Mesa* (a table) is feminine. So again we should put (*yo*) *la hallé*.

The accusative *él* has two forms : *le* and *lo*. The distinction between them is not strictly observed, but the best course we can adopt is to put *le* when the meaning is " him ", *i.e.*, when the pronoun stands for a *male* person, and to put *lo* when the meaning is " it ", *i.e.*, when the pronoun stands for a thing for which the Spanish noun is masculine. " I found him " (the doctor) = *le hallé*. " I found it " (the money) = *lo hallé*.

In recent exercises we have been using the perfect tense, formed by the present tense of *haber* combined with a past participle—*e.g.*, *he hallado*, meaning, as we saw, sometimes " I have found " and sometimes " I found ". We can form what is called the pluperfect tense by combining the imperfect of *haber* with the past participle : *había hallado*, which means : " I (he) had found ". Both these tenses are called compound tenses. The object pronoun comes before the verb in a simple tense of one word. It does so also in a compound tense. *He hallado* forms part of one tense, so the object pronoun comes not only before the past participle, but before the auxiliary as well.

La hemos hallado = we have found her.

In a negative the " not " (*no*) comes after the subject pronoun (if it is put in), but in front of the object pronoun.

(*Yo*) *no la he hallado* = I have not found her.

So far the examples given have only concerned the direct object. The rules regarding the position of the indirect object are the same. Normally a verb does not have an indirect (dative) object unless it also has a direct one. For instance : " I go to him " would not involve the dative of the pronoun at all, but merely the prepositional. It would be translated *voy a él.* Even in such a sentence as " I speak to him " or " I said to him ", though no direct object is in evidence, it is implied, since whatever words you said to him constitute the direct (accusative) object. We should therefore say : *le hablo* and *le dije.* In the sentence : " she wrote me a letter " the real meaning is : " she wrote a letter (direct) to me (indirect) ". We should therefore put : *me escribió una carta.* Another use of the dative pronoun is to represent the person for whose benefit or profit something is done : *e.g.,* " I bought them some apples " = *les he comprado manzanas.*

Ser is often used with an adjective in the formation of impersonal verbs; for instance, " it is impossible ", " it is evident ". These would be followed generally either by an infinitive or by a " that " clause introduced by *que.* With such expressions the dative pronoun is freely used.

It is evident to me that he works hard = *me es evidente que trabaja mucho.*

It is difficult for me to learn Spanish = *me es difícil aprender el español.*

Here are some other common impersonal verbs :

Es preciso = it is necessary; *es lástima* = it is a pity; *es verdad* = it is true; *es mentira* = it is a lie.

Is it true ? etc., can be rendered without alteration of the words, either the tone of voice or the written interrogative signs sufficiently indicating that a question is being asked : *¿ Es verdad ?*

The neuter *ello* (it) never refers to definite nouns, but to adjectives or statements. For instance : " He says that eating snails is good for the health, but I do not believe in it " = *no creo en ello* (*i.e.,* in the eating of snails as a step towards good health). Similarly, when you hear a row in the street, you say " What is it ? "—meaning " What is it all about ? "—without reference to some definite noun. So in Spanish *¿ Qué es ello ?* Again, " I believe it " (referring to some statement) = *Lo creo.* This *lo* is, of course, not to be confused with the accusative *lo* or *le* of *él* referred to previously, and standing for a definite masculine noun. There is a good deal more to be said about object pronouns, particularly in the matter of distinguishing between *le* meaning " him " and *le* meaning " you ". But this lesson has already given you a lot to think about, and we will leave further points for the next one. Meanwhile, refer constantly to the table when in doubt, and you will soon master the various forms. The exercises below will give you a good deal of practice.

Vocabulary

venir = to come.	*¿ cómo ?* = how ?
suceder = to happen.	*nada* = nothing.
prometer = to promise.	*sé* = I know.
satisfecho = satisfied, pleased.	*regalo* = present.
gusto = pleasure.	*entender* = to understand.
interesante = interesting.	*estudiar* = to study.
bien (adv.) = well.	

Exercise 11(a)

1. Mi padre me ha dado un reloj de oro.   2. Voy a hacer una visita a mi primo : ¿ quiere Vd. venir conmigo?   3. ¿ Por qué ha venido Vd. sin ella ?   4. Me es siempre imposible entender lo que nos dice el médico.   5. ¡ Qué casa tan deliciosa !   ¿ Cómo la llama Vd. ?   6. ¿ Dónde está la hija de Vd. ?   No (lo) sé, pero yo la llamaré.   7. He perdido mi bolsillo.   ¿ Lo ha visto Vd. ?   8. Sí.   Lo he hallado en la calle y lo he dado a su marido.   9. Me es preciso trabajar mucho para ganar mi vida.   10. ¿ Escribe Vd. a su madre?   No.   Le escribí el sábado.   11. Los hijos del general están muy satisfechos porque les ha comprado un auto.   12. El profesor pronunció un discurso muy interesante :   lo escuchamos con mucho gusto.   13. El abogado me dice que el hijo del médico está en Madrid. ¿ Es verdad ?   14. Es mentira.   Mi vecino le ha visto esta mañana.   15. ¿ Qué ha sucedido a Carlos?   16. ¿ Qué le ha sucedido ?   Nada.   Está muy bueno.   17. Aquellas mujeres no tienen dinero.   Les he dado dos pesetas.   18. ¿ La carta de Vd. ?   No la he recibido.   19. Me es imposible estudiar mientras Vds. hablan.

Exercise 11(b)

1. I am going to see the farmer : do you want to come with me? 2. Why has she not come with him? 3. He says that he will buy her a present. 4. Where did you find my handkerchiefs? We found them underneath the table in your room. 5. Here are the books which I bought him. 6. I used to have a gold pencil but I sold it on Saturday. 7. I did not give them a present because they were not polite. 8. I saw her this morning while I was walking towards the river. 9. We will write to them to-morrow. 10. It is difficult for us to listen to the birds. 11. If you give (*da*) him a car he will sell it. 12. He used to speak to us every day. 13. It is true that I did not receive the present which he had promised me. 14. He says that the train has left the station, but I don't believe it. 15. Where are your neighbours? We have not seen them. 16. It is impossible for us to understand what you say. 17. I do not know what (that which) has happened to them. 18. It is true that he sold his house, but I did not buy it. 19. He lost his money and he had not found it when I went into his room this morning. 20. Why have you not sold them?

LESSON XII

OBJECT PRONOUNS—REFLEXIVE VERBS

It was pointed out, in the lesson on possessives, that *su* may mean his, her, its, your, their. To make the meaning clear, the appropriate personal pronoun was substituted for *su* and *de* put before it : e.g., *el sombrero de él* (*de Vd.*) instead of *su sombrero*.

A similar device is also used with object pronouns. *Le*, for instance, as a glance at the table shows, might be the masculine accusative of *él* or the dative of either *él* or *ella*. In other words, it may mean him, to him, or to her. But this is not all. Since *Vd.*, the usual translation of "you", is third person, *le* may also mean "you" or "to you". Obviously this is liable to lead to confusion, for *le veo* may mean either " I see him " or " I see you ". Fortunately the difficulty is easily overcome.

When the NOUN object of a verb is a person, we put the preposition *a* before it. *Yo veo a la mujer (al hombre)* = I see the woman (the man). Adapting this practice to pronouns, we make the meaning of *le* clear by writing *le veo a él* if it means " I see him ", and *le veo a Vd.* if the meaning is " I see you ".

NOTE, however, that the *le* MUST be put in. You cannot simply say : *veo a Vd.* It is true that you would put *voy a Vd.* = I go to you, but that is quite different. " To go " is complete in itself : it has no object at all. But in " I see you " the pronoun is the object : the *le* is essential, the *a Vd.* an accessory to make the meaning clear. The *le* comes in its normal position before the verb, the *a Vd.* after the verb (though, in cases of great emphasis, it may be put at the beginning of the sentence). But the normal order is this : *no le he mandado a él* = I have not sent him.

This repetition of the object in the prepositional form of the pronoun is not confined only to sentences in which *le* occurs : it is used with the other object pronouns as well. You see, at best, *me, nos*, etc., are very weak-sounding and short. They will not convey the most meagre degree of emphasis, so, to make them more robust, the repetition method is employed, using the various forms of the pronoun used after prepositions which we already know. " It seems to me " might be simply *me parece*, but the phrase would acquire far more " body " if it were rendered *me parece a mí*. Again, using another impersonal verb, *importar* (to matter, to be important), " what does it matter to us ? " would be : *¿ qué nos importa a nosotros ?*

REFLEXIVE VERBS

In the majority of sentences the subject and object of a verb refer to different persons or things, as in such phrases as " I see you," " he sees me ", or " I kill him ". But sometimes the subject and object refer to the SAME person or thing : *e.g.*, " I kill myself ". Verbs of this kind are called reflexive verbs. A fencing foil that is flexible will bend under pressure until the tip of the blade meets the hilt. So here the object " bends back ", as it were, and refers to the subject.

The pronoun *le* means many things, as we have seen, but it is not reflexive. *El le mata* means that he (A) kills him (B). It does not mean he kills himself. For this we want *se* (as in French), which is both singular and plural and covers all third-person forms in reflexive verbs. Since *Vd.* is grammatically third person, *se* will also mean yourself or yourselves, in addition to himself, herself, itself, themselves and oneself. The ordinary object pronouns do duty for the other persons. The present tense of the verb *matar* (to kill) used reflexively would therefore run as follows :

yo me mato = I kill myself.
(*tú te matas*) = (thou killest thyself).
Vd. (*él, ella*) *se mata* = you (he, her) kill(s) yourself, (himself, herself).
nosotros nos matamos = we kill ourselves.
(*vosotros os matáis*) = (you kill yourselves).
Vds. (*ellos, ellas*) *se matan* = you (they) kill yourselves (themselves).

Such verbs, of course, can be used also in the ordinary way : *i.e.*, not reflexively. *La mató* (*a ella*) = he killed her. In their compound tenses reflexive verbs follow the same order of words as other verbs.

El no se ha defendido = he has not defended himself.
¿ No se ha lastimado el niño ? = hasn't the child hurt himself ?

You must remember that the word " myself " is not always reflexive. In the sentence " I see myself ", myself is the object referring to the same person as the subject, and is therefore reflexive. But if you said " I saw him myself ", " him " is the object and " myself " is only an intensification of the subject, and would be rendered by *mismo* (*-ma, -mos, -mas*). So the first would be *me veo*, and the second *yo mismo le he visto*, though there are alternative ways of putting it.

" He speaks of me " is *habla de mí*.   " I speak of myself " is *hablo de mí*. In other words, the forms of reflexive pronouns after prepositions are the same as those of ordinary personal pronouns after prepositions. But just as in reflexive verbs we use *se* in the third person, where in an ordinary verb we should put *le, la, los or las*, so also the reflexive form of the third person after prepositions is *sí*. "He speaks of himself" = *habla de sí*. "You (they) speak of yourselves (themselves)" = *Vds. (ellos) hablan de sí*.

Just as *mí* and *tí* governed by *con* become *conmigo, contigo*, so does *sí* take the form *consigo*.

Are you talking to yourself? = *¿ Habla Vd. consigo ?*

Reflexive pronouns can, of course, be indirect (dative) as well as direct (accusative) objects.

Me he comprado un regalo = I have bought myself (dative) a present (accusative).
Ella se enseñó el inglés = she taught herself English.

The Conditional

In an earlier lesson we learned that the imperfect indicative could be formed by adding certain endings to the STEM. The imperfect endings of the *er* verbs were identical with those of *ir* verbs. In the conditional, *ar, er* and *ir* verbs all have the same endings that *er* and *ir* verbs have in the imperfect. The conditional (I should or would take, eat, live) is formed by adding these endings to the INFINITIVE.

Present Conditional

yo tomar-ía	comer-ía	vivir-ía
(tú tomar-ías)	(comer-ías)	(vivir-ías)
Vd. (él) tomar-ía	comer-ía	vivir-ía
nosotros tomar-íamos	comer-íamos	vivir-íamos
(vosotros tomar-íais)	(comer-íais)	(vivir-íais)
Vds. (ellos) tomar-ían	comer-ían	vivir-ían

Vocabulary

aguardar = to wait for, expect. *ocultar* = to hide.
quitar = to take off. *detrás de* = behind.

OBJECT PRONOUNS—REFLEXIVE VERBS 73

robar = to steal.
ladrón = robber.
guardia civil (masc.) = policeman.
mozo = porter.
llevar [1] = to carry.

sobretodo = over-coat.
zapato = shoe.
baúl = trunk (luggage).

Exercise 12(a)

1. Aquí está el regalo que le he comprado a Vd. 2. El se ha comprado un sobretodo. 3. Cuando llegaron los guardias civiles se ocultó el ladrón detrás de la puerta. 4. El ladrón me ha robado el sombrero. 5. El se quitó los zapatos. 6. Le aguardaré a Vd. delante de la iglesia. 7. No me parece a mí que estos libros son muy interesantes. 8. No sé por qué esta pobre mujer se ha matado. 9. Le prometí a él que Vd. le aguardaría. 10. ¿No los recibiría Vd. a ellos? 11. ¿No la ha llamado Vd. a ella? 12. Ella se llama Mercedes. 13. Yo llamaré a Juan : está en el jardín. 14. El me ha dado a mí el dinero que le prometió a Vd. 15. ¿Sabe Vd. lo que le ha sucedido a ella? Ha perdido el tren. 16. ¿Qué le importa a ella? 17. No creo que estos niños se han lastimado. 18. Su madre está mala pero ella misma está buena. 19. Este hombre es muy inteligente, pero habla siempre de sí. 20. Llevaron consigo sus baules.

Exercise 12(b)

1. Didn't you see us this morning? 2. I shall buy myself a car. 3. We have bought him a present. 4. He hid himself underneath the table. 5. We shall expect you (plural) to-morrow. 6. Did you not expect me to-day? 7. It seems to me that you do not listen to him. 8. We did not promise them any presents. 9. He took off his overcoat (refer to previous exercise, sentence 5). 10. I will take off your shoes. 11. Has the policeman hurt himself? 12. I myself killed the robbers. 13. It doesn't matter to me. 14. I will call him myself. 15. My eldest brother is called John. 16. They promised that they would wait for me. 17. Why have you given him the letter which I wrote to you? 18. It is not true that she

[1] *Llevar* means to carry from one place to somewhere further off, *traer* to bring nearer to the speaker.

killed herself. 19. He talked of himself but I did not listen to him. 20. He does not give me as many presents as he buys you.

LESSON XIII

THE OBJECT PRONOUN (*concluded*)

Hitherto we have dealt only with a single pronoun object. But it is quite possible for both the indirect (dative) and direct (accusative) objects of a verb to be pronouns. " He has given it to me " is a case in point. Here the same general principle still holds good. Both pronouns come before the verb. But what about the order ? Are we to put *lo me ha dado* or *me lo ha dado* ? Actually the latter is correct. Hence the following rule :—

When there are two object pronouns the DATIVE comes before the ACCUSATIVE (though, to be strictly accurate, in reflexive verbs *se* comes first of the two, whatever its case).

Nos lo prestará = he will lend it to us.

Now for the next step. *Le* means " to him " or " to you ". It follows that in many sentences both direct and indirect objects will be of the third person. Instead of " he will lend it to us ", we also want to be able to say " I will lend it to him " or " I will lend it to you ". We should thus expect to put : *yo le lo prestaré*. But here we are wrong. The two short words both beginning with the same letter sound awkward and confusing, so this further rule is made :—

. When both objects are in the third person, the dative (which will by the previous rule come first of the two) is rendered by *se*, whether for singular or plural. Therefore, for " I will lend it (acc.) to him (dative) ", we write : (*yo*) *se lo prestaré*. This change from *le* to *se* takes place only when both object pronouns are in the third person.

Se, then, stands here for *le*, and *le* may mean either " to him " or " to you ". So, as in the previous lesson, we add the appropriate form of the pronoun preceded by *a* to make the meaning clear. Thus the final result is : *(yo) se lo prestaré a él (a Vd.*, etc.). *Se* used REFLEXIVELY can, of course, be intensified like the other object pronouns :—

Me engañó a mí = he deceived me.
Se engañó a sí = he deceived himself.

The *se* used in *se lo prestaré* is not reflexive, but a substitute for *le*, so the addition is *a él* (or *a Vd.*), not *a sí*, as in the reflexive sentence.

One further point. Both pronouns can come before the verb only if the direct object is of the third person. If it is of the first person or second (though this will not arise for us, since we translate " you " by *le*, which is third person), then the dative object must come after the verb.

For instance : " they will introduce her to me " = *me la presentarán*, because " her ", the direct object, is of the third person. But for : " they will introduce me to her " we should have to put : *me presentarán a ella*. This necessity does not often arise, but it is as well to know how to cope with it.

The ordinary translation of " I will give it to your brother " is *lo daré al hermano de Vd*. But it is quite common to find a dative pronoun inserted : i.e., *se* (substituted for *le*) *lo daré*, and then *al hermano de Vd*. This *se* is quite unnecessary, since the dative object is a noun, not a pronoun; but you must be prepared to encounter it in your reading, and remember that the *se* is not to be translated.

There is one more case when the prepositional form of the pronoun is required, this time instead of, not as well as, the other. This is when there is no verb expressed.

For whom are you looking? = *¿a quién busca Vd.?* Suppose the answer is " him ". We might make a whole sentence and say : *le busco (a él)*. But if we simply say " him ", we cannot render it in Spanish by the one word *le*, because there is no verb *expressed* of which it can be the object. So we should use the prepositional form and say : *a él*.

Again : " He likes the cook more than me " = *quiere más a la cocinera que a mí* (and not *me*, because there is no verb expressed before which it can be put).

THE IMPERATIVE

When you command anyone to do anything, you are using the imperative. Furthermore, since you are addressing them, you are necessarily using the second person. The imperative proper therefore exists only in the second person singular and plural. Thus : " speak ! " is *habla*, or in the plural, *hablad*. Now, these are the *tú* and *vosotros* forms which we, as foreigners, are practically never going to use. Nevertheless, we do want to be able to order, or at all events ask, somebody to do something. The missing forms of the imperative that we want are borrowed from the present subjunctive. While we are at it, we also take the first person plural, which allows us to say : " let us speak, eat, live, etc.". We have then :

Speak (sing.) .	hable Vd.	coma Vd.	viva Vd.
Let us speak .	hablemos	comamos	vivamos
Speak (plural) .	hablen Vds.	coman Vds.	vivan Vds.

We shall find, in practice, that we seldom give commands, but we make requests. For this we shall want the imperative (*i.e.*, subjunctive) of *tener* and *hacer* (to do) in the expressions : *tenga Vd. la bondad de* = have the kindness to. *Hágame Vd. el favor de* = do me the favour of.

In this second sentence you will see that " do me " is rendered by *hágame*. In other words, the dative pronoun *me* is after the verb, not in front of it. What is the explanation ? It is this : The object pronoun of a verb in the infinitive or in the imperative affirmative follows the verb. The same holds good also of the gerund or present participle, but it will be as well to delay consideration of this for the moment. In the light of this new piece of information it should not be difficult to master the matter from the following examples :—

I see him (you) = *le veo a él* (*a Vd.*).
I want to write to him = *quiero escribirle*.

NOTE that the object pronoun is joined on to the infinitive and forms one word with it.

Have the kindness to (or, please) buy me a paper =
tenga Vd. la bondad de comprarme un periódico.
Escríbales Vd. al instante. = write to them at once.

When the direct and indirect objects are both pronouns,
they both follow the infinitive and imperative affirmative
with the dative first. They can be intensified, too, in the
normal way :—

Cómpremelos Vd. = buy them for me.
Enséñeselo Vd. a ellos = teach it to them.

(NOTE that the addition of the pronouns does not alter
the stress of the verb. In *compren* the stress falls on the
first syllable, in *cómpremelos*, as we still want the stress
on the first syllable, the accent mark must be supplied,
otherwise it would fall on *me*.)

When the imperative is NEGATIVE, the pronouns (as in
French) follow the general rule and come before the verb
in the ordinary way :—

Dénmelo Vds. = give it to me.
No me lo den Vds. = don't give it to me.

Since, grammatically, *dénmelo* means " may you give ",
rather than simply " give ", the *Vd.* is generally supplied.
This, of course, applies to all other imperative verbs.

VOCABULARY

página = page.	*fósforo* = match.
novela = novel.	*fumar* = to smoke.
en casa = at home.	*enviar* = to send.
dar = to give.	*sino* = but.

Sino means " but " in the sense of " but on the contrary ",
and is used after a negative statement.

Exercise 13(a)

1. Hágame Vd. el favor de leerme unas páginas de esta
novela. 2. ¿Está en casa el hermano de Vd? Quiero
hablarle de un asunto importante. 3. No me lo den Vds.
a mí, dénselo a él. 4. No hablo el español, pero ella ha

prometido enseñármelo. 5. Tenga Vd. la bondad de traerme esos fósforos, quiero fumar. 6. Estos cuchillos son míos. Mi padre me los envió de Madrid. 7. No sé dónde está mi amigo : me es imposible escribirle. 8. ¿Quién es esa muchacha ? Hágame Vd. el favor de presentarme a ella. 9. ¿Cuándo nos lo prestará Vd. a nosotros ? 10. Ellos quieren comprar mi casa, pero yo no quiero vendérsela. 11. Ocultémonos detrás de la puerta. 12. No nos ocultemos allí : sería mejor quedarnos aquí. 13. Los que engañan a los otros se engañan a menudo a sí mismos. 14. Aquí está su sobretodo. ¿Quiere Vd. prestármelo ? 15. No se lo hemos dado a Vd., sino a él. 16. No me haga Vd. a mí este favor, hágaselo a ella. 17. Si Vd. quiere comprar este auto yo se lo venderé. 18. No me presente Vd. a él, sino a ella. 19. Este caballo será mañana de Vd. Yo sé que él se lo ha prometido. 20. No me quite Vd. este periódico : quiero leerlo.

Exercise 13(b)

1. I will send them to you. 2. He wishes to give them to me. 3. Have the kindness to give them to him. 4. Do not send it to me, send it to him. 5. Let us walk as far as the river. 6. Is your friend at home ? 7. I wish to see him. 8. If you have not got this novel I will lend it to you. 9. I will not give it to him, but to you. 10. I will introduce you to her. 11. I will send them to you. 12. It is impossible for me to send it to you. 13. They have deceived themselves. 14. My matches are on the table in my room : please bring them to me. 15. He did not sell it to us. 16. Please introduce him to me. 17. It will not be easy to teach it to her. 18. I shall not lend them to you. 19. I will give them to you. 20. Do not sell it to him, sell it to me.

LESSON XIV

RELATIVE PRONOUNS

The commonest relative pronoun in Spanish is *que*. We have already encountered the word, both as a relative and as a conjunction (that), and with the meaning of " than " in comparisons. As a relative pronoun it is translated as who, whom, that, and sometimes as which. It applies to persons or things, and can be either the subject or object of a verb. But relative pronouns in Spanish (or French) can NEVER be left out, as they frequently are in English :—

The things (that) he says = *las cosas que dice.*
The book which is on the table = *el libro que está sobre la mesa.*
The man who is here = *el hombre que está aquí.*

Que, governed by a preposition, is used in reference to THINGS :—

The matters of which they spoke = *los asuntos de que hablaron.*

Que, governed by a preposition, cannot refer to people. It is much the same in English. We can put : " the man (that) I saw ". We cannot put : " the man from that I bought my car ". We must use " whom ". Similarly in Spanish, the relative governed by a preposition and referring to a person is *quien* (plural *quienes*).

NOTE that the absence of the accent sign distinguishes relative pronouns from interrogatives. Even when *a* has no dative force, but is merely inserted to distinguish the object, *a quien* is preferable to *que* :—

El hombre a quien he visto = the man (whom) I saw.
Es un hombre a quien no importa nada = he is a man to whom nothing matters.

" Who (whom) " used after some part of TO BE, following a noun or pronoun, is likewise *quien* (not *que*) :—

It is he who built this house = *es él quien ha edificado esta casa.*
It is I who killed him = *soy yo quien le he matado (a él).*

NOTICE, in passing, that " it is I " is not *es yo*, but *soy yo*. Similarly, " it is we " = *somos nosotros*, and the verb in the relative sentence following would be in the same person as that of the word to which *quien* (*quienes*) refers :—

Somos nosotros quienes le hemos matado.

Another form of the relative is *el cual* (*la cual*, *los cuales*, *las cuales*). This is substituted for *quien* or *que* in the following circumstances :—

Firstly, when the relative is governed by a preposition of more than one syllable, or by *por*. This last is included since *por que* would be mistaken for " because " :—

The river towards which we are walking = *el río hasta el cual andamos*.
The door behind which they hid = *la puerta detrás de la cual se ocultaron*.

Secondly, *el cual* is used when *que* does not stand next to, or at least very close to, its antecedent : *i.e.*, the word to which it refers. *El cual* has various different forms, *que* only one, so *el cual* is used to make the meaning of the relative clear, whenever it is separated from its antecedent.

Consider this sentence :—

The prince used to give audiences in the garden of the palace which belonged to his father.

Here " which " clearly refers to the palace and comes next to it.

So we can put : *el príncipe daba audiencias en el jardín del palacio que pertenecía a su padre*.

Now, with a slight alteration :—

The prince used to give audiences in the garden of the palace to which he invited his subjects.

Here " which " does not refer to the palace garden, but to the audiences. *Que* cannot be used, as it must refer to the noun nearest before it.

So we put : *el príncipe daba audiencias en el jardín del palacio a las cuales convidaba a sus súbditos*.

And thirdly : the prince used to give audiences in the palace gardens : which pleased his subjects very much.

Here what pleased his subjects was not the audiences, nor the garden, but the actual giving of the entertainment. " Which " refers to no definite noun, but to the whole idea, and we use *lo que* (" the which " or " that which ") already introduced in previous lessons. *El príncipe daba audiencias en el jardín del palacio : lo que (les) agradaba mucho a sus súbditos*.

Sometimes the sentence may be rearranged so as to

bring the relative next to its antecedent, in which case, of course, *que* can be used :—

> He had a house in the main street which gave on to the river.

Here, obviously, it is the house, not the street, which had the view on the river. So, altering the order slightly, we can say : *Tenía en la Calle Mayor una casa que daba al río.*

In dealing with interrogatives we saw that " which (which one) ? " was *¿ cuál (cuáles) ?*

> Which of the two houses will you buy ? = *¿ cuál de las dos casas comprará Vd. ?*

In indirect questions the interrogative *cuál*, not the relative *el cual*, is likewise used.

> I do not know which of the two houses I shall buy = *no sé cuál de las dos casas compraré.*

El cuál may be followed by a noun as in English. " Which house ? " is *¿ cuál de las casas ?* This is interrogative. The relative *el cual* with a noun is less common. But it might occur in such a sentence as this : He lived many years in Paris, in which city he had many friends = *Vivió durante muchos años en París, en la cual ciudad tenía muchos amigos.* But one could more easily say : *En París, ciudad en que* (or *en donde*) *tenía muchos amigos.*

It has already been pointed out that in relative sentences the subject frequently follows the verb. There are occasions when it cannot, though these are beyond the scope of this book. So for most practical purposes you may say that in relative clauses the subject is most elegantly placed after the verb.

The Relative " Whose "

Cuyo (*-a, -os, -as*) means " whose " or " of which ", and refers to either persons or things. Like *mi* and other possessives, it " agrees " with the thing possessed, and not with the owner. We can say in English either " the town whose streets " or " the town the streets of which ". In Spanish *cuyo* can only be used in the first way : *la población cuyas calles*, etc.

Cuyo, like *que*, relates to an antecedent immediately before it. If " whose " is separated from its antecedent, then *de quien* (*de quienes*) is used instead.

> These men were two of Napoleon's soldiers whose bravery was undeniable = *estos hombres eran dos soldados de Napoleón, de quienes el valor era innegable.*

Cuyo would refer to Napoleon, not to the two men.

"Whose ? " as an interrogative is, as we saw earlier, *¿ de quién* (*de quiénes*) *?* This is genitive, and means really " of whom ? " So, not interrogatively, does *cuyo*. Now, in a recent exercise we had the sentence : I will take off your shoes = *yo le quitaré a Vd. los zapatos*, and we put, in effect, " the shoes to you ", instead of " your shoes ". In Spanish the definite article (as in French) is used instead of the possessive before parts of the body or clothes. " He has cut his finger " becomes " he has cut the finger to himself " = *se ha cortado el dedo*. We have got to remember this in the translation of " whose ", referring to clothes or parts of the body. For : " the man whose wife is ill " we put : *el hombre cuya esposa está enferma* ; but in the sentence " the man whose leg I broke ", we cannot put *cuyo*, which is genitive and means " of whom ", because we have to say : " the man *to* whom I broke the leg " = *el hombre a quien he fracturado la pierna.*

This has been a fairly lengthy explanation, but relatives are always cropping up (like their namesakes in everyday life), and one must be in a position to deal with their eccentricities.

VOCABULARY

asombrar = to astonish.   *cirujano* = surgeon.
amputar = to amputate.   *cesta* = basket.
encontrar = to meet.   *frutos* = fruit (plural).
gobernador = governor.   *brazo* = arm.
agradable = pleasing, charming.   *molestar* = to annoy.

Exercise 14(a)

1. Los discursos que pronuncia el Profesor X son muy interesantes. 2. No he leído todos los libros de que él

hablaba. 3. ¿Quién tomó el lápiz con que yo escribía?
4. ¿Cómo se llaman aquellos dos niños que están andando
hacia la aldea? 5. Son los hijos del pobre zapatero a quien
los cirujanos amputaron ayer el brazo. 6. Son los hijos
del tendero, a los cuales Vd. envió ayer una cesta de frutos.
7. Ella tiene una casa muy agradable cuyas ventanas
superiores dan al jardín del gobernador. 8. Aquel profesor
ha leído todas las comedias de Lope de Vega : lo que me
asombra. 9. Aquellos hombres son los dos criados del
médico a cuya esposa hemos encontrado esta mañana. 10.
Aquella mujer es la cocinera de Carlos, de la cual yo le
hablé a Vd. 11. El ha leído la carta que recibí : lo que
me molesta. 12. ¿Es este el hombre en cuya tienda Vd.
ha entrado? 13. ¿Sabe Vd. cuál de estos libros me ha
prestado? 14. Los muchachos entre los cuales él se halló
eran amigos suyos. 15. ¿Es Vd. quien se ha cortado el
dedo? 16. Somos nosotros quienes cantábamos cuando
entró Vd. en el cuarto. 17. ¿De quién es este auto? No
es mío sino de mi hermano. 18. El hombre a quien
encontré ayer es panadero. 19. Le aguardaré a Vd. delante
de la iglesia cerca de la cual hay una posada. 20. El
general, el cual [1] nació en Madrid, vive ahora en Burgos.

Exercise 14(b)

1. He says that he has no money : which is (a) lie. 2.
That is not the man you met. 3. The soldier whose wife
you have seen comes from Toledo. 4. The soldier whose
leg the surgeon amputated is here. 5. The soldier whose
wife's arm (turn into : the soldier to whose wife) the
surgeon amputated is a friend of mine. 6. We live in a
house behind which there is a stable. 7. That girl is the
elder daughter of the lawyer whom you met. 8. The
daughter of the lawyer whom (referring to daughter) you
have seen this morning is married. 9. It was I who came
into your shop. 10. Aren't the houses cheap which give
on to the square? 11. I have not read the works on which

---

[1] Sometimes, even when the meaning is clear, you may find *el
cual* used instead of *que*. There is no need to worry about this, but
you may meet it in the course of your reading. This usage occurs
sometimes when the relative clause is as important as the main
sentence and divided from it by commas.

he gave us a speech. 12. I am going to pay a visit to the governor : which will be very pleasant. 13. The man in whose office I found myself used to be very rich. 14. It is not those workmen who are idle. 15. Our cook, who arrived yesterday from Madrid, is very talkative. 16. The matters of which you spoke are not important to me. 17. There is a house in this street which I want to buy. 18. My friends, in whose garden we are, want to teach me English. 19. I do not know which of these hats is yours. 20. Do you know which of these baskets are mine ?

LESSON XV

CONJUGATION OF REGULAR VERBS

This lesson marks the half-way stage in this little book. It will be as well, therefore, to devote the exercises to revision of some of the points dealt with so far. Thus, there being nothing new this time to introduce into the preliminary matter, we may profitably show in tabular form the full conjugation of the three classes of regular verbs. The indicative tenses we have already used. But they are here grouped together for convenience, and with them—for reference only at this stage—are the tenses of the subjunctive mood. All regular verbs are conjugated after the manner shown in the table. Those of the first conjugation (infinitive in -ar) have the endings under the heading 1, those of the second conjugation (infinitive in -er) the endings under heading 2, those of the third (infinitives in -ir) the endings under heading 3.

In using the table, remember the following points :—

1. The future indicative and the conditional are formed by adding the given endings to the infinitive (*tomar, comer, vivir*).

2. All other parts of the verb—*i.e.*, the remaining tenses of the indicative, all those of the subjunctive, the imperative, the past participle, the present participle (or gerund) —are formed by adding the given endings to the stem (*tom-, com-, viv-*).

3. The first and third persons singular of many tenses

are alike, so the pronoun subject will probably have to be inserted.

4. The first person plural of the present and past definite are also often exactly similar.

5. All compound active tenses are formed by combining some part of *haber* with the past participle of the verb in question. Perfect, *he hablado*, pluperfect, *había hablado*, future perfect, *habré hablado*, etc.

CONJUGATION OF REGULAR VERBS

Infinitive.			Past Participle.		Present Participle.	
1.	2.	3.	1.	2 & 3.	1.	2 & 3.
-ar	-er	-ir	-ado	-ido	-ando	-iendo

INDICATIVE MOOD.			SUBJUNCTIVE MOOD.	
Present.			*Present.*	
1.	2.	3.	1.	2 & 3.
-o	-o	-o	-e	-a
-as	-es	-es	-es	-as
-a	-e	-e	-e	-a
-amos	-emos	-imos	-emos	-amos
-áis	-éis	-ís	-éis	-áis
-an	-en	-en	-en	-an

Imperfect.		*Imperfect.*	
1.	2 & 3.	1.	2 & 3.
-aba	-ía	-ara	-iera
-abas	-ías	-aras	-ieras
-aba	-ía	-ara	-iera
-ábamos	-íamos	-áramos	-iéramos
-abais	-íais	-arais	-ierais
-aban	-ían	-aran	-ieran

Past Definite.		*Past.*	
1.	2 & 3.	1.	2 & 3.
-é	-í	-ase	-iese
-aste	-iste	-ases	-ieses
-ó	-ió	-ase	-iese
-amos	-imos	-ásemos	-iésemos
-asteis	-isteis	-aseis	-ieseis
-aron	-ieron	-asen	-iesen

Future.		*Future.*
1, 2 & 3.	1.	2 & 3.
-é	-are	-iere
-ás	-ares	-ieres
-á	-are	-iere
-emos	-áremos	-iéremos
-éis	-areis	-iereis
-án	-aren	-ieren

CONDITIONAL MOOD.	IMPERATIVE MOOD.		
1, 2 & 3.	1.	2.	3.
ía	—	—	—
ías	-a	-e	-e
ía	—	—	—
íamos	—	—	—
íais	-ad	-ed	-id
ían	—	—	—

VOCABULARY

tarde (fem.) = afternoon.
convidar = to invite.
por desgracia = unfortunately.
decir = to say, tell.
anteojos (plur.) = spectacles.

seguro = sure, certain.
situación = situation.
político = political.
dejar = to leave.
repisa de la chimenea = mantelpiece.

Exercise 15(a)

1. Voy a pasar unos días en casa de mi primo en Santander : él le ha convidado también a Vd. 2. Por desgracia me es imposible ir con Vd., por que mi madre está mala. 3. ¿A quién está buscando Vd.? A Juan. Quiero decirle que un pariente suyo llegará aquí esta tarde. 4. Son ellos quienes han roto las ventanas. 5. No es tan docto este profesor como lo que dice. 6. Nuestra casa no tiene tantas habitaciones como la de Vd. 7. Mi vecino dice que hay aquí más de veinte oficiales, pero no lo creo. 8. Me parece a mí que Vd. ha olvidado todo lo que había aprendido. 9. No le preste Vd. a él su reloj : es seguro que lo perderá. 10. Es la mujer más habladora a quien he encontrado jamás. 11. La botella no está llena de agua, sino de cerveza.. 12. ¿En cuál de los bancos está sentado

su primo? En el que compré ayer. 13. Esta novela no es buena, es la peor de las obras de Valera. 14. Háganos Vd. el favor de leernos este artículo sobre la situación política. 15. ¿Dónde están sus anteojos? Los he dejado sobre la repisa de la chimenea en mi cuarto. 16. ¿A quién aguardaba Vd. esta mañana? A un amigo mío. 17. No han llevado consigo sus baúles. Los han dejado en el tren. 18. El hombre más rico de la aldea es el que está sentado delante de la posada. 19. Yo no se lo enviaré a él. 20. Esta es la iglesia más célebre de la ciudad.

Exercise 15(b)

1. To which of these two boys will you give this knife? 2. The house towards which we were going gave on to a small garden. 3. There are three articles in this paper which I am going to read. 4. It will not be easy for me to send them to you. 5. How many baskets of fruit have you given her? 6. I have left my shoes in my room; have the goodness to bring them to me. 7. Let us listen to the birds. 8. I do not know how many bottles of beer he has drunk. 9. Every day he walked as far as the square. 10. Have you seen the thief for whom the police are looking? 11. The man whose car I bought is a very celebrated author. 12. The house behind which I found myself belonged to the doctor. 13. Whose is this overcoat? Yours or his? 14. It is not these workmen who are so skilful. 15. This is the most pleasant city in Spain. 16. It is true that I have bought myself a watch, but it was very cheap. 17. In front of which door shall I wait for you? 18. It is certain she will cut her finger. 19. We shall not remain here more than two days. 20. It is impossible for us to read while you talk.

LESSON XVI

FIRST READING LESSON

The time has now come to tackle a bit of real Spanish. Hitherto you have only had to cope with bits specially prepared for you and made to suit your limited vocabulary.

This being your first attempt at translation, you must

be ready to take the trouble to turn up a good many words in the vocabulary at the end of the book, but you will find that, with practice, your range of words will rapidly increase.

You might think that, with the aid of a Spanish dictionary, you could translate any passage without knowing any grammar at all. But this is not so. The dictionary does *not* give every word that you are liable to meet, particularly in the case of verbs.

Take the simple word *repliqué*, for instance. You will not find it in the dictionary. But you should by this time know enough grammar to recognise it as the first person singular of the past definite of a first conjugation verb. You will, therefore, be able to find it in the vocabulary in the form *replicar*, and the rest is easy.

It will not always be quite so simple. There is *encuentro*, for example. This looks like the first person of a verb. So it is. There is no verb *encuentrar*, but there is *encontrar*, which we have already used. The verb is irregular, or at least peculiar, in certain tenses, and it, together with others like it, will be dealt with in succeeding lessons. Some verbs, of course, are disgustingly irregular. We have our share of them in English (why should *went* be the past tense of *go*?). In this passage the word *dispongo* appears. The thing to do in this case is to turn to the table of irregular verbs, where you will quickly run it to earth as the present indicative of *disponer*. *Dijo*, likewise, can be traced to *decir*. You may find this difficult at first, but you will quickly get the hang of it.

Translation may be done in two ways—*literal* and *free*. In the literal translation the meaning is given from the Spanish word by word, and the English will read stiffly, and sometimes seem hardly intelligible. The free translation, on the other hand, takes the meaning of a passage as a whole and turns it into good English. You will appreciate this difference better when you come to read in Part II the two translations of the first extract.

Don't be afraid of being too literal at first. You will soon be able to pay more attention to the style of your English. A dictionary, if you have one, is useful; but it is a bad thing to be a slave to it. In any case, use your wits to try to discover the meaning of a word before checking your interpretation (or guess !) by referring to the vocabulary at the end of the book, or to your dictionary.

The Verb "Deber"

The ordinary meaning of *deber* is *to owe* :—

Me debe grandes sumas de dinero = he owes me large sums of money.

The infinitive used as a noun means *duty* :—

Hemos hecho nuestro deber = we have done our duty.

But *deber* is also used, before an infinitive, as a kind of auxiliary, to express the idea of duty, obligation or a mild form of necessity. In this sense it is generally equivalent to *ought, should, must* :—

Debo ir a la estación = I must go to the station.
Vd. debe escribirle = you should write to him.
Debía aguardarme = he was to wait for me.
Debí salir para Madrid = I had to (was obliged to) start for Madrid.

Deber also conveys the idea of inference, probability or supposition, as the word *must* does sometimes in English :—

El tren debe haber llegado = the train must have arrived.
No debe ser difícil hacerlo = it should not be difficult to do it.
Vd. no debería hablarle = you ought not to speak to him.

Translation I

By a ruling of the Spanish Academy the use of the written accent on words of one letter (*a, o*) is abolished. But in many books it is still retained, and the student should bear this in mind.

" Buenos días, Señor," me dijo el dependiente al mismo tiempo que entraba en la oficina de Turismo Español.

Mi abuelo era de Valencia y yo me parezco a él por lo que toca a las facciones y al color de la tez. Por lo tanto mucha gente a quien encuentro por vez primera cree que soy español. Me gustaría muchísimo hablar bien el español y en consecuencia no perdí la oportunidad de emplear dicha lengua dirigiéndole la palabra.

" ¿ En qué puedo servirle ? " continuó el dependiente.

" Buenos días," repliqué. " Esto es lo que me trae a mí aquí. Quiero pasar las vacaciones en España pero no dispongo de mucho tiempo."

" Muy bien, Señor. Entonces lo importante es llegar allí rápidamente."

" Eso es. Pero no quiero ir en aeroplano. Es demasiado caro."

" ¿ Qué parte de España desea visitar ? "

" En primer lugar voy a Barcelona."

" ¿ Le gustaría ir en barco ? "

" No. Siempre me mareo mucho. ¿ No hay un tren directo desde París ? "

" Seguramente, Señor. El expreso sale de la estación de Quai d'Orsay a las 8.0 de la noche y llega a Barcelona poco después de las 12—un viaje de diez y seis horas."

" Excelente. Sin duda un billete de ida y vuelta será más barato. Pero no estaré mucho tiempo en Barcelona. Deme Vd. pues por favor un billete sencillo de segunda clase. Pienso salir el viernes de la próximá semana."

After you have translated the above and carefully compared your version with that given in Part II, you should be able to do the following exercise without much difficulty.

Vocabulary

ya = already.	*modo* = way, method,
comercio = commerce.	manner.
ejercicio = exercise.	*agradable* = pleasant.
gracias (fem. plur.) = thanks.	*falta* = mistake.

Exercise 16

1. I have the pleasure to introduce you to my cousin. 2. The pleasure is mine, but I have already met this gentleman. 3. Where is Mr. Gomez ? He is not here. He had to start for Madrid at ten o'clock. 4. How many times have you read this book ? 5. We must not spend much time here. 6. When do you think of starting for London ?

7. We very much like going by aeroplane; it is the most pleasant way of travelling (infinitive). 8. I do not know what he said to me. The worst (of it) is that he does not pronounce his words well. 9. It is evident that Mr. Lopez is very skilful in all that concerns commerce. 10. Good afternoon, miss. How are you? Very well, thanks. And you? 11. There is a young lady at the door who wants to speak to the doctor. 12. Who is that gentleman? He is a friend of Mr. Fuentes. 13. It is not pleasant to find oneself alone and friendless. 14. I have taken a first-class return ticket. 15. We were to meet them near the church, at seven o'clock. 16. Many people tell me that I am like my father. 17. Shall we go by boat? I do not want to (say: want it) because I am always seasick. 18. I do not know how much money he owes me. 19. How many times have you written to him? 20. It cannot be easy to do all these exercises without a mistake.

LESSON XVII

COMMON IRREGULAR VERBS

There are comparatively few Spanish verbs that are irregular. Unfortunately some of the number are very common. For that reason the most important forms of the most widely used are given here. But do not run away with the idea that there are an enormous number of alarmingly irregular verbs. Many verbs are slightly eccentric, but, apart from those shown below, few are fantastically temperamental.

IRREGULAR FUTURE TENSES

In regular verbs the future is formed by adding -*é* to the infinitive, the conditional by adding *ía* to the infinitive. If the future of a verb is irregular, the conditional will have the same irregularity. But the endings of each are all according to rule. So, if you know the future, you also know the conditional. Below is a *complete* list of irregular Spanish futures and conditionals. There are no others.

Infinitive.	*Future.*	*Conditional.*
querer (to wish)	querré	querría
haber (to have)	habré	habría
tener (to have)	tendré	tendría
venir (to come)	vendré	vendría
hacer (to do, make)	haré	haría
decir (to say)	diré	diría
poder (to be able)	podré	podría
poner (to put)	pondré	pondría
saber (to know)	sabré	sabría
salir (to leave)	saldré	saldría
valer (to be worth)	valdré	valdría
caber (to be containable in)	cabré	cabría

It will be seen that the irregularity in most of these consists merely in the suppression of the vowel of the infinitive ending with, in some cases, the insertion of a *d.* In short, nothing very alarming.

The other tense most liable to present irregularities is the past definite. Here again some of these same verbs are the offenders. As we shall not be using the familiar *tú* and *vosotros* forms, they are omitted, for convenience, from this table. Some of these tenses have already been illustrated, but there will be no harm in reprinting them here.

Past Definite

	(yo)	(él)		
tener (to have)	tuve	tuvo	tuvimos	tuvieron
haber (to have)	hube	hubo	hubimos	hubieron
estar (to be)	estuve	estuvo	estuvimos	estuvieron
ser (to be)	fuí	fué	fuimos	fueron
ir (to go)	,,	,,	,,	,,
andar (to walk)	anduve	anduvo	anduvimos	anduvieron
venir (to come)	vine	vino	vinimos	vinieron
saber (to know)	supe	supo	supimos	supieron
ver (to see)	ví	vió	vimos	vieron
dar (to give)	dí	dió	dimos	dieron
poder (to be able)	pude	pudo	pudimos	pudieron
poner (to put)	puse	puso	pusimos	pusieron
querer (to wish)	quise	quiso	quisimos	quisieron
decir (to say)	dije	dijo	dijimos	dijeron

hacer (to do, make)	hice	hizo	hicimos	hicieron
caber (to be containable in)	cupe	cupo	cupimos	cupieron
traer (to bring)	traje	trajo	trajimos	trajeron
conducir (to lead, drive)	conduje	condujo	condujimos	condujeron

Here again there is an easily discernible pattern about the departures from the regular. *Hizo* is only so spelt because to leave the *c* would produce a *k* sound. Also *i* is inadmissible in a third person plural termination after *j*. Taking these into account, the extent of the irregularities is even further reduced.

The imperfect tenses of *tener, haber, estar, andar, venir, saber, poder, poner, decir, dar, caber, hacer, querer, traer* and *conducir* are all regular. That of *ser* (*era*) is already known to us. That of *ir* is *iba, ibas, íbamos, iban*.

There remain the present tenses of a few of these common irregular verbs :—

dar	doy	da	damos	dan
ir	voy	va	vamos	van
venir	vengo	viene	venimos	vienen
hacer	hago	hace	hacemos	hacen
poder	puedo	puede	podemos	pueden
querer	quiero	quiere	queremos	quieren
decir	digo	dice	decimos	dicen
ver	veo	ve	vemos	ven

Both *ir* and *venir* are used in the present tense, as in English, to show that something " is going " to happen in the near future. Both, likewise, require *a* before a following infinitive. " To go to see " and " to go AND see " are both translated by *ir a ver*.

Translation II

Llovía cuando salí de Londres. Pero en llegando a Dover me encontré con que el tiempo había aclarado. El sol brillaba. Hacía calor y yo estaba contento de ver que la mar estaba tranquila. La travesía de Dover a Calais duró solamente una hora y a eso de las seis me encontraba en París. Como sólo pensaba estar fuera de casa quince días, no tenía equipaje facturado, sino sólo una maleta, la cual pasé por la ventana del vagón a un mozo. Fué a buscar un taxi, el cual me condujo a la estación de Quai d'Orsay. El tren no debía salir hasta las ocho, por tanto cené en el restaurant de la estación.

La oficina de turismo me había reservado un asiento de frente a la locomotora y estaba contento de encontrar, cuando el tren salió, a sólo otro pasajero en el compartimento : un caballero español que me dijo que volvía a Barcelona después de haber pasado tres semanas en Francia.

Teniendo en cuenta que yo era extranjero, me hablaba despacio y podía yo entender mucho de lo que me decía. Como yo estaba cansado después del viaje desde Londres, muy pronto me acosté en el asiento, la cabeza descansando en una almodaha alquilada por cuatro francos a un oficial de la Compañía de ferrocarriles. No dormí muy bien, pero no lo sentí, y cuando desperté me encontré con que el tren pasaba por el corazón de los Pirineos.

Exercise 17

1. That gentleman is the only son of Mr. Galdos whom you met yesterday. 2. On arriving at the station I will come and see you. 3. After having read the paper I went to my friend's house. 4. He told us what he wanted to do. 5. He says that it will be cold to-morrow, but I do not believe it. 6. The train will leave the station at eight o'clock. 7. We were not talking of political matters, but of something else. 8. I bought this car from a friend of mine, who did not know (how) to drive. 9. He did not bring me the book I wanted, but another. 10. As I was only going as far as the church I did not take my overcoat. 11. Yesterday he did not wish to come and talk to you : to-day he is glad to do so (it). 12. He did me the favour of lending me five pesetas. 13. We must see you again. 14. I cannot find the suitcase you gave me. 15. Can you not reserve us rooms which give on to the garden ? 16. He told me all that he knew of the matter. 17. Please speak more slowly, it is impossible for me to understand

you. 18. I do not like hired motor-cars. 19. Will you come and look for my spectacles? I cannot see well without them. 20. He saw me, but I did not see him.

LESSON XVIII

THE INFINITIVE

One of the difficulties in French is to know how to translate *to* after a verb and before another in the infinitive. In Spanish the problem is not so acute. Many widely used verbs take a direct infinitive : *i.e.*, with no preposition. Such are, for instance : *poder, querer, desear, temer* (to fear), *sentir* (to feel, to regret), *oír* (to hear), *esperar* (to hope, to expect), *saber, ver, hacer, mandar, necesitar, deber, servirse* (to have the kindness to, " please "), *prometer* (to promise), *permitir* (to allow), *gustar* (to like), *parecer, pensar* (to think, intend) : *e.g., sírvase tomar asiento* = please (to) take a seat.

Add to these IMPERSONAL expressions formed by *ser* and an adjective. *Es fácil hacerlo.* But *es tiempo de salir* (*tiempo* is a noun, not an adjective).

Many expressions NOT used impersonally, consisting of *estar* or *ser* and an adjective, require *de* before the following infinitive : *Estoy contento de verle. No soy capaz* (capable) *de hacerlo.*

In many other cases the preposition to be used can be determined by the English :

No tardaré en venir = I will not delay in coming.

Of verbs requiring *a* before an infinitive the commonest are : *aprender* (to learn), *empezar* (to begin), *convidar* (to invite), *enseñar* (to teach), and *persuadir* (to persuade).

Me convidó a cenar = he invited me to have supper.

NOTE also : *ponerse a* = to begin to, to set to work to; also *echar a* = to start to : *echó a correr* = he started to run. On the other hand, *dejar de correr* = to leave off running (*dejar*, when meaning to let, to allow, takes a direct infinitive).

The verb *tener* is used, in many expressions, with a noun and *de* before the following infinitive :—

Tener tiempo de, to have time to ; *tener la intención de*, to intend to ; *tener la bondad de*, to have the kindness to ; *tener el gusto de*, to have the pleasure of ; *tener la ocasión de*, to have an opportunity to ; *tener medios de*, to have the means to, etc.

NOTE, in passing, certain expressions in which *tener* is used, where the English use " to be " :—

Tener hambre (*sed*), to be hungry (thirsty) = lit. to have hunger, thirst (as in French also). *Tener calor* (*frío*), to be hot, cold. (*Hacer frío*, etc., applies to the weather, not to people.) *Tener miedo* (*sueño*), to be afraid (sleepy). *Tener razón*, to be right. *No tener razón*, to be wrong.

Another phrase to note is *tener que* + infinitive. This means " to have to " :—

Tengo que hacerlo = I have to (must) do it.
Tengo muchas cosas que hacer = I have many things to do.

We have already seen that *hacer* is used impersonally in expressions concerning the weather. It is also used impersonally with regard to time :—

Hace dos años que = it is two years since.
Hacía dos años que = it was two years since.
It is six weeks since he arrived = *hace* (present) *seis semanas que llegó* (past).
It will be six weeks to-morrow since he arrived = *mañana hará seis semanas que llegó*.

In each of the above examples the " arriving " is over. But in many sentences the action begun in the past is still going on : *e.g.*, " we have been living here for six weeks " (and still are). As the process is not yet complete, the Spanish use the present tense, the literal translation being : " it makes six weeks that we live here " = *hace seis semanas que vivimos aquí*. Similarly, in " we had been living here for six weeks " (when something happened), the Spanish use the imperfect for the English pluperfect and say, in effect, " it made six weeks that we were living there " = *hacía seis semanas que vivíamos allí*. Of course, in " we lived there for six weeks " the construction is quite straightforward, since the event is wholly over : *vivimos* (past definite) *allí durante seis semanas*. *Hacer* can also be used to translate " ago ". " I saw him two days ago " = *le vi hace dos días* (" I saw him it makes two days." Note the order). But, " it is six weeks since I was in Madrid " (and I'm not there yet) = *hace seis semanas que estuve en Madrid*. *Hace seis semanas que estoy en Madrid* would, of course, mean " I have been in Madrid for six weeks " (and am still there).

Haber may also be used impersonally to mean "ago", under the form *ha*. In such cases it always follows the expression of time :—

Poco ha = a little while ago.

As this construction is obsolete, that with *hace* is better.

Translation III

El dependiente de la Oficina de turismo me había dicho que había dos rutas para Barcelona. Podía pasar la frontera por Port-Bou o por Puigcerdá. Escogí la última y me alegré de haberlo hecho. El escenario era magnífico. A los dos lados de la vía, las montañas bañadas por los rayos del sol que hacía poco había salido, se elevaban a gran altura. En las cumbres había restos de nieve y arroyuelos se deslizaban por sus lados para unir sus aguas al naciente río, cerca de la vía del tren. El tren pasó por la pequeña república de Andorra, la cual hasta hace poco tiempo no tenía casi ninguna comunicación con España y Francia.

Pronto llegamos a La Tour de Carol, el último pueblo del lado francés. Entonces el tren pasó la frontera y se paró en la estación de Puigcerdá. Todos los pasajeros salimos del tren y nos dirigimos a la Aduana. Un oficial me miró el pasaporte y me revisó el equipaje. Me preguntó si tenía algo que declarar. Le dije que no tenía más que los cigarrillos que tenía en la pitillera y me permitió volver al tren. Después de media hora de espera el tren salió de la estación y poco a poco nos fuimos alejando de las montañas. Miré el paisaje y me entretuve anotando los nombres de las estaciones. El tren se paró en muchas de ellas. El compartimento donde yo iba, estaba ahora lleno y yo hacía cuanto podía para entender lo que decían mis compañeros de viaje. No era muy fácil, puesto que muchos de ellos hablaban el Catalán, que es muy diferente del Español. Por fin el tren llegó. Entré en un taxi y me dirigí al hotel donde había reservado una habitación.

VOCABULARY

el juez = judge.
alcalde = mayor.
traje = suit.
el calcetín = sock.
llevar = to wear.
instrumento = instrument.
reir = to laugh.
música = music.

cierre de cremallera = zip fastener.
bolsa (para tabaco) = tobacco pouch.
poner la radio = to turn on the wireless.
ponerse (la ropa) = to put on (clothes).

Exercise 18

1. What instrument of music have you learned to play? 2. I have been waiting for them for two hours. 3. She and I did as much as we could to teach him to sing. 4. After spending six hours without eating we were very (use *mucho*) hungry. 5. He invited me to have supper in his parents' house. 6. I bought this tobacco pouch two years ago. 7. I am very fond of music : have the goodness to turn on the wireless. 8. He put on the suit which he had bought from his cousin. 9. " You are wrong," said the judge, starting to laugh. 10. We had been waiting two hours, when the mayor entered the room. 11. I should very much like to wear socks with zip fasteners. 12. There they are ! Can't you see them? 13. I used to have a car, but I sold it two weeks ago. 14. Please take a seat. They will not be long (delay) in coming. 15. How long have you (how much time makes it that you) been looking at the mountains? 16. There used to be robbers in this neighbourhood, but there aren't any (*los*) now. 17. We were pleased to find that the sun was shining. 18. It is useless to tell me that you have nothing to declare. 19. Will you allow me to see you again? 20. I promised to lend him money, but I have no intention of doing it.

LESSON XIX

INDEFINITE PRONOUNS

alguien = somebody,
anybody.

alguno = some, any.

algo = something, anything.

nadie = nobody, not anybody.

ninguno = none, no, not any.

nada = nothing, not anything.

Of these only *alguno* and *ninguno* are variable in form. Their feminine and plural are formed according to the regular rule for adjectives ending in *o*.

Alguien, algo, nadie and *nada* are invariable. They stand alone : that is, they cannot be used to qualify nouns. They are pronouns, not adjectives.

Alguien is used of people, not of things. It can be preceded by any preposition and, since it always refers to people, requires the usual *a* before it when it is the object of a verb :—

¿ Ha ido él con alguien ? = did he go with anyone?

Veo a alguien = I see someone.

Algo means " something " or " anything ". It applies to things, not people :—

¿ Ha visto Vd. algo ? = did you see anything?

As an adverb it means " rather " or " somewhat " :—

Ella es algo habladora = she is somewhat talkative.

An adjective following it is occasionally preceded by *de* :—

He oído algo (de) interesante = I heard something interesting.

Referring to persons *alguno* means " some ", " any ", " a few ", " somebody ", etc., and, as direct object, requires *a* before it. It may be used with or without a noun :—

Busco a alguno = I am looking for someone.

Busco a algunos amigos = I am looking for some friends.

Alguno, used without a noun, differs from *alguien* in that it denotes someone already mentioned or referred to.

With reference to things, *alguno* means " some ", " any ",

" a few ". It is more definite and emphatic than *unos*, but, like it, is liable to be omitted in Spanish, where the English " some " or " any " would be retained :—

> *Algunos amigos míos* = some of my friends.
> *¿Tiene Vd. vino? Sí, tengo* = have you any wine? Yes, I have (some).

The negatives *nadie*, *ninguno* and *nada* correspond to *alguien*, *alguno* and *algo* respectively.

When these words FOLLOW a verb, they require *no* before the verb to make the negative complete. If they come BEFORE a verb or are used without one, the *no* must be omitted :—

> *No veo a nadie* = I see no one.
> *No dijo nada* = he said nothing.
> *¿Qué ha dicho Vd.? Nada* = what did you say? Nothing.
> *¿Tiene Vd. vino? No tengo ninguno* = have you any wine? I have none.

Alguien and *algo* are NOT used in negative sentences. *Nadie* and *nada* replace them :—

> I did not say anything = *no dije nada* (not *algo*).

After *sin* (without) and *antes de* (before) *nadie* and *nada* are likewise used instead of *alguien* and *algo* :—

> *Sin decir nada* = without saying anything.

Alguno and *ninguno* coming before a MASCULINE singular noun drop the final *o* :—

> *¿Tiene Vd. algún buen vino?* = have you any good wine?
> *No tengo ningún dinero* = I have no money.

but :

> *No veo a ninguno de sus amigos* = I see none of his friends.

Negatives.—As already shown, *no* comes before the verb in a simple (one word) tense and before the auxiliary in a compound (two or more words) tense. Object pronouns come between *no* and the verb. *No me lo ha enviado.*

Like *nada* and *nadie*, *nunca* (never) requires *no* when

following a verb. Preceding a verb or standing without one, it is used without *no* :—

No gasta nunca su dinero, sino siempre el mío = he never spends his money but always mine.

¿ *Le ha visto Vd. jamás ? Nunca* = have you ever seen him ? Never.

Ni means " neither " or " and not " :—

No he tomado el libro de Vd. ni quiero leerlo = I haven't taken your book, nor do I (and I do not) wish to read it.

After *ni* the negatives *nadie, ninguno, nada* must be used for *alguien, alguno* and *algo* :—

No tengo un auto, ni quiero comprar ninguno = I have no car, nor do I wish to buy one (lit. none).

" Neither—nor " is expressed by *ni—ni.* If these come after the verb, *no* is required before it. If they come in front of the verb, *no* is omitted, as with other negative phrases :

No tengo ni vino ni cerveza.
Ni el hermano de Vd. ni el mío. han llegado, or : *no han llegado ni el hermano de Vd. ni el mío.*

Phrases such as " neither do I " are rendered in Spanish by *ni yo tampoco* (lit. " nor I as little ").

NOTE also *de ningún modo* = by no means, not at all.

Remember that the English habit of answering a question with some such phrase as " Yes, I did " or " No, I didn't " is not to be copied in Spanish. If the question is " Did you see him ? " you must make your answer either a plain " yes " or " no ", probably accompanied by *señor* (or whichever form is appropriate), or you must make a complete sentence and say : *Sí, señor, le he visto* or *No, señor, no le he visto.* Another common affirmative is *ya* (already), in such a phrase as : Yes, I should think so ! = *ya lo creo.*

Translation IV

El hotel donde yo me hospedaba estaba situado en una gran avenida conocida por las Ramblas, que se dirige desde el puerto hasta una magnífica plaza llamada Plaza de Cataluña. El proprietario hablaba francés y también un poco de inglés, pues Barcelona es una ciudad cosmopolita, pero le dije que me hablara español pues estaba decidido a mejorar el conocimiento de la lengua. Sonriendo me dijo que era una idea excelente. Entonces subí a mi habitación que estaba en el segundo piso, me lavé, deshice la maleta y bajé al comedor. Había tomado una taza de café antes de pasar la frontera, pero desde entonces no había comido nada ; tenía pues mucha hambre. Tuve un excelente almuerzo, que consistió en entremeses, pescado, pollo, cocinado a la manera española, ensalada, queso y frutas. Yo de vinos no entiendo mucho, y le dije al camarero que me trajera una botella de vino blanco de marca recomendable. Y en efecto, era admirable.

Después de comer descansé un rato en mi habitación. Y salí después para ver algo de la ciudad. Entré primero en una librería donde compré una guía de Barcelona con un mapa. Estudiando el plano, me sorprendió el ver que gran parte de la ciudad es de tipo moderno, las calles se alargan en líneas rectas como las de una ciudad de los Estados Unidos.

La parte en que yo me encontraba era el barrio más antiguo de Barcelona y contenía muchos pintorescos edificios e iglesias. Me dirigí primero a lo largo de las Ramblas hacia el puerto, dominado por una gigantesca estatua de Cristobal Colón.

A poca distancia estaba un barco correo que debía salir aquella noche para Mallorca (Islas Baleares). Había también otros muchos barcos, pues Barcelona es uno de los puertos más importantes de España.

Exercise 19

1. I will tell the maidservant to bring down the suitcase.
2. He went out of the room without saying anything.   3. Is there anything new in the paper?   4. When I looked out of (*por*) the window there was someone in the garden.
5. Neither she nor her sister knows (how) to swim (*nadar*).
6. I will lend you this book, I have many others in my library.   7. If you will (are willing to) wait a little while, I will tell Mr. Gutierrez that you are here.   8. I have nothing to say to you.   9. I did not know what he wanted to do. Neither did she.   10. We have no friends in this

city : which is a pity. 11. I will never speak to you again.
12. I have never met that gentleman nor do I wish to know
him. 13. Before leaving for London, did he not say anything to you? 14. Is there anyone there? I cannot see
anybody. 15. How long have you been looking for him?
Since eight o'clock. 16. We shall have to buy a little
coffee. 17. Few men speak more than two languages.
18. Did you meet anyone? Yes, three gentlemen. 19. My
brother never writes to anybody. 20. Wasn't she afraid?
By no means.

LESSON XX

THE PASSIVE VOICE

The passive voice most commonly indicates that an
action has been completed : there is no further " action "
to expect. It is formed by any tense of *ser* followed by the
past participle of the verb in question. The participle
agrees with the subject as though it were an adjective :—

They are married = *ellos son casados.*

Remember that a past participle used with *haber* does
not agree.

Ella se ha cortado la mano = she has cut her hand.

But in a compound PASSIVE tense the participle still
agrees with the subject. There may be a part of *haber* in
the tense, but there will also be a part of *ser*. *Había sido,*
for instance, together forms a tense of *ser*, not of *haber*, and
so with the addition of another past participle the auxiliary
is still *ser* rather than *haber*. This sounds involved, but is
easily made plain by example :—

Los caballos han sido vendidos = the horses have been
   sold.

The point is that the horses *were* sold; the part of *haber*
is merely an accessory helping to indicate when the selling
took place. The whole tense is passive, not active, *ser*
being the essential, *haber* only helping to form a particular
tense of it. In passives the word " by " frequently occurs
to indicate the doer of the action, or, in one word, the *agent*.

If the action is material or physical, " by " is translated by *por*. If mental—*i.e.*, due to a process of thought or emotion—it is often rendered by *de* :—

> *El pajaro fué muerto por el muchacho* = the bird was killed by the boy.
> *El oficial era aborrecido de los soldados* = the officer was detested by the soldiers.

Actually, however, the passive is avoided in Spanish, whenever possible. Each of these two sentences would better be rendered in the active with the agents as subjects :—

> *El muchacho mató el pájaro. Los soldados aborrecieron al oficial.*

Remember, in passing, that the past participle with *estar* is purely adjectival. It conveys no idea of action, but only one of state :—

> *La puerta está abierta* = the door is open (state).
> *La puerta es abierta* = the door is opened (action).

But we have just made the point that the passive is avoided whenever possible. If the sentence were " the door is opened by John ", we can turn the whole thing into the active and write : *Juan abre la puerta.* How are we to avoid the passive, however, if the doer of the action is unknown? The answer is that the reflexive verb *abrirse* is used, and we put : *se abre la puerta*. Literally this means " the door opens itself ". But as doors do not behave so energetically of their own accord (except in haunted houses or when the latch is faulty), there is no possibility of the expression being misunderstood. So *se abre la puerta* is the correct way of saying " the door is opened ", when we do not know who is actually doing it.

We use this same construction for a large number of expressions that in English are impersonal passive. For instance : " it is said that ", " it is forbidden to go in ". We do not know who is doing the talking or the forbidding, and we avoid the passive by the reflexive, putting : *se dice* and *se prohibe entrar* (or *la entrada*). Again : " that is not done this way " = *eso no se hace de este modo*.

These reflexive forms are also used when the English

avoid a passive by using some such indefinite subject as
" one ", " they ", " you ", " people ", etc. (the French *on*).
" What is one to do ? " or " What is to be done ? " is
changed, for example, into : What must itself to do ? =
¿ *qué se debe hacer ?*

> How does one get into the palace ? = ¿ *cómo se entra en
> el palacio ?*

Similarly, a Spanish shopkeeper, anxious to inform
tourists that English was spoken in his establishment,
would write on his notice : *Aquí se habla inglés* (lit. English
speaks itself here). So with others : *se necesita un manda-
dero* = errand boy (is) wanted.

As an earlier example we said that " the bird was killed
by the boy " should be turned into " the boy killed the
bird ", the agent in the passive becoming the subject in the
active. If the agent was unspecified, we said that the
reflexive should be used. But this will not meet every
case without modification. For " the king was killed by
his enemies ", we might put (actively) *los enemigos del rey
le mataron*. Now, according to our rule, if the sentence
were " the king was killed ", no agent being specified, we
ought to put : *se mató el rey*. This turn of phrase was well
enough for a door, but it will not do for a human being. A
door cannot open itself, so there was no possibility of misunderstanding, but a man can kill himself, and *se mató el rey*
would be far more likely to mean " the king killed himself "
than " the king was killed ". Clearly some other phrase is
needed. We can still use the reflexive and put the equivalent of " it was killed to the king ", translating " it was
killed " by *se mató*, just as " it is said " became *se dice*.
Thus the whole phrase is *se mató al rey*.

Similarly : " he was robbed of all his money " becomes
" it robbed itself to him of all his money " = *se le robó
todo su dinero*. It follows that this construction is only
needed with living beings, not with things. Inanimate
objects are (with apologies to eminent scientists) incapable
of acting for themslves. For instance : *se revisó la maleta*
must unmistakably mean " the suitcase was examined ".
It cannot be interpreted as meaning " the suitcase examined
itself ", for even the most gifted piece of luggage is incapable

of doing more than falling off the rack on to your head, and then through the jolting of the train rather than by its own malevolent activity. But " the judge was seen " would be *se vió al juez*, since *se vió el juez* would mean " the judge saw himself ".

It is important to remember that many verbs used without an object in English require one in Spanish. *Acostar*, for instance, means " to put (someone) to bed ". It cannot mean " to go to bed ". For this we have to say, as it were, " to put oneself to bed " = *acostarse*. Similarly *llamar* = to call someone, *llamarse* = to be called (lit. to call oneself). There are other cases where the need for the reflexive is not obvious to the English-speaking person, but essential in Spanish. Some common verbs of this type are : *pasearse*, to go for a walk ; *sentarse*, to sit down ; *enojarse*, to grow angry ; *engañarse*, to be deceived or mistaken. Most of these can, of course, be used as ordinary transitive verbs, as well as reflexives. Compare :—

Creo que él me engaña = I think he is deceiving me.
Creo que él se engaña = I think he is making a mistake.
Creo que se le engaña = I think he is being deceived.

In the last we have the reflexive being used for the passive : *i.e.*, " it is deceived to him ", though there is no exact translation in English of this turn of phrase.

This formation of passives is so unlike the English practice that you will find it a little odd. But a glance at a Spanish book or paper will show you how very frequently it is used. Nor, when you have mastered the principle, will you find it difficult to deal with.

Translation V

Habiendo consultado mi plano, me dirigí a la Plaza de Toros. En esta época del año no había corridas de toros, y aunque hubiera habido, no estoy seguro de que hubiera ido a ver ninguna. Pero me interesaba mucho ver la arena. Un portero a quien le dí una peseta de propina me permitió entrar. Lo que más me sorprendió fué la pequeña extensión del lugar. El círculo no tenía mucho más que 60 yardas de diámetro. Retratos de famosos toreros adornaban las paredes y el programa de la última fiesta me demostraba que habían sido lidiados (muertos) seis toros durante la corrida de la tarde. Yo pienso que es un deporte cruel, pero lo mismo son las cacerías de zorros y ambos se distinguen por la habilidad y valentía. Además nadie puede juzgar una cosa sin haberla visto. El exterior era muy hermoso. El edificio era de ladrillo rojo con dos torres estilo morisco.

El paseo me había fatigado y me senté en una de las mesas de la parte de fuera de un café. Pedí un vaso de cerveza y no había comenzado aún, cuando un limpia-botas se acercó y empezó a limpiarme los zapatos. Se fijó en que uno de mis tacones estaba usado y antes que tuviera tiempo de protestar lo había quitado y estaba preparando otro para ponérmelo. Esto lo hizo en menos de cinco minutos. Me divirtió mucho todo ello y le pagué las treinta pesetas que me pidió. Compré también una corbata a un vendedor que recorría los cafés. Creí encontrar las calles llenas de mendigos pero no había ninguno, y las calles estaban tan limpias como las de cualquiera de las ciudades en que estuve antes. Comencé a pensar que muchas de las ideas que tenía acerca de España eran falsas. Ni tampoco encontré, a pesar del pobre conocimiento que yo tenía de la lengua, a nadie que dejara de hacer lo posible para contestar a las preguntas que le hacía.

Por fin miré a mi reloj de pulsera y pensé que sería mejor volver al hotel para cenar.

VOCABULARY

arrojar = to throw.	*estimar* = to respect.
bosque = wood.	*oscuro* = dark.
creer = to think, believe.	

Exercise 20

1. We never understand the questions the professor puts to us. 2. Having finished his work he went to bed shortly after 10. 3. This gentleman is respected by all those who know him. 4. Every three days he used to invite me to come and see him. 5. I am not sure if I shall have the opportunity to speak to them. 6. I was walking through the old quarter of the city looking for a bookshop. 7. I thought I was right, but it is evident that I was mistaken.

8. Before sitting down he took off his hat. 9. Books and newspapers are sold here. 10. It is well known that it is I who have set fire to the house. 11. This poor child was thrown through the window. 12. They hid themselves because they were afraid. 13. They were hidden (by someone unknown) in the darkest part of the wood. 14. We were tired when we arrived. 15. I think the train is going to stop. 16. Please call the police, they have robbed me. 17. Let us sit down awhile, I am very hot. So am I (and I also). 18. It is very warm at this period of the year. 19. Have they seen the judge? Nobody knows where he is. 20. He told me that they have not written the letters.

LESSON XXI

ADVERBS

Many adverbs are formed in Spanish from adjectives and past participles by the addition of *mente*, equivalent to the English *ly*. This *mente* comes from the Latin *mens*, meaning "manner". Thus *nuevo* (adjective) becomes *nuevamente* (adverb), meaning " newly ", literally, " in a new manner ", the *o* of *nuevo* becoming *a*, since *mens* in Latin is feminine. So adjectives ending in *o* and past participles (which all end in *o*) may be turned into adverbs by adding *mente* to the feminine singular form. Thus *perfectamente* (perfectly), *decididamente* (decidedly).

This applies also to adjectives having no distinction in form between the masculine and feminine singular: *felizmente* (happily), *fácilmente* (easily).

It is to be noted that adverbs formed by the addition of *mente* are pronounced as two words, both the adjective and the *mente* portions retaining their original accent, whether written or spoken : *cortés* (courteous, polite), *cortesmente* (politely).

Adjectives which do not end in *o*, but which yet have a distinctive feminine form, cannot add *mente*. The adverb effect is supplied instead by using the phrase *de una manera* (" in a manner ") and adding the adjective, making it feminine to agree with *manera*. Inquisitively = *de una manera preguntona* (not *preguntonamente*).

In the same way, where the addition of *mente* is permissible, but would result in a very long or clumsy sound, the adverb is not used, but a noun substituted preceded by *con*, just as we often put " with ease " instead of " easily ", and invariably " with difficulty " instead of any such word as *difficultly*. For instance, "independently " might be *independientemente*. But this is a terrible mouthful, and *con independencia* would be much more elegant. Similarly *con paciencia* instead of *pacientemente*, and *con orgullo* instead of *orgullosamente*, etc.

De un modo or *de una manera*, plus an adjective, or two adjectives, will also often help to avoid ugly sounding phrases : *e.g.*, silently and swiftly = *de un modo silencioso y rápido*.

When several adverbs modify the same word and occur in rapid succession, only the last actually takes the *mente*, the others assuming the ending they would have were *mente* tacked on to them : *Habla clara y enfáticamente* = he speaks clearly and emphatically; or *habla de una manera clara y enfática* ; or, again, *habla claramente y con énfasis*. You have therefore various possibilities open to you. The great thing to aim at is the avoidance of a jingle of unpleasing sounds.

An adverb may modify an adjective. In this case it comes before the adjective : *extremadamente feo* = extremely ugly. If it modifies a verb, the adverb usually comes IMMEDIATELY after the verb : *mira atentamente el retrato*, or, *mira con atención el retrato* = he looks attentively at the portrait.

In compound tenses the adverb follows the past participle in Spanish. It cannot come between the auxiliary and the participle as it often does in English : I have often read this book = *he leído a menudo este libro*.

Mejor and *peor* are the comparatives of the adjectives *bueno* and *malo*. They are also the comparatives of the adverbs *bien* and *mal*. Adverbs, otherwise, form their comparative, as do adjectives, by the insertion of *más* (more) or *menos* (less) before them : *más rápidamente, menos claramente*.

With adverbial expressions made up of *con* and a noun *más* (*menos*) comes before the noun : *con más* (*menos*) *diligencia* = more (less) diligently.

With adverbs proper there is no distinction between comparative and superlative. Adjectives put the definite article or a possessive before the comparative to obtain the superlative, but adverbs (single words, not, of course, *con* + noun phrases) make no change :—

Fastest (adverb) = *más aprisa*.
He had worked most diligently = *había trabajado más diligentemente*. Or, of course : *con la mayor diligencia* (*la* inserted because *mayor* is an adjective, not an adverb).

The word " fast " is, in English, either an adjective (a fast train) or an adverb (he runs fast). In Spanish likewise there are certain words which are sometimes adjectives and sometimes adverbs :—

alto = high, tall (adj.) ; aloud (adverb).
claro = clear (adj.) ; clearly (adverb).
temprano = early (adj.) ; early (adverb).

Note also the following adverbial phrases :—

De vez en cuando = from time to time.
A más tardar = at the latest.
Cuanto antes = as soon as possible.
A más no poder = with all one's might.
De propósito = on purpose.
Hasta mañana = good-bye until to-morrow (lit. until to-morrow).
Hasta luego = good-bye for the moment (until shortly).

CHANGES OF SPELLING IN THE INFLECTION OF CERTAIN VERBS

The introductory lesson showed that the pronunciation of certain letters—*c* and *g*, for example—varies according to the vowel that follows. We must bear this in mind in dealing with certain verbs. The present of *hablar* is *hablo*, the past definite *hablé*. But what of *tocar*? The present is *toco*, but if we write *tocé* for the past definite, we shall not get a *k* sound but a *th* sound for the *c*. This would alter the pronunciation altogether. Obviously the hard sound will have to be retained throughout; so, to preserve the sound, we alter the spelling and put *toqué*.

This does not mean that the verb is irregular at all. It is merely a modification made necessary, to preserve the "hard" sound, by the Spanish rules of pronunciation.

Followed by *a*, *o*, or *u*, both *c* and *g* have the hard sound, seen in the English words "cat" and "gate".

Before *e* and *i* they change their pronunciation (as does the English *c* in "centre" or "city"). From this fact we can easily make a rule.

Verbs whose infinitives end in *car* or *gar* change the *c* and *g* to *qu* and *gu* respectively before *e*.

Past Def.	. .	toqué (tocaste)	tocó	tocamos	tocaron
Pres. Subj.	.	toque (toques)	toque	toquemos	toquen
Past Def.	. .	pagué (pagaste)	pagó	pagamos	pagaron
Pres. Subj.	.	pague (pagues)	pague	paguemos	paguen

Likewise, though the reasons (to the ear) for the change are less obvious, verbs in *zar* change *z* into *c* before *e*: *alcanzar* (to attain, reach), *rezar* (to pray).

Translation VI

En muchos lugares de España hace mucho calor muy a menudo. Por esta razón durante el mediodía se cierran las tiendas y la gente permanece en casa dos horas poco más o menos. Para rehacerse de esta perdida de tiempo, continúan el trabajo hasta más tarde de lo que se acostumbra en Inglaterra y cenan en lugar de a las siete, a las ocho o más tarde. Por tanto las representaciones en los teatros no comienzan hasta las nueve y mucha gente se va a la cama después de media noche.

Barcelona es una ciudad comercial y sus habitantes son activos trabajadores. Allí nunca hace mucho calor. Sin embargo me encontré con que la cena en los restoranes, se sirve raramente antes de las ocho. Tuve pues mucho tiempo antes de cenar y me senté en un café para tomar una copa de Jerez.

Las Ramblas son una gran avenida a cuyos dos lados pasan los tranvías. En el largo paseo que se extiende por la mitad, hay kioscos donde se pueden comprar periódicos, flores y tabaco. Me divirtió el ver que también se vendian loros. Yo observaba todo esto con el mayor interés, mientras los habitantes, terminado su trabajo, paseaban arriba y abajo, riendo y hablando.

Mi habitación en el hotel daba a esta calle, que todavía, cuando me acosté, estaba llena de gente. Pero el ruido no me molestaba, y dormí bien. A la mañana siguiente, los cantos de los gallos me despertaron; al parecer mucha gente los tiene en los tejados y en los balcones de sus casas.

Me vestí rápidamente y tomé el desayuno. Leí los periódicos durante unos minutos y pensando cómo iba a pasar el día, decidí ir por tren a Sitges, un pueblecito en la costa, no lejos de Barcelona. Después de Sitges pensé visitar Tarragona, una de las ciudades más antiguas de España.

VOCABULARY

entregar = to deliver, hand over.
explicar = to explain.
pintor = painter.
cuidado = care.
correcto = correct.

amo = master, " boss ".
pegar = to beat, thrash.
conducir = to drive.
asegurarse (*de*) = to make sure (of).

Exercise 21

1. Do not touch that ! You will break·it and you will have to pay for it. 2. I arrived home without seeing anybody. 3. Do not beat the poor boy. He has worked with all his might. 4. Deliver the letter to him as soon as possible. 5. You should (must) drive more carefully. 6. He has only been learning Spanish for six months, but he writes it clearly and correctly. 7. From time to time I looked out of the window to make sure that he was still there. 8. Do not speak so fast. No one can understand you. 9. The trams passed on both sides of the avenue which extended from the river to the station. 10. Sometimes it is very hot in this city and one has to stay indoors. 11. The servant was waiting patiently for his master. 12. Many people were looking admiringly at the works of the famous painter. 13. On arriving at Madrid, I explained to my parents that it had not been possible for me to return earlier. 14. Nevertheless, I found that it was not easy for me to make up for this loss of time. 15. He has lost most

(the greater part) of his money. 16. Of all these books the one I like most is that one. 17. You will have to dress quickly in order not to miss the train. 18. Walking along the avenue, I was thinking how I was going to spend the morning. 19. Silently I approached (*acercarse a*) the house where the thieves had concealed themselves. 20. After spending two years in a boarding-house, we decided to set up house in Burgos. 21. One must work diligently to earn one's living.

LESSON XXII

ORTHOGRAPHIC CHANGES IN VERBS

Other types of verb, in addition to those mentioned in the previous lesson, make changes of spelling in certain forms. These, likewise, do not amount to irregularities and are easily grasped.

Verbs in -*ger* and -*gir* change *g* into *j* before *o* and *a* : e.g., *escoger*, to choose ; *dirigir*, to direct.

Pres. Ind. escojo	escoge	escogemos	escogen.
dirijo	dirige	dirigimos	dirigen.
Pres. Subj. escoja	escoja	escojamos	escojan.
dirija	dirija	dirijamos	dirijan.

The reason for this change is obvious, since *g* has a different sound when followed by *e* or *i* from what it has when followed by *a* or *o*, so, to keep the sound of the verb consistent throughout, the change from *g* to *j* becomes necessary. This simple fact realised, the verbs present no difficulty.

Verbs in -*cer* (or -*cir*) preceded by a CONSONANT change *c* into *z* before *o* and *a* : e.g., *vencer*, to conquer.

Pres Ind. venzo	vence	vencemos	vencen.
Pres Subj. venza	venza	venzamos	venzan.

Verbs in -*cer* or -*cir* preceded by a VOWEL insert *z* before the *c* when followed by *o* or *a* : e.g., *parecer*, to appear; *lucir*, shine.

Pres. Ind. parezco	parece	parecemos	parecen.
luzco	luce	lucimos	lucen.
Pres. Subj. parezca	parezca	parezcamos	parezcan.
luzca	luzca	luzcamos	luzcan.

By exception, verbs in *-ducir* (*conducir*, etc.), besides making the above changes, alter the *c* of their stem into *j* in the past definite (and in tenses derived from it : imperfect, future and conditional subjunctive). The endings of the past definite of *conducir*, etc., are irregular : *conduje* (not *í*), *condujo* (not *ió*), *condujimos*, *condujeron* (not *ieron*). This is rather similar to the same tense of *decir* (*dije*, *dijo*, etc).

There follow three further instances of orthographical changes which are not of such frequent occurrence, but which must be put on record.

Verbs in *-guir* and *-quir* drop the *u* in favour of plain *g* and *c* before *o* and *a* : e.g., *distinguir*, to distinguish ; *delinquir*, to sin, transgress.

Pres. Ind.	distingo	distingue	distinguimos	distinguen.
	delinco	delinque	delinquimos	delinquen.
Pres. Subj.	distinga	distinga	distingamos	distingan.
	delinca	delinca	delincamos	delincan.

We have seen that such verbs as *pagar* take the form *pagué* (pronounced *pag-ay*) in the past definite. Verbs in *guar* (pronounced *goo-ar*) require the diæresis over the *u* before an *e* to prevent the two letters from being merged into one sound, as in *pagué* : e.g., *averiguar*, to ascertain.

Past Def. averigüé (goo-áy) averiguaron.
Pres. Subj. averigüe averigüemos averigüen.

An UNACCENTED *i* coming between two vowels is changed into *y* : e.g., *leer*. He read = *leyó*, but : he was reading = *leía* (*i* accented). Similarly *caer* = to fall. I fell = *caí* ; he fell = *cayó*.

Imperfect subjunctives, *leyera*, *cayera*, etc.

RECIPROCAL VERBS

It has been shown that a reflexive verb is one in which both the subject and the object of the verb refer to the same person or thing : *yo me encontré* = I found myself. We know, too—this as a passing reminder—that many verbs intransitive (*i.e.*, used without an object) in English, are not so in Spanish, the Spaniard getting over the difficulty by using a reflexive verb, the object pronoun being untranslated in English. We can say : " the train stopped ".

But the verb *parar* is transitive, and must have an object, so the Spaniard says : *el tren se paró* (literally, the train stopped itself).

Occasionally a verb has one meaning when used transitively, and a slightly different one when used reflexively. For example :—

> *Enfadar* = to anger (someone); *enfadarse* = to get annoyed.
>
> *Levantar* = to lift (something) up; *levantarse* = to get up.
>
> *Morir* = to die; *morirse* = to be dying.
>
> *Ir* = to go; *irse* = to go away.
>
> *Reir* = to laugh; *reirse* (*de alguno*) = to laugh at someone.

A few verbs can be used with or without the reflexive pronoun without difference of meaning : e.g., *quedar* or *quedarse* = to remain.

But there is another use of reflexive verbs. When two people meet and talk, the probability is that they talk to one another, and not to themselves. *Se hablan*, therefore, will mean : " they talk to one another ". Similarly *se vieron* might mean : " they saw themselves " (perhaps in a looking-glass). But the obvious meaning is that they saw each other. Verbs with this meaning of mutual action are called reciprocal, and this, apparently, is but an enlarged use of the reflexive. But what about *se felicitaron*? As a reflexive, this means : " they congratulated themselves ". But it might also mean : " they congratulated each other ". Both meanings are perfectly sensible. It follows, then, that where the meaning is not unmistakably reciprocal, we shall have to find means to show that the ordinary reflexive meaning is not intended.

The Spanish make this distinction by adding suitable forms of *uno* and *otro*, and say, in effect, " they congratulated themselves the one the other ". In other words, the one congratulated the other. " The other " is thus the object of the verb, and therefore requires *a* before it. So the sentence runs : *se felicitaron el uno al otro*. If they were women, not men, we should, of course, put *la una a la otra*. If four or more were concerned, with some males among them, we should use the masculine plural, and put

los unos a los otros. This usage is not necessary if the reciprocal, not the reflexive, meaning is the only one that
makes sense. Another possible way of doing it would be to
put : *se felicitaron mutuamente* (mutually).

NOTE finally the phrase " to have just ". For this the
verb *acabar*, to finish, is used : " I have just seen him "
is turned into " I finish from seeing him " = *acabo de verle.*
Similarly, " I had just seen him " = *acababa de verle.*

The point to remember is that the second verb is in the
infinitive in Spanish, though the past participle is required
in English.

Translation VII

Sitges no es un pueblo grande. Se encuentra solamente
a cuarenta kilómetros de Barcelona; es decir, aproximadamente veinticinco millas, y el viaje por tren no dura más de
tres cuartos de hora.

Cuando llegué allí, me dirigí por una estrecha calle, a lo
largo de la cual se alineaban pintorescas casas, a un paseo
adornado con palmeras. Pequeños barcos de pesca pintados
de rojo yacían en la arena, que se extendía en una magnífica curva a dos millas de distancia. El mar era de un azul
profundo y mucha gente se estaba bañando.

Aquello era muy agradable, pero no quedé mucho
tiempo, pues este pueblecito era uno de los muchos que se
pueden encontrar en la costa mediterránea, y yo ansiaba
ver cuanto podía de las históricas ciudades de España.
Así pues, volví a la estación y tomé el siguiente tren para
Tarragona, que se halla a sesenta millas de Barcelona.

En el puerto había varios barcos mercantes. Los
examiné un poco y me dirigí a la calle que conduce a la
parte más antigua de la ciudad, encontrándome a poca
distancia un pequeño parque con naranjos y pequeñas
paredes con tejas de colores. A un lado ví una gran línea
de montañas. Al otro lado se extendían enormes murallas,
las cuales datan del tiempo de los Romanos, quienes
hicieron de esta ciudad su primera posesión en España.

Se veía que los habitantes no estaban acostumbrados a
visitas de turistas, pues me miraban extrañados cuando
pasaba a lo largo de las calles. Pero no presté atención a
esto, pues mi interés por todo lo que veía era muy grande.

Al fin ví con gran pena que había llegado la hora de bajar la cuesta que conduce a la estación y volver a Barcelona.

Vocabulary

obedecer = to obey.
lámpara = lamp.
muelle = quay.
norte = north.

extinguir, apagar = to put out, extinguish.
luz = the light.
coger un resfriado = to catch a cold.

Exercise 22

1. I have known this gentleman for a long time. 2. Aranjuez is only about 40 kilometres from Madrid. 3. I do not always obey the " boss ", which makes him very angry. 4. Do not put out that lamp. I shall not be able to see anything. 5. While I was reading, the light went out. 6. Do you like that carpet? I have just bought it. 7. Where did you buy it? At Fernandez' shop. 8. All the passengers had gone to bed when the steamer put to sea. 9. He believed that we had gone away in order to annoy him. 10. I had just returned from Bilbao when you came to see me. 11. Finding himself near the harbour he made his way along the quay. 12. I will ask (beg) him to choose me (that he may choose me) an interesting book. 13. Don't you see him? He is making his way along the street. 14. The servant led me to a room on the second floor. 15. Whom were you laughing at? At John's brother. 16. The two robbers killed one another. 17. We were all looking at one another wonderingly. 18. Going by train to the north of Spain I always catch a cold. 19. I shall remain here until about six o'clock. 20. No, I have not seen Charles. I think he is getting up.

LESSON XXIII

THE NUMERALS

Cardinal Numbers

0.	cero.	21.	veinte y uno.
1.	uno (un), una.	22.	veinte y dos.
2.	dos.	23.	veinte y tres.
3.	tres.	24.	veinte y cuatro.
4.	cuatro.	30.	treinta.
5.	cinco.	31.	treinta y uno.
6.	seis.	40.	cuarenta.
7.	siete.	41.	cuarenta y uno.
8.	ocho.	50.	cincuenta.
9.	nueve.	60.	sesenta.
10.	diez.	70.	setenta.
11.	once.	80.	ochenta.
12.	doce.	90.	noventa.
13.	trece.	100.	ciento (cien).
14.	catorce.	101.	ciento uno.
15.	quince.	102.	ciento dos.
16.	diez y seis.	200.	doscientos.
17.	diez y siete.	300.	trescientos.
18.	diez y ocho.	500.	quinientos.
19.	diez y nueve.	700.	setecientos.
20.	veinte.	900.	novecientos.

1000. mil.

The following points are to be noted :—

1. Numbers from 17 to 29 are very often written in the contracted form *dieciseis, diecinueve, veintidós,* etc. But from 31 to 99 inclusive the orthodox long form is preferred : *treinta y uno, setenta y seis,* etc.

2. 500, 700 and 900 are irregular : *quinientos* (not *cincocientos*), *setecientos* (not *sietecientos*), *novecientos* (not *nuevecientos*). 200, 300, 400, 600, 800 are regular : *seiscientos* etc.

3. The cardinal numbers are all invariable, except *uno*, the compounds of *ciento*, and *millón* (a million), which is,

regarded as a noun and is followed by the preposition *de* before a noun or pronoun.

4. *Uno*, identical with the indefinite article, agrees with the noun to which it refers, dropping the *o* when preceding a *masculine* noun : *Un perro. Veinte y un (veintiún) soldados. Cincuenta y una vacas.*

5. *Ciento* drops the *-to* before a noun or before *mil*. When followed by smaller numerals *ciento* must be written in full : *Cien buenos caballos. Cien casas. Cien mil libras esterlinas* (£100,000), but : *ciento cuarenta botellas.*

The multiples of *ciento* agree in gender and number with the nouns to which they refer : *Doscientos barcos. Sete-cientas mujeres.*

6. In the formation of compound numbers *y* (and) couples the last two, provided that the last number is less than ten. Elsewhere *y* is not used : 75, *setenta y cinco.* 240, *doscientos cuarenta* (40 is more than 10, so *y* is omitted). 8,367, *ocho mil trescientos sesenta y siete.*

7. In English we say nineteen hundred or one thousand nine hundred. In Spanish counting in hundreds ceases at 900. Thereafter *mil* (invariable) is used : 1783 = *mil setecientos ochenta y tres.*

8. *Un* is never used before *ciento* or *mil* except when misunderstanding might arise. A hundred is simply *ciento (cien).* But 201,000 is *dos cientos y un mil*, because *dos cientos mil* would mean 200,000.

9. *Ciento* and *mil* can take a plural form when used as collective nouns, *e.g.* :—

Some hundreds of miles = *algunos cientos de millas.*
Many thousands of books = *muchos miles de libros.*

Unas cien millas would mean " some (about a) hundred miles ".

The FOUR SEASONS are : *la primavera* (spring), *el verano* (summer), *el otoño* (autumn), *el invierno* (winter).

The DAYS of the WEEK are : *el domingo* (Sunday), *el lunes* (Monday), *el martes* (Tuesday), *el miércoles* (Wednesday), *el jueves* (Thursday), *el viernes* (Friday), *el sábado* (Saturday).

MONTHS of the YEAR :—

January, *enero*.	July, *julio*.
February, *febrero*.	August, *agosto*.
March, *marzo*.	September, *septiembre*.
April, *abril*.	October, *octubre*.
May, *mayo*.	November, *noviembre*.
June, *junio*.	December, *diciembre*.

NOTE that days of the week and months of the year, except when at the beginning of a sentence, are written in Spanish with a small letter.

The days of the week require the definite article, except in the dating of letters, etc. :—

El domingo es día de descanso = Sunday is a day of rest.
Hasta el sábado = until Saturday.

The preposition *on*, so frequent in English before days of the week, is NOT translated in Spanish :—

I will visit you on Monday = *le visitaré a Vd. el lunes*.
I do not work on Sundays = *no trabajo los domingos*.

DATES

What day of the month is it ? = *¿ a cuántos estamos ?* (lit. at how much are we ?). The answer will, therefore, normally begin : *estamos a* (we are at), equivalent to the English : " It is the —— "

Cardinal numbers are used in Spanish for the dates of the month, except for the first, when the ordinal (*primero*) is used. The definite article comes before the numeral. But in dating letters the article is omitted. If the month and year are expressed, they are linked up with the date by the preposition *de* :—

Madrid, 4 de agosto de 1938 (letter-heading), but : *el primero de febrero* = (on) the first of February.
El veintidós de julio de mil novecientos treinta y siete = July 22nd, 1937.

If the month is not stated, it is usual to insert *día* BEFORE the numeral :—

We shall start on the 12th = *partiremos el día doce*.

Some Useful Expressions of Time

ayer = yesterday.
anteayer = the day before yesterday.
mañana = to-morrow.
pasado mañana = the day after to-morrow.
ayer por la mañana (*tarde*) = yesterday morning (afternoon).
mañana por la mañana (*tarde*) = to-morrow morning (afternoon).
anoche = last night.
al anochecer = at dusk.
por la mañana (*tarde*) [1] = in the morning (evening).
por la mañana temprano = early in the morning.

Translation VIII

A algunas personas les entusiasma escribir cartas. Yo lo detesto, especialmente cuando estoy en vacaciones. Pero a pesar de todo debía comunicar a mis padres cómo me encontraba. Compré pues antes de salir de Tarragona algunas tarjetas postales. Cuando se necesitan sellos en España es muy raro que se tenga que ir a la oficina de Correos. Se pueden comprar en los cafés y hoteles.

De regreso a Barcelona le pregunté al proprietario del hotel lo que costaba enviar una postal a Inglaterra.

"Tres pesetas cincuenta céntimos," me respondió.

Compré una docena de sellos del valor requerido y rápidamente escribí unas cuantas postales.

Después encendí un cigarrillo y comencé a hacer planes. Era muy agradable estar en Barcelona, pero en el término de una semana debía volver a Inglaterra. Sabía que Barcelona no era una ciudad como las del resto de España, y como yo quería ver tantos aspectos del país como pudiese, resolví ir a Madrid.

A la mañana siguiente fuí a la oficina de turismo del Paseo de Gracia y oí al dependiente recomendar a una anciana señora ir a Madrid en avión.

"Tengo mucho miedo," decía ella.

---

[1] *La madrugada* = midnight to sunrise; *la mañana* (sunrise to noon); *la tarde* (noon to sunset); *la noche* (strictly, until midnight, but used more loosely).

"No hay por qué, señora," le contestó. "Nuestros pilotos son todos muy hábiles. Los asientos son muy confortables y los aparatos son del más moderno tipo."

No había pensado ir volando, pero después de escuchar esta conversación, la tentación me pareció irresistible.

"¿Me pueden reservar un asiento en el avión de Madrid para mañana?" pregunté, cuando la buena señora hubo declarado que nada la induciría a abandonar el suelo terrestre.

"Sólo queda un asiento, justamente," me dijo. "Cuesta 2,500 pesetas incluyendo el transporte de la oficina al aerodromo."

"Esto me conviene," le dije. "¿Puede usted decirme donde puedo cambiar dinero?"

"En la ventanilla de allí señor."

"El cambio hoy es a 167 pesetas," me dijo el empleado cuando le pedí que me cambiara £15 en dinero español. "Tenemos comisión de una peseta por lo que son 166. Aquí tiene Vd. 2490 ptas. 2 (dos) billettes de 1000 ptas., 4 (cuatro) de 100 ptas. y nueve monedas de diez pesetas."

· Vocabulary

noticia = news.	*emplear* = to employ.
aparejarse = to get ready.	*ferrocarril* = railway.
nacer = to be born.	*compañia* = company.
dentro (de) = within.	*ahogarse* = to drown.
irse al fondo = to sink.	*escuela* = school.

Exercise 23

1. As I had not received the letter I went to the post office. 2. As soon as the news had been received, all the inhabitants got ready to defend the city. 3. Cervantes was born on September 29th, 1547. 4. Some 100,000 persons are employed by the railway companies of this country. 5. More than 7 million people live within 5 miles of Trafalgar Square. 6. 257 passengers were drowned when the mail-boat sank, not very far from the Spanish coast. 7. This week 490 horses were sold. 8. They have stolen 540 pesetas from me. 9. On Saturdays I never go to school. 10. What will the date be to-morrow? It will be (the) 20th. 11. To-day we are going to Toledo, we shall not

return before the day after to-morrow. 12. We went last night to the harbour, from where the mail-boat was due to leave for Majorca. 13. They have told me that he drinks a whole bottle of sherry every day. 14. One can't go into the palace on Tuesdays. 15. I have nothing left (there remains to me nothing) of all you gave me the day before yesterday. 16. This street is called " the Avenue of the 2nd of May ". 17. It seems to me that the spring is the most delightful season (*estación*) of the year. 18. I have never read the " Thousand and One Nights ". 19. I did not lose £100, but £101. 20. We shall be in Madrid until October 10th.

LESSON XXIV

THE NUMERALS (*continued*)

The ordinal numerals are as follows :—

1st, primero.	11th, undécimo.
2nd, segundo.	12th, duodécimo.
3rd, tercero.	20th, vigésimo.
4th, cuarto.	21st, vigésimo primo.
5th, quinto.	30th, trigésimo.
6th, sexto.	40th, cuadragésimo.
7th, séptimo.	100th, centésimo.
8th, octavo.	200th, ducentésimo.
9th, noveno.	500th, quingentésimo.
10th, décimo.	1000th, milésimo.

This list of ordinal numbers is incomplete. In theory any number existing as a cardinal has a corresponding ordinal form. In practice, owing to their undue length and clumsiness, the ordinal numbers higher than 10th are seldom used, and may therefore be largely disregarded.

For instance, " the 41st page " might be *la página cuadragésima prima*. But it would always be expressed as page 41 = *la página cuarenta y una*.

Ordinal numbers are adjectives, and agree in gender and number with their nouns.

Primero and *tercero* drop the *o* when coming immediately before a masculine singular noun, or when separated from it only by an adjective :—

> *El primer año* = the first year.
> *El tercer día* = the third day.

Simple ordinals—*i.e.*, up to 10th—come before their noun. Compound ordinals (should you happen to use them) generally follow the noun. Cardinal numbers USED AS ORDINALS follow the noun. Used in the ordinary way as cardinals, they come before it :—

> *El quinto tomo* = the 5th volume.
> *El siglo diez y nueve* = the 19th century.
> *Diez y nueve perros* = 19 dogs.

We have already seen that cardinals are used in expressing dates of the month (*el primero* excepted). With the names of kings ordinals are used, WITHOUT THE ARTICLE, up to 10th. Above that they are replaced by cardinals :—

> *Carlos quinto* = Charles the fifth.
> *Luis catorce* = Louis the fourteenth.

NOTE the following collective numerals : *un par*, a pair; *una docena*, a dozen; *una veintena*, a score; *un centenar*, a hundred; *un millón*, a million.

These are nouns, not adjectives, and require *de* before the following noun : *una docena de huevos* = a dozen eggs.

Fractional numerals down to 1/10 correspond roughly to the ordinals : $1/3$ = *un tercio*; $1/4$ = *un cuarto*; $1/10$ = *un décimo*; $2/3$ = *dos tercios*; and so on.

One may also write : *las dos terceras partes*, especially when the thing of which we have two-thirds is then mentioned.

From 1/11th onwards the cardinal is used with the termination *avo* : $1/12$th = *un dozavo*; $1/100$th = *un centavo*; $\frac{1}{2}$ = *medio*. *La mitad* is the noun. The fairy-story monarch who was always so ready to give away half of his kingdom (regardless of the wishes of his subjects) would talk about *la mitad de su reino*. If he was going to cut off someone's head (another favourite relaxation) at 2.30, he would refer to the fatal hour as : *las dos y media*. Which brings us to the subject of time.

For this the cardinals are used, preceded by the feminine article to agree with *hora(s)* understood.

What time is it = *¿ Qué hora es ?* (not *está*).
It is one o'clock = *es la una.*
It is two o'clock = *son las dos.* (Note the change in the number of the verb.)
At five o'clock = *a las cinco.*
It is only six = *son sólo las seis.*

Points of time between the hour and the half-past are rendered by the addition of *y* and the number of minutes (*minutos*); between the half-hour and the hour by using *menos* (less) and subtracting the given number of minutes from the hour ahead.

Three-twenty = *las tres y veinte minutos.*
Three-forty = *las cuatro menos veinte minutos.*

The word *minutos* is often left out in conversation, particularly when used with *menos*.

One-thirty = *la una y media.*
Two-fifteen = *las dos y cuarto.*

NOTE that *medio*, being an adjective, agrees with *hora* understood, while *cuarto*, a noun, does not.

Eleven o'clock in the morning (at night) = *las once de la mañana (noche).*
It is nearly four o'clock = *son cerca de las cuatro.*

" To strike " of a clock is *dar*, which agrees in number with the hour :—

¿ Han dado las diez ya ? = has it struck ten?
Va a dar la una = it is going to strike one.
Acaban de dar las dos = it has struck two.

NOTE the following phrases :—

El año pasado (last year); *el año que viene* (next year).
Llegará el viernes próximo = he will arrive next Friday.

Próximo pasado means the one (month, etc.) just past.

In business style where we use " ult.", " prox.", etc., the word *mes* is usually omitted :—

El seis del actual = the 6th inst.
El veinte del último (or *del próximo pasado*) = the 20th ult. (of last month).

A week and a fortnight are reckoned as eight and fifteen days, both the beginning and closing days of the period being counted in (as also in French).

To-day week (fortnight) = *de hoy en ocho* (*quince*) *días*.
Within a week = *dentro de ocho días*.

AGE

We say : " to be ten years old ", the Spaniard " to have ten years ".

How old are you ? = *¿ cuántos años* (or *qué edad*) *tiene Vd. ?*
I am eighteen = *tengo diez y ocho años*.

In Spain a birthday is not celebrated, but rather the day of the Saint after whom the person is named. The actual anniversary of one's birth is called either *el día en que cumple años* or simply *su cumpleaños*. One's Saint's day is either *el día de su santo* or simply *sus días*.

MEASUREMENTS

We say : " this street is five yards wide ". The Spaniard as in dealing with age, uses *tener*, and puts the equivalent of " this street has five metres of width " = *esta calle tiene cinco metros de anchura*. Similarly with height (*altura*), length (*extensión*), depth (*profundidad*).

When there is no verb connected with the measurement—*e.g.*, " he lived in a house sixty feet high ", the adjective is used, the phrase being changed into " he lived in a house high of sixty feet " = *vivió en una casa alta de sesenta pies*. Similarly *ancho* (broad), *largo* (long), *profundo* (deep), *espeso* (thick).

After the verb *ser* numerals indicating weight, price, dimension, etc., are preceded by *de* :—

La distancia es de doce kilometros.
El precio del caballo es de treinta libras esterlinas = the price of the horse is £30.

Translation IX

Pasé el resto de la mañana explorando el viejo barrio de Barcelona. Fuí a la Catedral. El exterior era magnífico, pero el interior estaba demasiado oscuro para permitirme apreciar sus bellezas. Después fuí a ver los viejos palacios, de los cuales el más interesante es el de la Generalidad, cuartel general del gobierno.

Anteriormente fué un palacio real, pero España es ahora una república y Cataluña es hasta cierto punto un estado independiente. Los guardias de la parte exterior llevan un uniforme muy curioso que poco más o menos data del siglo catorce. En un patio interior se ven fuentes y naranjos. Cerca de la Generalidad se encuentra el palacio de justicia con una tortuga tallada en la pared, símbolo irónico de la lentitud de la justicia, lo que podía referirse también a otros paises además de España.

Por la tarde subí en funicular a la cumbre de Montjuich, que está dominando la ciudad y contemplé los edificios y jardines, restos de la gran exposición que allí tuvo lugar hace algunos años.

Hay allí un ferrocarril aéreo que va del Montjuich directamente al puerto y, cogiendo un billete de ida y vuelta, allí me dirigí.

Los barcos, desde la altura del ferrocarril, me parecían pequeñísimos y pensé al poco rato que al día siguiente me encontraría a mucha más altura sobre la tierra. Me había divertido cuando la anciana señora había rehusado el viajar en avión, pero en aquel momento yo mismo no pude menos de pensar que nunca había viajado en un aeroplano. Quizá después de todo, había sido un poco precipitado.

– Por esta razón, cuando llegué al hotel estaba deprimido; pero una buena cena y una copa de clarete reanimaron mi espíritu y me encontré pensando tranquilamente en mi viaje. Pero a pesar de eso no dormí tan bien como acostumbro y estaba ya despierto cuando los gallos, desempeñando su oficio de despertadores, empezaron a cantar.

Vocabulary

morir = to die.	*todo el mundo* = everybody.
suceder = to succeed.	*cada uno* = everybody.
ocupar = to occupy.	*la clase* = class.

área = area.
cuadrado = square (adj.).

cuento = story.
capítulo = chapter.
principio = beginning.

Exercise 24

1. The palace occupies an area of more than 500 square feet. 2. My daughter is only ten years old, but she is the first of her class. 3. The distance from Barcelona to the frontier is more than a hundred kilometres. 4. This story is to be found in the seventeenth chapter of the book. 5. To-morrow week we shall depart for Salamanca, the capital of the province. 6. The river is thirty metres wide and five metres deep. 7. That lady is not a Spaniard but a Frenchwoman. 8. We shall have to return to Madrid within five days. 9. The train is due to start at 2.45. 10. My uncle's library contains hundreds of books. 11. Henry IV (*Enrique*) of France was killed in 1610. 12. I cannot help thinking of what has happened to him. 13. It had just struck seven when I reached the harbour. 14. More than two dozen people were making their way towards the church. 15. I don't like this book. I have read from the first chapter to p. 92 without coming across (*encontrar*) anything interesting. 16. Charles IV succeeded Charles III on August 12th, 1788. 17. Everybody knows that a day is the seventh part of a week, and that ten is the half of twenty. 18. Louis XIV was 77 years old when he died in 1715. 19. I shall stay here until a little before 6.0. 20. During the summer of last year I went for the second time to San Sebastian, a delightful town.

LESSON XXV

PARA AND POR

These two prepositions are so important that they must have a lesson to themselves. Their uses may be summarised as follows :—

Por (1) indicates the agent by whom an action is performed. As already pointed out, *de* is required if the action is mental.

Este libro fué escrito por Blasco Ibañez.

(2) The reason or motive for some action :—

Por esta razón no puedo acompañarle a Vd. = for this
reason I cannot accompany you.
Por miedo = for fear.
Por falta de = for lack of.

(3) Indicates manner or means :—

Por tren = by train.
Por la ventana = through the window.
Por las calles = through the streets.

(4) Indicates unaccomplished action :—

Está por decir = it is yet to be said.
El tren está por salir = the train has yet to start.

(5) Means " in favour of ", " instead of ", or " as a " :—

Le dejaron por muerto = they left him for dead.
Estoy por él = I am in favour of him.
He venido por él (en vez de él) = I have come instead of
him.
Pasó por profesor = he passed as a teacher.

(6) With verbs of motion, but not before places, it
indicates the object of a mission :—

Le mandé por el médico = I sent him for the doctor.
Va por vino = he goes for wine.

(7) Corresponds to the English " per " in measure, rate
or number :—

A seis por ciento = at six per cent.
Gana cinco pesetas por día = he earns five pesetas a day.

(8) Is used in speaking of exchanges :—

Le daré mis caballos por aquel auto = I will give you my
horses (in exchange) for that car.
Palabra por palabra = word for word.

Para (1) expresses the destination or purpose for which
anything is intended :—

Salgo mañana para Londres = I leave to-morrow for
London.

Estudia para abogado = he is studying to be a lawyer.
Un libro escrito por el profesor para sus discípulos = a book written by the teacher for his pupils.

(2) It is used with verbs of motion before places :—

Partir para España = to start for Spain.
(*Viajar por Francia* = to travel through France.)

(3) Indicates purpose :—

Como para vivir = I eat in order to live.

(4) Indicates that something will shortly happen, especially with *estar* :—

El tren está para salir = the train is about to start.

(5) Denotes aptitude, readiness or utility :—

Madera para sillas = wood for chairs.
Sello para fechar cartas = letter stamp.

(6) Denotes a point or limit of future time :—

Para entonces estarán hechos = by then they will be done.

(7) Has the meaning or idea of " considering that " :—

Hace calor para diciembre = it is hot for (considering that it is) December.
Para ser extranjero habla bien el español = he speaks Spanish well for a foreigner.

When followed by an infinitive to denote purpose, *para* denotes certainty as to the result, *por* merely intention without conviction of success.

Trabajo por ganar la vida, for instance, would imply that I endeavour to gain my living, whereas *trabajo para ganar la vida* would mean that I work in order to live, and succeed in doing so.

Translation X

Me vestí precipitadamente hice la maleta y desayuné. Después pagué la factura. El servicio estaba incluido, un sobrecargo del 10 por ciento había sido añadido a los gastos, pero le dí al camarero 5 pesetas, con lo que se quedó muy satisfecho.

Le dije al proprietario que me bajaran la maleta y el portero buscó un taxi. Entré en él y el portero le dijo al chófer que me llevara a las oficinas del L.P.A.E.

Estaba contento de ver que no hacía viento, pero sin embargo estaba un poco nervioso. Me habían dicho que los pasajeros podían llevar consigo 15 kilógramos de equipaje, pero como mi maleta pesaba un poco más, tuve que pagar 5 pesetas de diferencia. Me miraron el pasaporte y el billete, después me pesaron. Cuando el oficial se aseguró que mi cámara fotográfica estaba en mi maleta y no en mi bolsillo, entré en el autobús, donde ya otros doce pasajeros esperaban.

Salimos al poco rato y llegamos al aeródromo. Entramos en un aeroplano cuyas alas estaban pintadas de amarillo y rojo, los colores nacionales de España. El piloto y el telegrafista ocuparon sus asientos, los motores comenzaron a marchar y el avión empezó a moverse por el campo aumentando su velocidad. Sostuve mi respiración un momento cuando un ligero bamboleo me advirtió que habíamos abandonado el suelo.

Yo no soy uno de esos que pueden estar en la punta de una roca escarpada, y mirar hacia abajo, pero muy pronto me acostumbré a la sensación. En 5 minutos estaba ya gozando, a pesar del hecho de que una o dos veces cuando el avión entró en uno de esos vacíos de aire, pareció que iba a caer rápidamente. Subimos muy alto y volamos sobre una alfombra de nubes con un sol resplandeciente. Poco después las nubes desaparecían y miré hacia abajo donde una gran extensión de terreno se veía. Parecía llano, aunque hay considerables cadenas de montañas entre Barcelona y Madrid. Por fin el avión comenzó a descender y por un momento sentí la impresión que se experimenta al bajar en un ascensor. Aterrizamos con un golpe muy perceptible. El avión se paró y salí con un zumbido sordo en mis oídos causado por el ruido de los motores, para hacerme recordar que acababa de tener mi primera experiencia del aire.

VOCABULARY

cerrar = to close.   *talento* = talent.
batalla = battle.   *partido* = party, faction.

tropa = troop.
librero = bookseller.
puesto que = since, seeing that.

asustarse = to be frightened.
necesitar = to need.
tarde = late.

Exercise 25

1. When he had killed the policeman the robber fled in order to hide himself in the woods. 2. The king had his enemies killed. 3. I hold him to be (for) a painter of the greatest talent. 4. It is said that a battle is about to take place between the troops of the two parties. 5. That remains to be seen. It seems to me that neither (*ninguno*) of the two has enough money to pay the soldiers. 6. My sister is ill, so I have come instead of her. 7. We sent my brother for the doctor, who says there is no cause for alarm (there is not for what to alarm oneself). 8. I have told my bookseller to send me all the books written by Palacio Valdés. 9. The house whose door is painted red belongs to a friend of ours who is ninety years old. 10. I need some money in order to buy a house. My cousin has promised to lend it to me at 3 per cent. 11. It is impossible for me to pay you so large a sum (a sum so large), seeing that I only earn £3 a week. 12. When I was studying to be a doctor, I lived in Paris. 13. As soon as the plane had begun to move, I closed my eyes. 14. For a child of eight he writes very well. 15. I was on the point of leaving when you came to see me. 16. He passed as one of the most intelligent men in the village. 17. For lack of time I have not read the paper this morning. Will you tell me what has happened? 18. I will do it for you with great pleasure. 19. In spite of the heat (that it made), we decided to go on foot. 20. You will have to dress hurriedly in order not to arrive late at the station.

LESSON XXVI

RADICAL CHANGING VERBS

We have already encountered certain verbs which are definitely irregular, in that in certain tenses there is an alteration of the stem of the verb : such are *haber*, *venir* and *ser*. The commonest irregularities of these verbs have been pointed out, but to meet all contingencies a fuller table of them will be found before the vocabulary at the end of the book.

We have also met other verbs which are not irregular, but which, owing to the rules governing Spanish pronunciation, make slight modifications in their spelling so as to preserve their sound consistently throughout a tense.

Now we come to another group of verbs which cannot exactly be classed as irregular, since their terminations are all according to rule. But these verbs are peculiar, in that they change the vowel of the stem whenever the accent in pronunciation falls upon the stem vowel.

This state of affairs occurs only in the first, second and third persons singular and the third person plural of the present indicative and present subjunctive—also in the second person singular of the imperative; but this will not trouble us, as, to all intents and purposes, we do not require the familiar second person form. Elsewhere the accent falls on the termination, and not on the stem, so no alteration takes place.

The easiest way to deal with this irregularity will be to divide the various offending verbs into groups according to their stem vowel and infinitive ending. From the look of a verb it is impossible to tell whether it is a radical changing one or not. Actually one soon becomes familiar with the commonest ones, but, for safety's sake, in the vocabulary at the end of the book you will find the first singular of the present indicative of any radical changing verb enclosed in brackets after the infinitive. Naturally the list will not be complete, as the vocabulary is not a dictionary of the Spanish language, but merely a list of the words occurring in this book. Still, you will find it helpful, owing to the impossibility of recognising one of these verbs at sight. For instance : *alcanzar* has a present indicative, *alcanzo*. One therefore naturally expects *empezar* to take the form *empezo*. But this is wrong. The correct form is *empiezo*, present subjunctive *empiece*. One would expect *empieze*, but we have got to remember, as was pointed out in dealing with orthographic changes in certain verbs, that *z* is changed into *c* before *e*, and *z* is not allowed to be used before *e* or *i*. Actually there would be no difference in sound, but the change is required by a rather arbitrary law governing the rules of the language. This point, though, has been dealt with. Any verb, whether radical changing or not, has to conform to the rules of spelling and pronunciation. In this lesson we are concerned with this common but irregular change in the stem vowel in four persons of the present indicative and subjunctive.

CLASS I (*a*) consists of *ar* and *er* verbs which change the stem vowels *e* and *o* into *ie* and *ue* respectively. But remember, once again, that this alteration only takes place in those persons of the present indicative and present subjunctive where the stress falls on the stem vowel. Examples : *cerrar*, *perder*.

Pres. Ind.	Pres. Subj.	Pres. Ind.	Pres. Subj.
cierro	cierre	pierdo	pierda
(cierras)	(cierres)	(pierdes)	(pierdas)
cierra	cierre	pierde	pierda
cerramos	cerremos	perdemos	perdamos
(cerráis)	(cerréis)	(perdéis)	(perdáis)
cierran	cierren	pierden	pierdan

Common verbs of this class are :—

empezar, to begin.   *recomendar*, to recommend.
comenzar, to commence. *sentarse*, to sit down.
pensar, to think.   *entender*, to understand.
negar, to deny.   *defender*, to defend.

CLASS I (*b*). Stem vowel *o*. *Costar* (to cost). *Morder* (to bite).

Pres. Ind.	Pres. Subj.	Pres. Ind.	Pres. Subj.
cuesto	cueste	muerdo	muerda
(cuestas)	(cuestes)	(muerdes)	(muerdas)
cuesta	cueste	muerde	muerda
costamos	costemos	mordemos	mordamos
(costáis)	(costéis)	(mordéis)	(mordáis)
cuestan	cuesten	muerden	muerdan

Common verbs of this class are :—

encontrar, to meet.   *colgar*, to hang up.
acordarse, to remember. *almorzar*, to lunch.
volar, to fly.   *llover*, to rain.
acostarse, to go to bed. *volver*, to return.

It should be remembered that such a verb as *oler* (to smell—*i.e.*, to emit a smell) will take the form *huelo*, since, again according to the rules of the language, no word can begin with *ue*.

NOTE also that *jugar* (to play), *forzar* (to force) and *torcer* (to twist) can be included in this class, taking the forms *juego*, *fuerzo* and *tuerzo* respectively.

CLASS II consists of *ir* verbs with *e* and *o* as the stem vowel. In the present indicative and present subjunctive these change (when accented on the stem) to *ie* and *ue* respectively. In addition, this class makes an additional change in the past definite and present subjunctive. When the stem syllable is NOT accented AND is immediately followed by two vowels or by *a*, the *e* and *o* become *i* and *u* respectively.

It is worth remembering for reference that the imperfect subjunctive, past subjunctive and future subjunctive are all formed from the past definite stem, and therefore, since two vowels occur throughout in their terminations, they also make the change from *e* and *o* to *i* and *u*.

The same applies to the gerund (present participle) of this class. Typical verbs: *sentir* (to feel); *dormir* (to sleep).

Pres. Ind.	Pres. Subj.	Pres. Ind.	Pres. Subj.
siento	sienta	duermo	duerma
(sientes)	(sientas)	(duermes)	(duermas)
siente	sienta	duerme	duerma
sentimos	sintamos	dormimos	durmamos
sentís	sintáis	(dormís)	(durmáis)
sienten	sientan	duermen	duerman

Past Def.:	sentí	sintió	sentimos	sintieron.
Past Def.:	dormí	durmió	dormimos	durmieron.
Imp. Subj.:	sintiera	durmiera	(*i* and *u* throughout).	
Past Subj.:	sintiese	durmiese	(*i* and *u* throughout).	
Fut. Subj.:	sintiere	durmiere	(*i* and *u* throughout).	
Gerund:	sintiendo	durmiendo.		

Common verbs of this class are :—

mentir, to lie.

convertir, to convert, change.

advertir, to notice.

herir, to wound.

morir, to die.

consentir, to consent, agree.

CLASS III consists of *ir* verbs with the stem vowel *e*.

Here again the stem vowel *e* changes to *i* when accented. It also changes to *i* whenever the termination begins with one of the strong vowels (*a, o, e*). In the past definite stem the stem vowel becomes *i* when the termination begins with a diphthong. Typical verb : *servir* (to serve).

Pres. Ind. :	sirvo	sirve	servimos	sirven.
Pres. Subj. :	sirva	sirva	sirvamos	sirvan.
Imperf. Ind. :	servía	servía	servíamos	servían.
Past Def. :	serví	sirvió	servimos	sirvieron.

Common verbs of this class are :—

> *despedirse*, to take leave.   *pedir*, to ask, beg.
> *elegir*, to elect.   *repetir*, to repeat.
> *vestirse*, to dress.

Remember that all these verbs behave quite normally in the imperfect indicative, future and conditional.

This does not quite exhaust the subject (though it may have exhausted you !). Still, this book does not set out to be a formal grammar, and enough has been said in this lesson to illustrate the most commonly met examples of root changing in otherwise regular verbs.

As no other grammatical points have been touched on in this lesson, the exercise, while introducing verbs of these various types, may profitably be devoted to revision of earlier material.

Translation XI

Después de haber salido del autobús que me condujo del aerodromo a la oficina de la compañia de aviación de Madrid, le pedí al oficial que me recomendase un hotel donde los precios no fueran muy elevados. Mé señaló varios ; busqué un taxi para ir al primero, el cual no se hallaba muy lejos del Prado ; el Prado es una de las más famosas galerías de pintura del mundo.

El taxi se paró a la puerta del hotel, bajé y le dije al chófer que esperara un momento. Entré y le pregunté al gerente del hotel si tenía vacante una habitación para una persona.

" ¿ Piensa Vd. estar mucho tiempo ? " me preguntó.

" No. Sólo necesito una habitación para tres noches."

" En ese caso le podemos dar a Vd. una habitación en el segundo piso. Si Vd. quiere la pensión completa, cuesta 500 pesetas."

" Esto está muy bien," le dije.

Pagué al conductor del taxi, y el mozo del hotel cogió mi maleta, subimos en el ascensor y llegamos a mi cuarto.

Era demasiado tarde para la comida y no tenía hambre; pedí pues una taza de café y leí un periódico que alguien había dejado en una de las mesas del salón. De pronto me fijé en la cartelera de espectáculos y ví que en uno de los teatros representaban " El pueblo de las mujeres ".

Siempre es interesante asistir a un teatro en una nación extranjera, pero tambien es muy difícil para un extranjero el comprender de lo que se trata. Pero yo había leído esta obra traducida al inglés y por tanto creí que podría seguir la trama de la comedia sin dificultad.

Me levanté pues del sofá y le dije al gerente si podría telefonear al teatro para que me reservaran una localidad.

" Seguramente, Señor. ¿Cuándo quiere Vd. ir? "

" Me gustaría un asiento para la representación de esta noche. Pero no quiero palco, algo que sea más barato."

El gerente descolgó el receptor.

" Central, póngame con el 47,98."

Esperó un momento.

" ¿Tiene Vd. entradas para esta noche? " continuó. " ¿Qué localidades quiero? Solamente una. ¿Tiene Vd. alguna en el patio de butacas? Bueno. ¿Cuánto es? ¿100 pesetas? Muy bien. Gracias."

Colgó el aparato y se volvió a mí.

" Señor, la representación empieza a las nueve."

VOCABULARY

darse prisa = to hurry (up).   *guerra* = war.
alquilar = to hire.   *prisionero* = prisoner.

Exercise 26

1. My father always goes to bed before 11 p.m., but he does not sleep well. 2. Hurry up! The train is beginning to move. 3. I think (of) hiring a car for six weeks. How much does it cost to do so (it)? 4. Do not hang up the receiver. I want to invite your friend to accompany us to

the theatre. 5. One never meets anyone in this street. 6. It is well known that the prisoner wounded three policemen, of whom one died before nightfall. 7. At what time do the shops shut on Thursdays? At half-past six. 8. Lunch was served yesterday at noon instead of at one o'clock. 9. They dressed rapidly so as not to arrive late at the station. 10. He begged me to recommend him a hotel near the centre of the city. 11. For six weeks I have been learning to play the piano. 12. Until a little while ago there were almost no foreigners in this country. 13. I asked him if he could come with us, but he went away without saying anything. 14. Did you see him as you were passing through the streets? No, I didn't. 15. I noticed that the door was open, which surprised me. 16. My two sisters meet one another every four days at the house of Mrs. Martinez. 17. I have not got your money now, but I will give it to you next Tuesday. 18. Good-bye for the moment; we shall be very glad to see you at 4.15. 19. More than a hundred people died of hunger in this town during the last year of the war. 20. To-morrow morning we shall have to have breakfast before eight o'clock.

LESSON XXVII

USE OF THE ARTICLES

In many instances the use of the definite and indefinite articles is the same in Spanish as in English. These therefore can be passed over without comment. There remain certain usages differing from the English practice, in part or wholly, and these will be dealt with in this lesson.

In both languages the name of a beast, plant, etc., requires the article before it in the singular when it is regarded as a representative of the species concerned :—

The dog is useful to man = *el perro es útil a los hombres*.

In Spanish the article is also required in the plural, which is not generally the case in English :—

Los perros son útiles a los hombres = dogs are useful to men.

Las águilas son aves de rapiña = eagles are birds of prey.

In both languages likewise the article is required before epithets attached to a proper name :—

Alfonso el Sabio. Pedro el Cruel. Alejandro el Grande.

Names of oceans, seas, rivers, mountain ranges and single peaks require the article in Spanish :—

El Pacífico. Los Pirineos. El Ebro. El Vesuvio.

In Spanish (but rarely in English) the definite article is required before any noun, singular or plural, used in a general sense or as representative of an entire class :—

El hombre es mortal. Los caballos son animales inteligentes.

The same applies to abstract nouns or verbal infinitives :—

El excesivo beber perjudica a la salud = excessive drinking is bad for the health.
La codicia es un pecado mortal = greed is a deadly sin.

Abstract nouns, qualified by an adjective, require the indefinite article when they are the objects of a verb, though not usually when governed by a preposition :—

Demuestra un entusiasmo excepcional = he shows exceptional enthusiasm : but—*con gran cuidado* (with great care).

In *modern* Spanish the definite article is not used before the names of most countries :—

Inglaterra tiene muchas posesiones coloniales.
España es una república.
El rey de Inglaterra ha vuelto de Francia (the king of England has returned from France).

Certain countries, continents, provinces, towns require the definite article even after prepositions. Most of these are to be found in the East or in the Americas : *la China, el Japón, el Asia, la America del Sur, la America del Norte, la Florida, el Brasil, el Ecuador, el Perú, la Argentina, la Habana.* In Europe practically the only example is *La Coruña* (Corunna). In any case the article is required if the name of the country is qualified by an adjective :—

El Asia Menor (Asia Minor).
La Gran Bretaña (Great Britain).

As a general rule the article should be repeated before each noun. If two or more nouns are closely connected in meaning or are connected by *o* (or), the article is preferably omitted before all except the first. In enumerations (*i.e.*, a rapid string of words) the article is generally omitted altogether for the sake of vividness :—

Tenemos un baúl y una maleta = we have a trunk and a suitcase.

El jefe o presidente de la sociedad = the head or president of the society.

El entusiasmo y celo del Gobernador = the Governor's enthusiasm and zeal.

Hombres, mujeres, niños—todos se ahogaron = men, women and children—all were drowned.

In actual practice the Spanish do not like using three nouns connected merely by " and ". For instance : " the doctors, the bishops and the lawyers congratulated themselves " would most elegantly be rendered by using *tanto— como* : *tanto los médicos como los abogados y los obispos se felicitaron, tanto* and *como* here having roughly the meaning of " both "—" as well as ".

The article is not required before the proper names of people or animals, unless they are qualified by an adjective : *Pedro*, but *el viejo Pedro*.

In proverbial sayings (which in most languages are liable to override the strict rules of grammar), together with chapter headings, book titles, etc., the article is omitted. Its omission in cases of apposition has already been dealt with.

Perro ladrador, poco mordedor = a dog that barks much bites little (*i.e.*, his bark is worse than his bite).

Gramática sucinta de la lengua española = a short Spanish grammar.

The article is omitted after such verbs as " to be ", " to become ", " to seem ", " to call ", " to name ", if they are followed by some word denoting rank, nationality, dignity, office, etc. :—

Es hijo de un sastre = he is the son of a tailor, but : *es el hijo mayor del sastre* (qualified by an adjective).

There are no adjectives in Spanish to express the substance of which a thing is made. Phrases such as " an iron bridge ", " a marble statue " must be turned into " a bridge of iron ", " a statue of marble ", no article being required before the second noun :—

Una estatua de mármol.

The same form is found frequently in the Spanish equivalent of English compound nouns :—

The seaport = *el puerto de mar* ; the table-spoon = *la cuchara de mesa.*

The same principle applies in compound nouns consisting in English of a participle and a noun, the infinitive being used in Spanish for the English participle :—

The sewing machine = *la máquina de coser.*

If the second word expresses the use or purpose for which the first is intended, *para* is used instead of *de* :—

El estante para libros = the book-case.

Sometimes the compound word is formed from a derivative of the main word.

azúcar, sugar. *azucarero*, sugar-bowl.
tinta, ink.   *tintero*, inkstand.

When an adjective qualifies two singular nouns of different gender, the adjective is in the masculine plural :—

El libro y la mesa son buenos.

If one of these nouns is singular and the other plural, the adjective is plural and agrees in gender with the nearest :—

El libro y las mesas son buenas.

If both nouns are plural the adjective takes the gender of the nearest, which should, if possible, be the masculine one :—

Las mesas y los libros son buenos.

The order of two singular nouns can often be changed : *e.g., La mesa y el libro son buenos.* (The adjective has to be made plural since there are two nouns and it sounds better to have the masculine noun the nearer to the adjective.)

Translation XII

Llegué al teatro muy temprano y un acomodador me señaló mi asiento. Estaba contento de lo bien que veía, el escenario. Tuve que esperar media hora hasta que empezó la función, pero no me aburrí; estuve muy entretenido observando la entrada de los espectadores. Poco tiempo después un señor se sentó junto a mí y reconociendo, evidentemente por mi traje, que era extranjero me preguntó si era la primera vez que visitaba Madrid. Le contesté que sí y que tambien era la primera vez que asistía a un teatro español.

" Los autores de esta obra, los hermanos Quintero, han escrito muchas obras buenas. ¿No es verdad? " le pregunté.

" Sí, más de cincuenta. Los dramáticos españoles son muy prolíficos. Pero los autores modernos en este sentido no pueden ser comparados con Lope de Vega, quien, dicho sea de paso, nació en Madrid.

" Su vida estuvo llena de acontecimientos. Fué hijo de un pobre comerciante, pero un noble se interesó en el muchacho y le envió a estudiar a la Universidad de Alcalá. Cuando era aún un hombre joven fué desterrado de Madrid por 5 años. Entonces navegó en la ' Armada Invencible ' enviada por el Rey Felipe II. Volvió sano y salvo y aun escribió un poema contra Drake. Después comenzó a escribir comedias. Para el fin de su vida había escrito más de 1,800, de las cuales 450 han sobrevivido. Por otra parte, sus obras fueron escritas en verso, no en prosa. Muchas de ellas fueron comedias de ' capa y espada ' tratando del honor y de las costumbres de la nobleza en aquellos días. Dramáticos de todos los paises han tomado modelo de sus tramas : las obras de Calderón fueron tambien muy populares.

" Pero los dramas de ambos pertenecen a una época pasada. Los escritores de hoy día son observadores de la vida real, y los hermanos Quintero son excelentes dramáticos ; sin embargo, algunos prefieren las obras de Benavente y Sierra. Si Vd. va a Sevilla, encontrará una fuente rodeada de bancos de piedra con estantes conteniendo las obras de los hermanos Quintero. No hay muchos hombres que se encuentren honrados con un monumento durante su vida."

No tuvo tiempo de contarme nada más aquel señor pues el teatro estaba ya lleno, no había un asiento vacante y el telón se levantó.

Vocabulary

acero = steel.
impropio = inapt.
ciencia = science.
piedra = stone.
grano = grain, bean.
castaño = chestnut.
volcán = volcano.
Nueva York = New York.
América del Norte = N. America.
isla = island.
nombre = name.
ilegible = illegible.
verde = green.

cuerda = rope.
bullicio = bustle.
Jorge = George.
tostar = to roast, toast.
oscuro = dark.
Nápoles = Naples.
clima(*m.*) = climate.
riguroso = severe.
cigarro = cigar.
máquina de escribir = typewriter.
cafeto = coffee tree.
colorado = red.
cáñamo = hemp.

Exercise 27

1. Vesuvius, one of the most famous volcanoes in the world, is situated in the centre of Italy, close to Naples. 2. Washington is the capital or principal city of the United States, but New York is the largest city in the New World. 3. Many of the buildings in various quarters of New York are extremely high. 4. I recognised by his complexion as well as by his clothes that he was a foreigner. 5. When he was only eight years old he began to study music, but afterwards he became an actor. 6. Old Charles went many times to Canada, didn't he? 7. The climate of North America is much more rigorous than that of Spain. 8. Havana, the capital of the island of Cuba, is known throughout the world for the cigars to which it has given its name. 9. Typewriters are very useful, especially nowadays when many people write in an almost illegible manner. 10. The coffee tree is a tree the colour of whose fruit changes from green to (*en*) red. 11. When the beans are roasted they

assume (take) a dark chestnut colour (colour chestnut dark). 12. King George VI has just returned from France, having spent four days in the French capital. 13. The general ordered stone walls to be constructed. 14. Shop-keepers, farmers, tradesmen—all do as much as they can to earn their living. 15. The two writers are excellent play-wrights, but neither the one nor the other can be compared with Benavente, who, by the way, lives now in Valencia. 16. Books which treat of the science of political economy are very numerous—the reading (of) them bores me very much. 17. It is easy to accustom oneself to the noise and bustle of modern life. 18. The name Pacific is inapt: the last time I went to Hong Kong I was very seasick. 19. Alexander the Great died at the age of thirty, having conquered (*conquistar*) the greater part of the known world. 20. Steel hawsers are stronger than hemp ropes.

LESSON XXVIII

THE SUBJUNCTIVE

The Subjunctive Mood is scarcely ever employed in modern English. It is true that we say : " if I were you " instead of : " if I was you ", but apart from that it is not often that the subjunctive is used. In Spanish its use, even among comparatively uneducated people, is far more widespread.

We have already pointed out that the indicative is the mood used to express knowledge, fact or certainty. It is used in principal clauses and in direct questions.

The primary use of the subjunctive is to express desire, doubt or some emotion. It may, as we shall see later, be employed in principal clauses. But it is more frequently to be found in dependent clauses : *i.e.*, in those which cannot stand alone but are dependent on some other word, such as a verb or a conjunction, before they can make complete sense.

The tense of the indicative to be used in any given sen-tence is generally clear enough from the meaning. But it is hopeless to try to give exact meanings to the tenses of the subjunctive. " May " or " might " are sometimes

THE SUBJUNCTIVE

indications of the subjunctive. But a sentence containing either of these words will quite possibly be in the indicative, while, on the other hand, a clause requiring the subjunctive may very well not contain either of them. We must therefore approach the matter from another point of view, ignoring the English of the sentence, and seeing what words and what circumstances call for the employment of the subjunctive in Spanish.

As a preliminary, since in this lesson we shall confine ourselves to the present subjunctive, it will be as well to recall that the present subjunctive of *ar* verbs is formed by adding to the stem the following endings : *-e*, (*-es*), *-e, -emos*, (*-éis*), *-en*. In *er* and *ir* verbs by adding : *-a*, (*-as*), *-a, -amos*, (*-áis*) *-an*. The characteristic vowel in the present indicative of *ar* verbs is *a*, in *er* and *ir* verbs *e*. In the present subjunctive these vowels change places.

Present Subjunctive :—

compre (compres) compre compremos (compréis) compren
viva (vivas) viva vivamos (viváis) vivan

Irregular verbs (as well as the more normal root-changing verbs) generally follow in the subjunctive their irregularity of the indicative.

Here, in some cases for the second time, are illustrated the present subjunctive of the commonest irregular verbs :—

tener	tenga	tenga	tengamos	tengan
haber	haya	haya	hayamos	hayan
querer	quiera	quiera	queramos	quieran
ser	sea	sea	seamos	sean
ir	vaya	vaya	vayamos	vayan
salir	salga	salga	salgamos	salgan
dar	dé	dé	demos	den
hacer	haga	haga	hagamos	hagan
ver	vea	vea	veamos	vean
venir	venga	venga	vengamos	vengan
pedir	pida	pida	pidamos	pidan

The perfect subjunctive of any verb is formed by combining the present subjunctive of *haber* with the past participle of the given verb. *Haya dicho*, etc.

USE OF THE SUBJUNCTIVE

1. The subjunctive is required in a clause dependent on a verb of commanding, demanding, telling, requesting, approving, permitting, suggesting or forbidding. It will be noticed that all these verbs have the effect, either strongly or mildly, of CAUSING something to be done or someone to act.

In these cases such a sentence as : " I will tell him to do it " is turned into : " I will tell him that he (should) do it ". *Le diré (a él) que lo haga.*

NOTE that " should " here is translated by the subjunctive, not by the conditional. It cannot be too strongly emphasised that it is impossible to give fixed meanings to the subjunctive.

Further examples of this use of the subjunctive are given below :—

Le pido a Vd. que me ayude = I beg you to help me.
Propongo que el Sr. X. sea elegido = I propose that Mr. X. be elected.
El juez ha mandado que se liberte al prisionero = the judge has ordered the prisoner to be set free.

CONTRAST the following sentences :—

Le dije que no tenía nada que declarar = I told him I had nothing to declare.
Le diré que se vaya = I will tell him to go away.

The first is merely a statement of fact. The second is an order, the final clause being subordinate to or dependent on the other. The first might be expressed : " I have nothing to declare," I said. The second would still remain a command : " Go away, I shall tell him ".

2. The second use of the subjunctive is in clauses governed by verbs expressing emotion—fear, sorrow, surprise, etc.

Temo que él esté muerto = I am afraid that he is dead.
Siento que se lo haya dicho a él = I am sorry that he has been told (of) it.

NOTE that when the subject of the second verb is the same as that of the first, the subjunctive is not used, an infinitive being substituted.

Estoy contento de verle a Vd. = I am glad to see you.

Es extraño que Vd. haya llegado sano y salvo = It is surprising that you (should) have arrived safe and sound.

3. Impersonal verbs, except those expressing certainty or marked probability, likewise require the subjunctive in the subordinate class.

Es importante que lo hagamos luego = it is important that we should do it at once.

Es dudoso que logren llegar a tiempo = it is doubtful whether they will manage to arrive in time.

But : *es cierto que llegarán a tiempo* = it is certain that they will arrive in time.

4. Similarly after verbs expressing denial, doubt or disbelief, the subjunctive is required. This applies also to verbs of thinking used interrogatively, for the mere fact that a question is asked shows that the speaker is in doubt, and the subjunctive is the mood of doubt or uncertainty. But if the question relates to the future, not to the present or past, the indicative is used.

El prisionero niega que haya asesinado a su enemigo — the prisoner denies that he has killed his enemy.

¿Cree Vd. que le haya asesinado ? = do you believe that he killed him ?

But : *¿Cree Vd. que le asesinará ?* = do you believe that he will kill him ?

5. Even after an ordinary relative pronoun the verb in the relative clause will be in the subjunctive if the pronoun refers to a person or thing either unknown or not definitely known. That sounds vague, but consider this sentence : " I am looking for a servant who speaks Spanish ".

Assuming this to mean that the search is for a certain person known to the speaker, who speaks Spanish, but is not to be seen for the moment, then the indicative is used because the identity of the servant is known, and the sentence would run : *Busco a un criado que habla español.*

But supposing that the would-be employer is on the look-out for a servant unspecified and unknown to him, perhaps, indeed, non-existent, who happens to be able to speak Spanish; then obviously the quest is very uncertain, and the subjunctive is needed. In this case, too, though it has nothing to do with the subjunctive, we shall find that the characteristic *a* before the object is omitted, the identity of the person being so vague as to make him unworthy of being distinguished from a thing. Thus we should write :—

Busco un criado que hable español.

Similarly, with indefinite expressions formed by adding *quiera* to relative pronouns or adverbs the subjunctive is wanted, and here there will very likely be a " may " in the English to suggest the subjunctive to us.

Quienquiera que sea = whoever he (may) be.
Cualquiera cosa que haya hecho = whatever he may have done.
Cuando quiera que lleguen = whenever they may arrive.

Translation XIII

El " Pueblo de las Mujeres " es una comedia muy divertida. Se refiere a un joven abogado de Madrid quien viene a trabajar a un pequeño pueblo de Andalucía. Mientras pasea por las calles ve a una muchacha que pasa por el otro lado, y da la coincidencia que se fija en que es bonita. Esto es lo bastante para las habladoras mujeres del lugar. Ellas están convencidas que el abogado se ha enamorado de esta muchacha y a pesar de sus negaciones (de él), ellas insisten en afirmar que él desea casarse con ella. Le hablan tan a menudo de su supuesto asunto de amor, que termina por creer que quizá sería bastante agradable el casarse con ella; y la comedia termina con su noviazgo.

Esta comedia es una entretenida y buena sátira de la vida provincial. Gracias a que conocía de antemano la obra, no encontré dificultad en apreciar sus agudezas y sus encantos. Además los actores que desarrollaron los principales papeles eran tan admirables que sus gestos y las expresiones de sus caras eran casi lo bastante para revelar el sentido de la comedia.

Era más de media noche cuando salí del teatro, pero no me sentía inclinado a irme a la cama. Hacía una noche estupenda. Las calles estaban muy bien iluminadas y anduve un rato mirando a los que pasaban y queriendo recordar lo que yo sabía de la historia de esta ciudad, la cual contiene alrededor de un millón de habitantes.

Felipe II fué quien estableció su corte en Madrid en 1561 e hizo de esta ciudad la capital de su reino. Fué el mismo rey quien construyó el monasterio de El Escorial, ese gran edificio, el cual decidí visitar al día siguiente. Los sucesores de Felipe II embellecieron la ciudad, sobre todo Carlos III. De su tiempo datan la Academia de Bellas Artes y el museo del Prado en el cual se encuentran algunos de los primeros trabajos de Velázquez y Goya; y sobre todo muchos cuadros de El Greco, Murillo y Ribera. Tendría que encontrar un rato para visitar el Prado. Antes de salir de Inglaterra me dijeron que no dejara de ver el Palacio Nacional situado en la Plaza de Oriente, el cual contiene entre otras cosas, la colección mas hermosa de armas y armaduras del mundo.

Mientras tanto no tenía idea en qué parte de la ciudad me encontraba, pues caminé un rato largo después de salir del teatro. Al fin le pregunté a un señor que me dijera el mejor camino para volver al hotel. Me indicó un tranvía que pasaba muy cerca de él (del hotel), esperé en la parada y tuve suerte de encontrar un asiento en un tranvía donde iba muchísima gente.

VOCABULARY

inquieto = uneasy.	*obispo* = bishop.
preciso = necessary.	*demandante* = plaintiff.
injuriar = to insult.	*acusado* = accused.
imperdonable = unpardon-	*asombrarse* (*de*) = to be sur-
able.	prised (at)
diputado = deputy.	*convencer* = to convince.

Exercise 28

1. Old María is very uneasy. She is afraid that her daughter may marry Mr. González. 2. I am sorry that you have forgotten what I told you last week. 3. I am waiting for someone who may be able to conduct me to the station. 4. I am waiting for my cousin who has promised to meet me here. 5. I do not wish to talk to that man. He always asks me to lend him money. 6. The deputy will propose that all shops be shut on Saturday. 7. It is

certain that the bishop will marry them.   8. It is necessary that we reach the frontier before nightfall.   9. We shall have to find him wherever he may have hidden himself. 10. It is doubtful whether this actor is capable of playing so important a part.   11. I shall end by believing that you do not wish to help us.   12. Do you think that we shall be able to convince him?   13. I will tell my clerk to go at once to the Air Company's office.   14. Do you deny that the accused has insulted the plaintiff in the most unpardonable manner?   15. We are sorry that it is impossible for you to attend the performance.   16. I was glad to notice that the theatre was full of people.   17. I will do everything possible to see you again.   18. I am surprised at what has happened.   19. I am surprised that you have not got used to working here.   20. I told them that I was not hungry.

LESSON XXIX

THE SUBJUNCTIVE (continued)

In the last lesson attention was drawn to the use of the subjunctive after certain verbs.   Now we must deal with the employment of this mood after certain conjunctions. Here, however, it is necessary to remind ourselves that the subjunctive will only be used if there is any idea of doubt or uncertainty in the dependent clause, or if the main verb has a definite "causing" effect.   For instance, in the sentence : "he drew up his troops so that they formed a hollow square", there is no subjunctive at all.   The whole sentence is merely a statement describing a particular military formation.   But in the sentence : "he drew up his soldiers so that they should form a hollow square to protect the supplies in the centre", we have a very different state of affairs, and the subjunctive would be required.

With this proviso in mind, here is a list of the chief conjunctions requiring the use of the subjunctive :—

Para que (in order that), *de modo que* (so that, in such a way that), *tanto que* (so much that), *supuesto que* (supposing that), *dado que* (granted that, assuming that), *a condición de que* (provided that), *a menos que* (unless), *aunque* (although), *no sea que* (lest). One can add to these most conjunctions of time—*hasta que, después que, antes que* (often in the form *antes de que*), and so on—provided that the verb following has the idea of uncertainty, not of fact.

SUBJUNCTIVE TENSES FORMED FROM THE PAST DEFINITE STEM

The imperfect, past and future subjunctives may all be formed from the past definite. All that has to be done is to drop the termination of the first person singular of the past definite, and then add the endings given in the table below. The same rule holds good with irregular verbs. If they are irregular in the past definite, the same irregularity is to be found in the stem of these three tenses of the subjunctive.

TABLE OF TERMINATIONS

Imperfect.		*Past.*		*Future.*	
ar	er & ir	ar	er & ir	ar	er & ir
-ara	-iera	-ase	-iese	-are	-iere
(-aras)	(-ieras)	(-ases)	(-ieses)	(-ares)	(-ieres)
-ara	-iera	-ase	-iese	-are	-iere
-áramos	-iéramos	-ásemos	-iésemos	-áremos	-iéremos
(-arais)	(-ierais)	(-aseis)	(-ieseis)	(-areis)	(-iereis)
-aran	-ieran	-asen	-iesen	-aren	-ieren

Except in conditional (" if ") sentences, which will be dealt with in the next lesson, the imperfect tense and past tense of the subjunctive (though, of course, not of the indicative) are virtually interchangeable, the preference generally being for the past subjunctive.

USE OF THE VARIOUS TENSES OF THE SUBJUNCTIVE

We know now most of the occasions on which the subjunctive is required in Spanish. But we have yet to find out which particular subjunctive tense may be required. In some cases there is no difficulty, the tense being readily ascertainable from the English.

The matter may be summed up as follows :—

1. When the main verb is in the present indicative, the present subjunctive is used in the dependent clause when the action described in this clause takes place at the same time as, or after, that of the main verb :—

Siento que no pueda venir = I regret that he is unable to come.

Dudo que llegue hoy = I doubt whether he will come to-day.

2. The perfect subjunctive can only be used after a main verb in the present or future indicative, and denotes an action completed before the time indicated by the main verb :—

Le acompañaré a Vd. luego que haya acabado mi trabajo = I will accompany you as soon as I have finished my work.

Of course, if the speaker is quite certain that he will finish his work, he would say *habré acabado* (future perfect indicative), the subjunctive indicating a possible doubt of his ability to do so.

Me asombro de que no haya llegado = I am surprised that he has not arrived.

3. If the main verb is in the present tense, an imperfect or past tense subjunctive refers to something prior to the time indicated by the main verb :—

Es posible que los Noruegos descubriesen América muchos años antes de la época de Cristobal Colón = it is possible that the Norwegians discovered America many years before the time of Christopher Columbus.

4. If the main verb is in the imperfect or past definite, the same tense of the subjunctive must refer to the same time or to a subsequent time relative to the main verb. This is difficult to express clearly in words, but examples should make the point plain :—

I am afraid that he will not arrive = *temo que no llegue.*
I was afraid that he would not arrive = *yo temía que él no llegase.*

I am sorry that there is no one here = *siento que no haya nadie aquí.*

I was sorry that there was no one there = *sentí que no hubiese nadie allí.*

5. So, to indicate a time previous to that indicated by a main verb in the imperfect or past definite, the pluperfect subjunctive must be used. This is often, though not invariably, pointed to by the presence of " had " in the English equivalent.

It seemed doubtful to me whether he ever wrote (had written) that book = *me parecía dudoso a mí que hubiese escrito jamás aquel libro.*

6. In English we often use the present for the future, e.g.—" I'm leaving tomorrow " for " I shall leave to-morrow ". But if such a phrase is preceded by a conjunction of time, the future indicative in Spanish would be wrong, since the future being uncertain, the subjunctive is needed : *cuando llegue* (not *llego* or *llegaré*). Sometimes the future subjunctive, not the present, may be needed. Compare the following :—

Le hice saber lo que habían dicho = I let him know what they had said.

Le haré saber lo que dijeren = I will let him know what they (may, will) say. (The conversation has not yet taken place, so that its purport is uncertain.)

The use of the subjunctive as a substitute for the imperative has already been dealt with. There remain one or two other cases where the subjunctive is used without any governing verb. For instance, such expressions as " come what may " = *venga lo que viniere.* *¡ Plugue a Dios !* (may it) please God !

In a direct command the present subjunctive is used for the imperative : *Entren Vds.* When it is indirect—*i.e.*, transmitted in the form of instructions to a third person—the subjunctive is preceded by *que* :—

Que no entre nadie = let no one come in.

The first person plural imperative " let us " is also

obtained from the subjunctive. Let us run = *corramos*. Let us hide ourselves = *ocultémonos*. Note that this person of the imperative of *ir* is irregular, *vamos* (not *vayamos*), but in the other persons *vaya, vayan*.

Translation XIV

El Escorial es un edificio sorprendente. Se encuentra a alguna distancia de Madrid y está rodeado de enormes montañas. Antes de ir allí, hice cuanto pude por aprender algo de su historia. Llegó a ser construido como sigue :

En el siglo diez y seis se libró una batalla cerca del pueblo francés de San Quintín. Durante la contienda, la artillería española destruyó una iglesia dedicada a San Lorenzo, y Felipe II. hizo voto de construir un monasterio en honor de este Santo. Les ordenó a sus arquitectos construir el edificio en forma de parrilla, para commemorar la manera cómo San Lorenzo fué martirizado. Un edificio en la fachada Este, el cual servía de residencia real, representa el asa de la parrilla, y las barras de la misma están representadas por edificios que se extienden en líneas rectas en el interior del cuadro formado por las paredes. La parte exterior contiene no menos de 1,100 ventanas y 15 puertas. Sobre la puerta principal se erige una estatua de San Lorenzo. Esta entrada da acceso al Patio de los Reyes y más lejos se encuentra una iglesia de granito, coronada por una enorme bóveda. En esta iglesia hay 48 altares, y en la capilla principal están las estatuas de Felipe II. y otros monarcas españoles.

Debajo del altar mayor está el panteón donde muchos de los reyes de España descansan (están enterrados). Ví los departamentos reales, incluyendo la sencilla y lúgubre habitación donde murió Felipe II., en 1598. Contemplé innumerables cuadros y obras de arte de todos los géneros. Sin embargo, y a pesar del esplendor del edificio, toda la atmósfera del lugar es indescriptiblemente triste y parece reflejar el frío y atormentado espíritu del hombre que lo construyó. Costó una suma inmensa y tardaron 22 años en completarlo. Era un edificio imponente, pero no me satisfizo tanto como otras cosas que ví en Madrid. El Manzanares, a orillas del cual Madrid está situado, no es un río importante. Sobre todo en verano se reduce a un diminuto riachuelo, pero hay sobre él uno o dos preciosos puentes, y en las proximidades algunas magníficas iglesias que datan del siglo XVII.

Pero lo que más llamó mi atención fué el Retiro, un parque parecido al de Bois de Boulogne de Paris con lagos, fuentes y jardín Zoológico, además de espaciosas avenidas. En invierno hace a menudo mucho frío en Madrid, pues la ciudad está a 635 metros sobre el nivel del mar. Pero en primavera y en otoño es delicioso y decidí volver allí tan pronto como tuviera una oportunidad.

VOCABULARY

ordenar = to order.
listo = ready, in readiness.
luego que = as soon as.
darse prisa = to hurry up.
restituir = to give back.
de madrugada = early (in the morning).
en caso de (que) = in case.

Exercise 29

1. He ordered his servant to wake him early, in order that he should have time to finish his work. 2. Do you think that it is going to rain? 3. Let us go to the theatre, unless you prefer to stay at home. 4. I was glad that they had not forgotten what I had said to them. 5. He asked me to hurry up, for he wanted us to arrive before nightfall. 6. He told me that it was important that we should hurry up, in case it should rain. 7. Let everything be in readiness for when he returns. 8. I will lend you my shoes on condition that you give them back to me to-morrow. 9. He promised to send me the book as soon as he had read it. 10. When he had read the newspaper he gave it to me. 11. Until I have received a letter from the " boss ", I shall stay here. 12. We were surprised that he had not written to us. 13. We feared that she was ill. 14. Do everything that he may tell you. 15. I will walk through the streets until I meet him. 16. Do you suppose that she has fallen in love with him? 17. It is possible that I shall buy a house in Burgos. 18. It is possible that he used to live in the United States. 19. As soon as he is dead I suppose that his house will serve as a museum. 20. He worked zealously in order that his children should not die of hunger.

LESSON XXX

CONDITIONAL SENTENCES

The primary function of the conditional is to denote futurity dating from a past time, just as the future indicative denotes futurity relative to the present. This sounds like mere verbiage, but example will make matters clear :—

Le prometo a Vd. que ella lo hará = I promise you that she will do it.

Le prometí a Vd. que ella lo haría = I promised you that she would do it.

The conditional, in this application of it, is thus always dependent on some past tense.

The commonest translation of the conditional is : " should " or " would ". But this is not a safe guide, since " should " or " would " may often be the translation of a verb in the subjunctive, in which case, naturally, the conditional cannot be used—*e.g.* :—

I was afraid that he would drop (let fall) the bottle = *temía que él dejase* (not *dejaría*) *caer la botella.*

The most important use of the conditional, however, is in " if " clauses. Now, the very fact that a sentence begins with " if " implies negation. The verb in the " if " clause therefore will be in the subjunctive, and the " should " or " would " in the other part of the sentence will be rendered by the conditional :—

Si yo fuese Vd. no lo haría = if I were you (but I am not) I wouldn't do it.

Si le hubiera visto, le habría hablado = if I had seen him (but I didn't) I would have spoken to him.

But : *si él viene, le hablaré* = if he comes I will speak to him.

(It might be argued that his coming is uncertain, but *si* (if) cannot take the present subjunctive or the future indicative. Hence the present indicative is required : meaning " whether " it can be followed by the subjunctive.)

It was stated in the previous lesson that the imperfect

and past subjunctives are interchangeable. There is one exception to this. For convenience we will refer to the Imperfect Subjunctive—*ara* or—*iera* as the " r " form and to the Past Subjunctive—*ase* or—*iese* as the " s " form. As we know, in the " if " clause involving the subjunctive, we can use either the " r " or the " s " form.

si tuviera (tuviese) dinero: if I had money. In the completing clause " would (should) " is likely to occur in English, and in Spanish we can use the conditional.

si tuviera (tuviese) dinero, lo compraría—if I had money I would buy it. As an alternative to this conditional we could use the " r " form of the subjunctive, but NOT the " s " form. In the " if " clause either: in the other the " r " only. So *si tuviera (tuviese) dinero, lo comprara*.

One last word. This substitution of the imperfect subjunctive for the conditional applies, quite apart from " if " sentences, to one or two common verbs. How often we find ourselves beginning a sentence with: " I should like to " ! One translation we have used is the impersonal *me gustaría (mucho)*. But quite the best one is *quisiera* (used for the conditional *querría*).

Translation XV

El día de mi marcha llegó. Por la mañana salí a dar un paseo final por la ciudad y compré algunos pequeños regalos para mis padres. Después me hice cortar el pelo. Volví al hotel, hice la maleta y tomé el almuerzo. Había tomado mi billete la víspera y, temprano, por la tarde, pagué mi cuenta y con gran pena cogí un taxi para dirigirme a la estación del Norte. Esta vez no conseguí un departamento para mí solo. Dos hombres estaban sentados ya y uno de ellos hablaba incesantemente a su compañero acerca de automóviles. No hacía mucho tiempo él había comprado un coche de segunda mano y había ido de viaje desde Madrid hacia el Sur de España. Por lo que yo pude entender, el viaje no había sido un éxito. Los frenos del coche no funcionaban bien. Había tenido un accidente, los neumáticos estallaron y por último se metió en una cuneta de la carretera. El otro hombre comenzó a hablar a su vez acerca de negocios. Al parecer era agente de bolsa y habló de dividendos y acciones y de la depresión económica. Terminó por leer en voz alta una carta del director de una sociedad anónima agregada. Su compañero procuraba escuchar atentamente mientras leía un periódico y yo miraba por la ventana. El otro continuaba hablando cuando volví del vagón-restaurant después de comer, pero por fortuna bajaron en Irún, ciudad fronteriza. Dormí bastante bien y me desperté cuando estábamos cerca de París. Cuando llegamos, tuve justamente tiempo para coger un taxi e ir a la Gare du Nord para coger el barco-tren, y llegamos a Dover poco después de las cinco. Me parecía extraño estar de vuelta en Inglaterra. Un hombre que viajaba en el mismo vagón que yo a Londres, viendo las etiquetas de mi maleta, me habló de España. Le dije que lo había pasado admirablemente allí y quería volver, pues había muchas cosas interesantes que quería ver.

" Por una cosa," dije, " porque no he visto la Alhambra." Un obrero que estaba en el asiento de enfrente, en una esquina, sonrió. " No lo podrá ver Vd. ahora. Es muy difícil reconocer Leicester Square, hoy día. Han derrumbado la Alhambra. En su lugar hay un Cine ! "

NOTE ON THE PARTICIPLES

The student may have noticed that in the foregoing pages reference has been made to a word ending in -*ando* or -*iendo* as the gerund OR present participle.

The truth is that the present participle in its strict form has almost disappeared from the language, existing only in the form -*ante* or -*ente*, and then only as an adjective (or occasionally a noun)—that is, without any participial force : e.g., *interesante* (interesting) ; *cesante* (a man who has lost his post).

But such a phrase as : " interesting himself deeply " would be *interesándose mucho* (not *interesántese*, which does not exist). In other words, the -*ando* or -*iendo* words combine the rôles of participle and gerund. Or, more simply, words in "-ing ", other than adjectives or infinitives (after certain prepositions), will be rendered in Spanish by a word in -*ando* or -*iendo*.

THE PAST PARTICIPLE

There are a certain number of verbs with two forms for the past participle. In such cases the irregular one— *i.e.*, not ending in -*ado* or -*ido*—is only an adjective, and is not used in the formation of a tense. For instance, *fijar* to fix, has *fijado* (reg.) and *fijo* (irreg.).

For " fixed prices ", *fijo* could be used, because the word here is an adjective—as in low (high) prices. But in the phrase " having fixed his attention ", fixed has a verbal force, and *fijado* would be used.

Other " adjective " past participles are *atento* (*atender*), *confuso* (*confundir*), *excluso* (*excluir*), *oculto* (*ocultar*), *tuerto* (*torcer*). But these verbs all have their regular past participle as well, and any possible confusion is lessened by the fact that in many cases the two forms would not be rendered in English by exactly the same word : for instance, *distinto* is quite " distinct " from *distinguido* (distinguished).

Exercise 30

1. I should like to have my hair cut, but we must hurry. 2. If you were a stockbroker, we should have plenty of (much) money. 3. If you had not bought a second-hand car, we should already have arrived at Barcelona. 4. I was afraid that we should have to start before breakfast. 5. I am glad to be back in England, but I shall go to Spain next year if I have enough money. 6. If I had not cut my foot, I would have come with you. 7. We shall just have time to go and see them. 8. He has just returned from the United States, after spending three years in New York. 9. What would you do if you were governor of the province ? 10. If you had asked me for my overcoat, I would have given it to you.

CONCLUSION

With this lesson we have come to the end of the road, or rather of the modest stretch of it which this book set out to cover. It is to be hoped that, as a result of the explanations given, the surface has been smoothed sufficiently to enable the student to continue his route without getting footsore. If he feels disposed to continue his journey, an interesting road lies ahead of him. Before setting out, however, he must bear in mind that this book, by its very nature, is not exhaustive. In particular, he must be prepared to find that the order of words in Spanish, especially in the relative positions of subject, verb and object, is much more variable than the foregoing pages have indicated.

At the point now reached a dictionary would be useful. There are a number of these, ranging from small pocket ones to *A Modern Spanish Dictionary*, published by the English Universities Press at 45*s*. There are also some good Spanish Grammars, the most comprehensive known to me being *Ramsey's Spanish Grammar*, marketed in England by G. Bell & Sons, Ltd., at, I think, 22*s*. 6*d*. There is also an admirable book, Harmer & Norton's *Manual of Modern Spanish* (University Tutorial Press, 15*s*.).

I think, however, that, armed with resolution, a dictionary and what he has already learned, he should be able to go ahead. In that case he cannot do better than read as many Spanish books as he can. The classics of any language, of course, are always worth reading. But modern Spanish differs a good deal from the tongue of Cervantes, and I would recommend the student to concentrate, to his own enjoyment and profit, on something more recent. Among the novels, those of Palacio Valdés, especially *La Hermana San Sulpicio* and *Marta y María*, are well worth reading. They are published in Madrid by the firm of Suárez, but are readily obtainable in England from such firms as the Librairie Hachette (127 Regent Street, W.1) or The Dolphin Book Co., Ltd., 14 Fyfield Road, Oxford, the proprietors of which latter are agents for all Spanish publishing houses.

The novels of Blasco Ibañez, though a little more difficult on occasion, by reason of the use of provincial dialect, should certainly be read, especially *Los Cuatro Jinetes del Apocalipsis, Sangre y Arena, Arroz y Tartana* and *Los Enemigos de la Mujer*. Then there are the delightful *Pepita Jiménez* by Juan Valera, and *El Sombrero de Tres Picos* and *El Final de Norma*, both by P. A. de Alarcón.

Some of the historical novels of Galdós, too, are interesting, and anyone who wants practice in reading dialogue could not do better than read the plays of Benavente, Sierra and the brothers Quintero. Azorín and Pío Baroja are two others whose works will well repay reading.

Messrs. Harrap have published a series of stories at 3s. 6d. with the Spanish on one page and the English version opposite. Such books are decidedly useful for studying style and turns of phrase. A more ambitious means of enlarging one's knowledge of a language is to buy a translation of some well-known work, and then turn a selected passage into Spanish, subsequently comparing the version with that of the original Spanish. The experience is liable to be a little depressing at first, but it is extremely valuable. But the student would be well advised to choose a work by Valera or Ibañez (their books have been translated into English) rather than *Don Quijote*, for instance, in which the language is to some extent obsolete.

At all events, there is no lack of good Spanish books to read. The great thing is to read as much as possible, and it will not be very long before the student finds himself not translating mentally as he goes along, but actually thinking in Spanish. Should he arrive successfully at that stage, this book will have more than fulfilled its intended purpose.

So, *amigo mío, vaya Vd. con Dios.*

PART II

KEY TO EXERCISES AND TRANSLATIONS

Exercise I

(*a*) 1. nosotros. 2. tú. 3. ellos. 4. vosotros. 5. yo. 6. nosotros. 7. ellos. 8. él. 9. vosotros. 10. tú.

(*b*) 1. toc-as. 2. trabaj-an. 3. habl-amos. 4. and-áis. 5. pas-a. 6. dejar-emos. 7. trabajar-ás. 8. vivir-é. 9. hablar-án. 10. comprar-éis.

(*c*)

yo compro	yo compraré.
tú compras	tú comprarás.
él compra	él comprará.
nosotros compramos	nosotros compraremos.
vosotros compráis	vosotros compraréis.
ellos compran	ellos comprarán.

Exercise 2(a)

1. The boy has a book. 2. The house has a door. 3. The friend will buy an apple. 4. Haven't you a table? 5. They haven't a book. 6. Will you take the apple? 7. I haven't a horse. 8. Shall we buy the table? 9. The woman hasn't a house. 10. When will he buy the book?

Exercise 2(b)

1. Nosotros tenemos una casa. 2. ¿No tiene Vd. un libro? 3. El muchacho tomará la manzana. 4. La mujer compra la casa. 5. ¿Tenéis vosotros un caballo? 6. La casa no tiene una puerta. 7. Ellos tienen una casa. 8. ¿No tomarán Vds. el libro? 9. ¿Tenemos (nosotros) una mesa? [1] 10. El hombre no tiene una casa.

[1] Note that, though the subject pronouns are frequently omitted when there is no possibility of misunderstanding, *Vd.* and *Vds.* must always be retained, because owing to their original meaning (Your Honour(s)) they are really nouns.

Exercise 2(c)

1. ¿No tiene ella la alfombra? 2. Vd. tomará el hacha. 3. ¿Dónde compraré yo el agua? 4. El hombre y la mujer no tienen un caballo. 5. ¿Tomaremos nosotros una hacha? 6. ¿No tiene Vd. una alfombra?

Exercise 3(a)

1. In the centre of the city there is a square. 2. The train will arrive immediately at the station. 3. The man takes a cup of coffee with his friends. 4. Our king has a palace in the city. 5. We have fifteen books. 6. The general arrives in the train with his wife. 7. Have you your bottle of wine? 8. I will speak to my friends. 9. Haven't you my hat? 10. In the station of our city there are ten trains. 11. The woman and her husband will arrive immediately in their car. 12. In the square of our city there is a church. 13. We have ten rooms in our house. 14. When shall we arrive at Madrid? 15. Have you my friend's books? 16. He will buy your house. 17. There isn't water in my bottle (*or*, there is no water). 18. My friend and his wife have a house in the square of the city.

Exercise 3(b)

1. Mi abuelo toma una taza de café con su mujer. 2. El soldado no tiene su botella de vino. 3. Mi amigo y su mujer tomarán luego el tren. 4. Su amigo (but, better, el amigo de Vd.) tiene una casa con ocho habitaciones. 5. (Nosotros) llegaremos a Madrid en nuestro automóvil. 6. Hay doce casas en la calle. 7. Ella comprará (unas) manzanas. 8. ¿Tiene Vd. vino en su botella? 9. Compraremos una casa en el centro de la ciudad donde hay una plaza. 10. Tienen dos automóviles, el médico tiene seis caballos. 11. ¿No comprará Vd. mi casa? 12. ¿Cuándo tomará Vd. su sombrero? 13. Las mujeres y sus maridos tomarán el tren. 14. Los reyes tienen sus palacios, nosotros tenemos nuestras casas. 15. Yo hablaré a mi marido y a [1] sus amigos. 16. ¿No comprará Vd.[2] (unos)

[1] In Spanish the preposition should be repeated before each noun to which it refers.

[2] The *pronoun* subject of a Spanish verb is generally omitted if the

lápices? 17. ¿Dónde hay una iglesia? 18. Compraré la casa de Vd. (*su casa*, if the meaning is quite clear), tiene siete habitaciones.[1]

Exercise 4(a)

1. I have not (got) the watch you wish to buy. 2. We (have) sold Charles's book yesterday. 3. I have written five letters to-day. 4. I haven't enough money to buy wine. 5. My brother has not arrived at Madrid. 6. Don't you wish to buy the doctor's car? 7. Have you seen the king? 8. We have spent the four pesetas that I (have) found to-day. 9. We will look for the general's daughter. 10. Have you not seen the knife which I lost in one of the rooms of your house? 11. I will call the boy who is talking in the street with John's uncle. 12. Do you want to buy some newspapers? I have a peseta in my pocket. 13. The generals have missed the train. 14. Have you seen the soldiers who have arrived from Madrid? 15. I have sold my books and I have enough money to buy two bottles of wine. 16. When did he write to his brother? 17. The woman has sent a letter to her son who has a house in Bilbao. 18. I am looking for the newspaper which John has lost.

Exercise 4(b)

1. ¿Tiene Vd. periódicos? 2. ¿Ha comprado Vd. los relojes? 3. ¿No han vendido ellos sus automóviles? 4. El hombre quiere llamar a su mujer. 5. ¿Ha visto Vd. al tío del médico? 6. ¿Tiene Vd. bastante dinero en su bolsillo para comprar manzanas? 7. ¿Ha visto Vd. hoy a Juan? 8. ¿Busca Vd. a su hermano? 9. ¿Mandará Vd. hoy la carta? 10. ¿Quiere Vd.[2] tomar una taza de

---

meaning is clear. But it is never wrong to insert the pronoun, and it *must* be put in when there is emphasis on it or contrast between one pronoun and another. Remember, also, that however clear the meaning may be, *Usted* and *Ustedes* can NEVER be omitted, because, strictly speaking, they are really nouns and not pronouns at all.

[1] Notice that with such a word as *habitación*, the accent mark disappears in the plural, as, owing to the addition of *es*, the stress falls according to rule.

[2] When we say : " Will you have some tea ? ", there is no idea of futurity : the meaning is : " Would you like ? " or " Do you want ? "

café? 11. Buscaré el periódico que ha perdido Vd.¹ 12. ¿Cuándo ha visto Vd. a los soldados? 13. El tío de Juan que llegará hoy de Madrid, ha perdido su dinero. 14. Tengo en mi casa diez libros que Vd. quiere comprar. 15. Yo tomaré las diez pesetas que tiene Vd. en su bolsillo. 16. No he tomado el periódico de Vd. (*su* would not make the ownership clear). 17. ¿No quiere Vd. llamar a Carlos? 18. ¿No ha visto Vd. a la muchacha? 19. ¿A dónde ha mandado Vd. a la mujer?

Exercise 5(a)

1. The man you saw is a shopkeeper. 2. The blue bottle (which) I bought is full of water. 3. My brothers are richer than the doctor. 4. Our cook is lazy : she does not work much. 5. Spanish women are always talkative. 6. I received to-day a letter from my daughter : she is in Barcelona. 7. Is the poor ² woman married? She is a widow. 8. The pupils are in the school, listening to the learned professor. 9. The workmen who are working in the fields are not very industrious. 10. The streets of many Spanish cities are very narrow. 11. I will listen to-day to the little birds which sing in the fields. 12. Where is the daughter of the brave General X? 13. She is in England with her mother, who always likes to travel. 14. The shopkeeper has no (lit. does not have) cheap watches : they are all (of) gold. 15. The daughter of my good friend Charles is very pretty. 16. A great French general has arrived here (in order) to visit the king. 17. Do you not wish to visit the palace of the Spanish kings? 18. My uncle is a farmer. He is not rich, but he is always happy. 19. The workmen are not polite, but they are very skilful. 20. The famous palace you are looking for is in King St.

In such cases the verb *querer* (to wish, want) is employed, and not the future tense of the other verb in the sentence.

¹ In sentences beginning with *que* (which, that, etc.) the verb often comes before the subject. It sounds better, but it is not a deadly crime to follow the English order, particularly at this fairly elementary stage.

² *Pobre* BEFORE the noun means wretched, unfortunate; AFTER it means poverty-stricken.

Exercise 5(b)

1. Las calles de la ciudad son largas. 2. Hoy he trabajado mucho, pero no estoy cansado. 3. El caballo blanco del obrero es pequeño. 4. No he visto a su hermano. ¿Dónde está? 5. Está en Inglaterra con su gran(de) amigo. Viaja mucho cuando tiene bastante dinero. 6. Los pájaros que cantan en los campos son muy hermosos. 7. Mi tío es un hombre docto, pero es holgazán. 8. Nuestra cocinera no está aquí : está en la iglesia que ha visitado Vd. hoy. 9. Vino blanco es mejor que café negro. 10. La hija de ella no es casada. 11. Los hombres que están en los campos son siempre felices. 12. La iglesia es pequeña pero muy hermosa. 13. Las botellas que han comprado Vds. están llenas de agua. 14. Escucho los pájaros : sus voces son muy melodiosas. 15. ¿Dónde está la hija bonita del labrador? 16. Buenos libros son baratos aquí. 17. Soldados alemanes están en la ciudad. 18. Obreros franceses son muy aplicados. 19. Somos médicos, mi hermano es de Madrid, pero yo soy de Bilbao. 20. La hermosa Inglesa no habla español, pero ha aprendido francés.

Exercise 6(a)

1. The apples which are on the table are mine. 2. This book is mine, that is my brother's. 3. These pencils are better than yours. 4. There are many (*mucho*, much, *muchos*, many) books in my room : the ones I bought this morning are on the bed. 5. Do you want this newspaper or that? 6. A relation of mine is in Madrid. 7. Have you seen Charles? Two friends of his will arrive to-day from Barcelona. 8. That car is not mine, it is John's. 9. That shopkeeper is richer than this one. 10. Where is my horse? Ours is here, yours is in the stable. 11. We are very pleased to-day : two cousins of ours have arrived here from England. 12. Is this bottle mine? No, it's hers. 13. My father and his (yours) have worked all day in the fields. 14. My house and our neighbours' are small. 15. Have you lost your handkerchief? No, this is mine. 16. Here are two watches; this is mine, that is yours. 17. I have given the money to Lewis and a friend of his. 18. My dog and hers are in the street. 19. Is this car

ours or yours? 20. Your horse and your servant's are in the stable.

Exercise 6(b)

1. Estas manzanas son mías, ésas son de Vd. 2. Su voz (*de ella* added, if context is not clear) es más melodiosa que la de su hermana. 3. Un vecino nuestro tiene una casa blanca con un tejado azul. 4. He leído mis cartas. No he leído las de Vd. 5. El reloj de oro, que Vd. ha hallado, es mío. 6. El dinero que he gastado es de Juan. 7. Carlos llegará aquí con dos amigos suyos. 8. La criada ha perdido mis pañuelos pero no los de Vd. 9. No tengo bastante dinero para comprar este auto : ése es más barato. 10. ¿Es de Vd. este periódico? 11. ¿Ha visto Vd. al labrador y a su hijo? Son amigos nuestros. 12. Estas manzanas son mejores que las que he comprado esta mañana. 13. Dos parientes suyos han comprado aquella casa. 14. Nuestra cocinera y la de nuestro vecino no quieren trabajar esta mañana. 15. Mi sombrero y el de Vd. están sobre la mesa. 16. Este no es mi libro, es de ella. 17. Hemos visto a nuestra madre pero no a [1] la de ella. 18. Un vecino mío ha vendido su casa : quiere comprar la mía. 19. No quiere comprar libros : los que tiene son buenos. 20. ¿Es de Vd. el caballo que está en la cuadra?

Exercise 7(a)

1. Which of my books have you read? The one which is on the table in your room. 2. What did you say to the lawyer? 3. How many streets are there in this city? 4. What is the number of your room? 5. Which pencils are mine? These or those? 6. We have lost the train. What a pity! 7. What a pretty girl! Who is she? 8. She is the daughter of a friend of mine. 9. Why haven't you finished your work? 10. Of what are you talking? Of matters which you do not understand. 11. Whose cows are those which are in that field? (They are) Charles's. 12. Where do you come from? From Madrid, but I live now in Burgos. 13. Who lives in your cousin's house? My uncle lives there, but my aunt is in England. 14. This

[1] The pronoun *la* stands for a person, so the preposition *a* is required, as before *madre* earlier in the sentence.

French officer always drinks white wine. 15. How much money have you in your purse? 16. To whom are you writing? To the doctor's son. 17. Those (the people) who are drinking in the inn are not my friends. 18. The train has left the station. 19. I wish to see the king. Where is his palace? 20. This soldier is very fond of (loves much) the cook, but she is married.

Excercise 7 (b)

1. ¿A cuál de los oficiales ha hablado Vd. esta mañana? A aquél. 2. ¿Cuál de estos autos es de Vd.? Este. 3. ¿De quién son esos caballos? No son míos. 4. ¿A cuál de sus hijos ha visto Vd.? 5. ¿Por qué no está Vd. trabajando? No trabajo porque estoy cansado. 6. Quiero ver al abogado. ¿Dónde está? No está aquí. 7. El pájaro está cantando en el jardín. ¡ Qué voz tan melodiosa ! 8. ¿A qué hombre quiere Vd. hablar? 9. ¿Cuál de las vacas ha comprado Vd.? La blanca. 10. He dado cinco pesetas a aquel labrador que está bebiendo en la posada con su hijo. 11. Somos madrileños, pero vivimos en Santander. 12. Ella está escribiendo a su primo. 13. ¡ Qué hombre ! Ha bebido cinco botellas de vino. 14. Tengo dos hermanas y un hermano. 15. ¿Cuántas iglesias hay en esta ciudad? 16. Ella tiene dos hijos. El que escribe a su amigo, es médico. 17. Dónde está el general? Está trabajando en su jardín. 18. Hay muchos trenes que salen de esta estación. 19. Aquellos hombres no viven aquí. Son de Valencia (or, son valencianos). 20. ¿A cuántos obreros ha visto Vd. en los campos?

Exercise 8(a)

1. These men are stronger than you. 2. Isn't this woman older than that one? 3. This beer is good; it is better than your white wine. 4. We have received less than five pesetas. 5. He spends more money than he says. 6. Is your car cheaper than ours? 7. We shall sell our house; it is very small. 8. These workmen are lazier than the ones who work in your garden. 9. My brother is in Madrid. To-morrow I shall be there too. 10. If you sell those books you will have enough money to buy the ones you want. 11. My friend will remain here more than a

week.[1] 12. One of my clerks is in my office : I have not seen the others this morning. 13. We have churches in this city larger than those of Madrid. 14. That lawyer is richer than the doctor. His house has more than twelve rooms. 15. To-morrow I shall be very tired, because I shall work all day in the fields. 16. The general says that his soldiers will not remain here more than two days. 17. These apples are not good; they are worse than yours. 18. When will you write to your cousin? 19. The rich are not always happier than the poor. 20. My neighbours are less well off than they say.

Exercise 8(b)

1. La hija de Vd. es más bonita que aquella muchacha. 2. ¿No es más grande la casa de ella que la nuestra? 3. ¿No son más holgazanes estos dependientes que los que trabajan en la oficina del primo de Vd.? 4. Aquellos tcnderos son más ricos de lo que dicen. 5. Mañana estaremos en Bilbao con un pariente nuestro. 6. ¿No (se) quedará Vd. aquí más de tres días? 7. Las calles de esta ciudad son más estrechas que las de Madrid. 8. ¿Ha perdido Vd. su pañuelo? Sí, pero tengo en mi bolsillo otro. 9. Escribe cartas más largas que yo. 10. Los caballos de la cuadra mía (more emphatic for purposes of contrast than *de mi cuadra*) son mejores que los de la suya (but, more clearly, *de la de él*). 11. Carlos es más grande que su hermano menor. 12. La casa de ella está en la calle Mayor, pero es más pequeña que la nuestra. 13. ¿Cuándo saldrá de la estación el tren? 14. Los que viven aquí son parientes míos. 15. Estos oficiales son menos valientes de lo que dice el general. (The Spanish often put the subject after the verb, even though the sentence is not interrogative, if to do so makes for a smoother sound. There is no need to bother overmuch about it, but it is worth while, in your reading, to keep an eye out for such changes.) 16. Buscaré a la tía de Vd. ¿No estará en el jardín? 17. Esta Inglesa tiene más dinero de lo que gasta. 18. Recibiremos mañana la carta que él ha escrito hoy.

---

[1] In Spanish, as in French, in reckoning a week in days, both the first and last are counted: *i.e.* eight not seven days. Similarly, a fortnight = fifteen not fourteen days.

19. ¿No es más aplicada aquella muchacha que la cocinera de Vd.? 20. Perderemos este tren, pero hay otros muchos que salen para Valencia de esta estación.

Exercise 9(a)

1. Barcelona is one of the biggest cities in Spain, but it is not so large as London. 2. These oranges are not as good as those I used to buy when I lived in Seville. 3. Used you not to have a very good car? 4. I used to travel a good deal when I was young. 5. My best friend is one of the most celebrated authors in the world. 6. When we were in England we used to write many letters. 7. We have not as many relations as you. 8. This woman, who is now so ugly, used in those days to be the best-looking girl in the village. 9. When we lived in Aranjuez my father took the train for Madrid every day. 10. In those days the city had many inhabitants. 11. The room where we were was my brother's. 12. Are not these matters as important as those of which you were speaking? 13. When I learned Spanish, I often forgot the most ordinary words. 14. This is the most delicious wine I have ever drunk. 15. She is not as industrious as her younger sister. 16. He used to drink a lot of beer, but he did not eat as much bread as I (did). 17. I used to talk to the doctor every day : he was a very intelligent man. 18. When we were young, we did not have enough money to travel. 19. I have not read the best works of the great Russian authors. 20. How many books have you? I haven't as many as he.

Exercise 9(b)

1. ¿Por qué es tan soberbia aquella muchacha? Por que su padre era uno de los hombres más ricos de la ciudad. 2. ¿Cuál de los trenes tomaba Vd.? 3. ¿Ha visto Vd. a aquella mujer? Era muy hermosa (or, *hermosísima*). 4. Su marido era de Málaga (or *malagueño*): tenía una casa en la Plaza Mayor. 5. ¿Cuántas botellas de vino bebía él todos los días? Más de seis. 6. Cuando vivíamos en Sevilla teníamos un auto. 7. Estos dependientes no son tan holgazanes como los de Vd. 8. He visto hoy al abogado : estaba en la oficina del primo de Vd. 9. Nuestra

cocinera no era tan habladora como la de ella. 10. Esta es
la casa más magnífica (hermosa) que he visto jamás.
11. Esta criada no era tan aplicada como la otra. 12. El
hermano mayor de mi amigo era muy rico, pero ha perdido
todo su dinero. 13. Yo buscaba esta mañana a mi hermano.
14. ¿Dónde estaba? Escribía cartas (or, *estaba escribiendo
cartas*). 15. Esta es la calle más larga de la ciudad.
16. Era el más hábil de mis obreros. 17. El era tendero,
cuando vivía en Londres. 18. Todos los días no recibía
menos de diez pesetas. 19. El hombre más rico de la
aldea era hijo de un labrador pobre. 20. En aquellos
días tenía menos dinero de lo que gastaba.

Exercise 10(a)

1. The learned professor delivered a speech about (on)
the works of Lope de Vega. 2. That celebrated author was
born in Madrid. 3. My cousin was sitting on a bench in
front of his house when the soldiers entered his garden.
4. How much money did you spend this morning? I
haven't spent more than two pesetas. 5. Every day I
used to walk as far as the river. 6. On Saturday I went to
the village to pay a visit to a friend of mine. 7. We went
to-day as far as the church. 8. According to what the
doctor says, she is well. 9. While I was calling the girl,
her sister came in with a friend of hers. 10. When we
reached the station we were very tired. 11. Without
doubt that lawyer had no money. 12. They hadn't much
money when they arrived here. 13. My friends were born
in a house near the square. 14. After two days we arrived
at the river we were seeking. 15. This shoemaker worked
hard to earn his living. 16. Every day he spent many hours
in his shop. 17. After the arrival of our relations we went
with them to the church. 18. We lived five years in the
most delightful city in Spain. 19. Didn't your brother
travel a great deal in France? 20. Yes. He spent two years
in Paris, but he is now in Seville.

Exercise 10(b)

1. ¿Cuándo llegaron Vds. a Londres? 2. Llegamos el
sábado, pero mi hermano ha llegado aquí esta mañana.
3. Yo hablaba con el zapatero cuando entró en la tienda el

primo de Vd. 4. ¿Ha visto Vd. a Carlos? Sí. Cuando fuí a la plaza estaba sentado en un banco en su jardín. 5. Después de la llegada del tren salimos de la estación. 6. Nací en Málaga pero pasé muchos años en Tarragona. 7. Nuestra casa no estaba lejos del río. 8. En aquellos días este dependiente era muy holgazán : pasaba muchas horas en la posada cerca de la plaza. 9. Mientras ella estaba en la calle el muchacho rompió las ventanas de su casa. 10. El profesor es muy inteligente y el sábado pronunció un discurso admirable. 11. Según lo que dice este oficial, los soldados estarán aquí mañana. 12. Todos los días andaba hasta la iglesia. 13. El sábado fuí hacia el río. 14. Hallaron el dinero que buscábamos. 15. Aquellos hombres que eran tan ricos como el tío de Vd. perdieron todo su dinero. 16. ¿No ha escrito Vd. a sus parientes? 17. Escribí a mi tía el sabado. 18. Sin duda trabajaron para ganar su vida. 19. Rompió la botella que estaba sobre la mesa. 20. ¿Cuántos años pasó Vd. en Francia?

Exercise 11(a)

1. My father has given me a gold watch. 2. I am going to pay a visit to my cousin : do you want to come with me? 3. Why have you come without her? 4. It is always impossible for me to understand what the doctor says to us. 5. What a delightful house ! What (how) do you call it? 6. Where is your daughter? I don't know, but I will call her. 7. I have lost my purse. Have you seen it? 8. Yes. I found it in the street and I have given it to your husband. 9. It is necessary for me to work hard in order to earn my living. 10. Are you writing to your mother? No. I wrote to her on Saturday. 11. The general's sons are very pleased, because he has bought them a car. 12. The professor delivered a very interesting speech : we listened to it with great pleasure. 13. The lawyer tells me that the doctor's son is in Madrid. Is it true? 14. It's a lie. My neighbour saw him this morning. 15. What has happened to Charles? 16. What has happened to him? Nothing. He is very well. 17. Those women have no money. I have given them two pesetas. 18. Your letter? I didn't receive it. 19. It is impossible for me to study while you are talking.

Exercise II(b)

1. Voy a ver al labrador. ¿Quiere Vd. venir conmigo?
2. ¿Por qué no ha venido ella con él? 3. Dice que le
comprará un regalo. 4. ¿Dónde halló Vd. mis pañuelos?
Los hallamos debajo de la mesa en su habitación. 5. Aquí
están los libros que le he comprado. 6. Yo tenía un lápiz de
oro, pero lo vendí el sábado. 7. No les he dado un regalo, por
que no estuvieron corteses. 8. La he visto esta mañana,
mientras yo andaba hacia el río. 9. Les escribiremos
mañana. 10. Nos es difícil escuchar los pájaros. 11. Si
Vd. le da un auto, lo venderá. 12. Nos hablaba todos los
días. 13. Es verdad que no recibí el regalo que me había
prometido. 14. Dice que el tren ha salido de la estación
pero no lo creo. 15. ¿Dónde están sus vecinos? No los
hemos visto. 16. Nos es imposible entender lo que dice
Vd. 17. No sé lo que les ha sucedido. 18. Es verdad que
él vendió su casa pero yo no la compré. 19. Perdió su
dinero y no lo había hallado cuando he entrado esta mañana
en su cuarto. 20. ¿Por qué no los ha vendido Vd?

Exercise 12(a)

1. Here is the present (which)I have bought you. 2. He
has bought himself an overcoat. 3. When the policemen
arrived the robber hid himself behind the door. (Note that
the subject does not necessarily precede the verb in a
Spanish sentence.) 4. The thief has stolen my hat (lit.
has stolen the hat to me). 5. He took off his shoes. 6. I
will wait for you in front of the church. 7. It does not
seem to me that these books are very interesting. 8. I do
not know why this poor woman has killed herself. 9. I
promised him that you would wait for him. 10. Would you
not receive them? 11. Did you not call her? 12. She
is called (lit. calls herself) Mercedes. 13. I will call John :
he is in the garden. 14. He has given me the money that
he promised you. 15. Do you know what has happened
to her? She has lost the train. 16. What does it matter
to her? 17. I do not think that these children have hurt
themselves. 18. Her mother is ill, but she herself is well. 19.
This man is very intelligent but he always talks of himself.
20. They carried their trunks with them (*con ellos* would not
refer to the subject of *llevaron* but to some other people).

Exercise 12(b)

1. ¿No nos ha visto Vd. a nosotros esta mañana?
2. Yo me compraré un auto. 3. Le hemos comprado a
él un regalo. 4. El se oculto debajo de la mesa. 5. Los
aguardaremos a Vds. mañana. 6. ¿No me ha aguardado
Vd. hoy? 7. Me parece a mí que Vd. no le escucha a él.
8. No les prometimos a ellos regalos. 9. Se quitó el
sobretodo. 10. Le quitaré a Vd. los zapatos. 11. ¿Se
ha lastimado el guardia civil? 12. Yo mismo maté a los
ladrones. 13. No me importa a mí. 14. Yo mismo le
llamaré a él. 15. Mi hermano mayor se llama Juan.
16. Prometieron que me aguardarían a mí. 17. ¿Por qué
le ha dado Vd. a él la carta que le escribí (a Vd.)? 18. No
es verdad que ella se mató. 19. Habló de sí pero no le
escuché. 20. No me da a mí tantos regalos como le compra
a Vd.

Exercise 13(a)

1. Do me the favour of reading me some pages of this
novel. 2. Is your brother at home? I want to talk to
him on an important matter. 3. Do not give it to me,
give it to him. 4. I do not speak Spanish, but she has
promised to teach it (to) me. 5. Have the kindness to
bring me those matches. I want to smoke. 6. These
knives are mine. My father sent me them from Madrid.
7. I do not know where my friend is : it is impossible for
me to write to him. 8. Who is that girl? Please introduce
me to her. 9. When will you lend it to us? 10. They want
to buy my house, but I do not wish to sell it to them. 11.
Let us hide behind the door. (Note that the *s* of
ocultemos is dropped before the addition of *nos*. This is
to make the sound pleasanter.) 12. Don't let us hide there :
it would be better to stay here. 13. Those who deceive
others often deceive themselves. 14. Here is your overcoat. Will you lend it to me? 15. We did not give it to
you, but to him. 16. Do not do me this favour, do it for
her. (Better : Don't do this favour for me, but for her).
17. If you want to buy this car I will sell it to you. 18.
Don't introduce me to him, but to her. 19. This horse
will be yours to-morrow. I know he has promised it to you.
20. Do not take this paper from me : I want to read it.

Exercise 13(b)

1. Se los enviaré a Vd. 2. Quiere dármelos. 3. Tenga Vd. la bondad de dárselos a él. 4. No me lo envíe Vd. a mí, envíeselo a él. 5. Andemos hasta el río. 6. ¿Está en casa el amigo suyo (or, de Vd.)? 7. Quiero verle. 8. Si Vd. no tiene esta novela se la prestaré. 9. No se lo daré a él, sino a Vd. 10. Se le presentaré a ella. 11. Se los enviaré a Vd. 12. Me es imposible enviárselo a Vd. 13. Se han engañado a sí (mismos). 14. Mis fósforos están sobre la mesa en mi cuarto : hágame Vd. el favor de traérmelos. 15. No nos lo vendió a nosotros. 16. Hágame Vd. el favor de presentármele a mí. 17. No será fácil enseñárselo a ella. 18. No se los prestaré a Vd. 19. Se los daré a Vd. 20. No se lo venda Vd. a él, véndamelo.

Exercise 14(a)

1. The speeches which Professor X delivers are very interesting. 2. I have not read all the books of which he was talking. 3. Who took the pencil with which I was writing? 4. What are the names of those two children who are going towards the village? 5. They are the sons of the unfortunate shoemaker whose arm the surgeons amputated yesterday. 6. They are the shopkeeper's sons to whom you sent a basket of fruit yesterday. 7. She has a very charming house whose upper windows give on to the governor's garden. 8. That professor has read all the comedies of Lope de Vega, which astonishes me. 9. Those men are the two servants of the doctor whose wife we met this morning. 10. That woman is Charles's cook of whom I spoke to you. 11. He has read the letter I received, which is very annoying. 12. Is this the man into whose shop you went? 13. Do you know which of these books you lent me? 14. The boys among whom he found himself were friends of his. 15. Is it you who cut your finger? 16. It is we who were singing when you came into the room. 17. Whose car is this? It is not mine, but my brother's. 18. The man I met yesterday is a baker. 19. I will wait for you in front of the church near which there is an inn. 20. The general, who was born in Madrid, now lives in Burgos.

Exercise 14(b)

1. Dice que no tiene dinero : lo que es mentira. 2. Aquél no es el hombre a quien encontró Vd. 3. El soldado a cuya esposa (mujer) Vd. ha visto es de Toledo. 4. El soldado, a quien el cirujano amputó la pierna, está aquí. 5. El soldado a cuya esposa el cirujano amputó el brazo es un amigo mío. 6. Vivimos en una casa detrás de la cual hay una cuadra. 7. Esa muchacha es la hija mayor del abogado a quien encontró Vd. 8. La hija del abogado a la cual Vd. ha visto esta mañana es casada. 9. Soy yo quien entré en la tienda de Vd. 10. ¿No son baratas las casas que dan a la plaza ? 11. No he leído las obras sobre las cuales nos pronunció un discurso. 12. Voy a hacer una visita al gobernador : lo que será muy agradable. 13. El hombre en cuya oficina me hallé era muy rico (riquísimo). 14. No son aquellos obreros quienes son holgazanes. 15. Nuestra cocinera, la cual (better than *que*) llegó ayer de Madrid, es muy habladora. 16. Los asuntos de que habló Vd. no me importan a mí. 17. Hay en esta calle una casa que quiero comprar. 18. Mis amigos en cuyo jardín estamos, quieren enseñarme el inglés. 19. No sé cuál de estos sombreros es de Vd. 20. ¿Sabe Vd. cuáles de estas cestas son mías ?

Exercise 15(a)

1. I am going to spend a few days at my cousin's house in Santander : he has invited you also. 2. Unfortunately it is impossible for me to go with you, because my mother is ill. 3. Whom are you looking for? For John. I want to tell him that a relative of his will arrive here this afternoon. 4. It is they who have broken the windows. 5. This professor is not as learned as he says. 6. Our house has not as many rooms as yours. 7. My neighbour says there are more than twenty officers here, but I don't believe it. 8. It seems to me that you have forgotten all you had learnt. 9. Do not lend him your watch : it is certain that he will lose it. 10. She is the most talkative woman I have ever met. 11. The bottle is not full of water, but of beer. 12. On which of the benches is your cousin sitting? On the one I bought yesterday. 13.

This novel is not good, it is the worst of the works of Valera.
14. Do us the favour of reading us this article on the political
situation. 15. Where are your spectacles? I have left
them on the mantelpiece in my room. 16. Whom were
you waiting for this morning? For a friend of mine. 17.
They have not brought their trunks with them. They
have left them in the train. 18. The richest man in the
village is the one who is sitting in front of the inn. 19.
I will not send it to him. 20. This is the most famous
church in the city.

Exercise 15(b)

1. ¿ A cuál de estos dos muchachos dará Vd. este cuchillo?
2. La casa hacia la cual andábamos daba a un pequeño
jardín. 3. Hay en este periódico tres artículos que voy a leer.
4. No me será fácil enviárselos a Vd. 5. ¿Cuántas cestas
de frutos le ha dado Vd. a ella? 6. He dejado mis zapatos en
mi cuarto, tenga Vd. la bondad de traérmelos. 7. Escu-
chemos los pájaros. 8. No sé cuántas botellas de cerveza
él ha bebido. 9. Todos los días él andaba hasta la plaza.
10. ¿Ha visto Vd. al ladrón a quien buscan los guardias
civiles? 11. El hombre cuyo auto yo compré es un autor
muy célebre. 12. La casa detrás de la cual me hallé pertenecía al médico. 13. ¿De quién es este sobretodo? De
Vd. o de él? 14. No son estos obreros quienes son tan
hábiles. 15. Esta es la ciudad más agradable de España.
16. Es verdad que me he comprado un reloj, pero era muy
barato. 17. ¿Delante de cuál de las puertas le aguardaré
a Vd? 18. Es seguro que ella se cortará el dedo. 19. No
quedaremos aquí más de dos días. 20. Nos es imposible
leer mientras Vds. hablan.

Translation I

Literal Version. "Good day, sir," to me said the
clerk at the same time that I entered in the office of Spanish
tourism.

My grandfather was from Valencia, and I appear myself
to him for the which touches to the features and the colour
of the complexion. For the so much much people whom
I meet for first time believe that I am Spanish. It would
please me very much to speak well the Spanish and in

consequence I did not lose the opportunity to use said language directing to him the word.

" In what way may I serve you ? " he continued.

" Good day," I replied.   " This is the which brings me here.   I wish to pass the holidays in Spain but I do not dispose of much time."

" Very well, sir.   Then the important is to arrive there quickly."

" That is.   But I do not wish to go in aeroplane.   It is too dear."

" What part of Spain do you desire to visit ? "

" In first place I am going to Barcelona."

" Would it please you to go in boat ? "

" No.   Always I sea-sick myself much.   Is there not a train direct since Paris ? "

" Certainly, sir.   The express goes out from the station of Quai d'Orsay at the 8 of the night and arrives at Barcelona little after the 12—a journey of 16 hours."

" Excellent.   Without doubt a ticket of go and return will be cheaper.   But I shall not be much time in Barcelona. Give me then by favour a ticket simple of second class. I think to start the Friday of the next week."

FREE VERSION.   " Good day, sir," the clerk said to me as I entered the Spanish tourist office.

My grandfather came from Valencia, and I take after him as regards features and complexion.   Therefore many people whom I meet for the first time think I am Spanish. I should very much like to speak Spanish well, and consequently I did not lose the opportunity of using this language in addressing him.

" What can I do for you ? " he continued.

" Good morning," I answered.   " This is what brings me here.   I want to spend the holidays in Spain, and I have not much time at my disposal."

" Very well, sir.   Then the important thing is to get there quickly."

" Quite so.   (That's it.)   But I don't want to go by aeroplane.   It's too dear."

" What part of Spain do you wish to visit ? "

" In the first place, I'm going to Barcelona."

" Would you like to go by boat ? "

" No. I'm always very sea-sick. Isn't there a through train from Paris? "

" Certainly, sir. An express leaves the Quai d'Orsay station at 8 p.m. and arrives at Barcelona shortly after noon—a journey of 16 hours."

" Excellent. No doubt a return ticket would be cheaper. But I shall not be long in Barcelona. So please give me a single second-class ticket. I am thinking of starting on Friday of next week."

NOTES. *Buenos días.* Similarly : *buenas tardes*, good afternoon; *buenas noches*, good-night; all three being plural in Spanish.

Buenas mañanas is NEVER used.

Señor. This brings us to the question of modes of address. Hitherto we have used the words *hombre*, *mujer* and *muchacho*. Actually in speaking to or of individuals these words would seldom be employed by a foreigner.

A gentleman, when we speak OF someone, is *un caballero* (lit. a horseman or knight). In speaking TO one, we should say : *señor*. This also means Mr., followed by a proper name. In speaking TO Mr. Martinez we should say: *Señor Martínez*. In speaking ABOUT him, we should put in the definite article and say : *el señor Martínez* (shortened, in writing, to *Sr*.). *Señor* (capital letter) in Bible or Prayer Book means *Lord*.

Similarly " a lady ", " Mrs." or " Madam ", is *señora* (abb. *Sra.*) ; an unmarried woman or girl is *señorita* (abb. *Srita.* or *Srta.*). *Señorito* is a diminutive (*i.e.*, Master John). Similarly a lady talking about her husband to a servant might refer to him as *el señorito* (Fetch the master's boots). Referring to his wife, a man would probably say *mi esposa*, to someone else's the more formal *señora*. A wife speaking of her husband would use *mi marido* (*mi esposo* is very formal). *La novia* means only " the bride ". *Don* and *Doña* are purely Spanish, and always used with a Christian name, though the surname may follow. Thus *Don Juan*, *Don Juan Tenorio*, *Señor Don Juan* and *Señor Don Juan Tenorio* are all possible forms of address. But the foreigner who wants to visit our old friend *Don Juan* would do best to use the simplest form, *Señor Tenorio*, and so in dealing with other less notorious personages. In referring to the relatives of someone he does not know well, he would make a good impression by inserting *señor*, etc., in speaking of them.

Has your mother arrived? = *¿ Ha llegado la Sra. madre de Vd.?*

Tocar, to touch ("to play" of instruments), also has the meaning of "as regards", "in what concerns", etc.

Por lo tanto = for the reasons given, therefore.

Vez. This means time in the sense of occasion. *Dos veces* = twice. *Tiempo* means a space of time. *Hora(s)* is used for times of day, though more often understood than expressed. *Por la primera vez* is less idiomatic than *por vez primera*, but grammatically correct. *Primero* drops the final *o* when preceding a masculine singular noun.

Repliqué. This change is necessary, because in *replicé* the *c* would have the sound of *th*. *Contestar* is, in fact, the more usual word for "to reply".

Note that *querer* and *desear* are followed by an infinitive without preposition. Note also that "of using" is *de usar* (not *usando*). The infinitive, NOT the gerund or present participle, is always used in Spanish after prepositions. The only exception is a particular and limited use of *en*.

Gustar. Many verbs are used impersonally in Spanish and with a personal subject in English. *Me gustaría* = lit. it would please to me—*i.e.*, I should like.

Mucho. This cannot have *muy* before it. It only has the superlative form *muchísimo*. Note that *gente* (people) is grammatically singular.

Lo importante. This construction, with some such word as "thing" understood, is very common.

Después is an adverb. *Después de* is the preposition, used when followed by a noun, pronoun or infinitive. Both refer to time. "Behind" or "after", of place, is *detrás de*.

Demasiado means too or too much (French *trop*). Too, in the sense of "also", is *también*.

The article is frequently omitted with *sin*. It is often used with nouns when English would have an adjective ending in "less". Doubtless = *sin duda*. Penniless = *sin dinero*.

Exercise 16

1. Tengo el gusto de presentarle a mi primo. 2. El gusto es mío, pero he encontrado ya a este caballero. 3. ¿Dónde está el Sr. Gómez? No está aquí. Debió salir para Madrid a las diez. 4. ¿ Cuántas veces ha leído Vd. este libro? 5. No debemos pasar mucho tiempo aquí. 6. ¿Cuándo piensa Vd. salir para Londres? 7. Nos gusta muchísimo ir en aeroplano : es el modo más agradable de viajar. 8. No sé lo que me dijo. Lo peor es que no pronuncia bien sus palabras. 9. Es evidente que el señor López es muy hábil en todo lo que toca al comercio. 10. Buenas tardes, señorita. ¿Cómo está Vd.? Muy bien, gracias. ¿Y Vd.? 11. Hay en la puerta una señorita que quiere hablar con el (Sr.) médico. 12. ¿Quién es aquel caballero? Es un amigo del señor Fuentes. 13. No es agradable hallarse sólo y sin amigos. 14. He tomado un billete de ida y vuelta de primera clase. 15. Debíamos encontrarlos cerca de la iglesia a las siete. 16. Mucha gente me dice que me parezco a mi padre. 17 ¿Iremos en barco? No lo quiero, porque me mareo siempre. 18. No sé cuánto dinero me debe. 19. ¿Cuántas veces le ha escrito Vd. (a él)? 20. No debe ser fácil hacer sin faltas todos estos ejercicios.

Translation II

LITERAL VERSION. It was raining when I left from London. But in arriving at Dover I met myself with that the weather had cleared. The sun was shining. It made hot and I was content to see that the sea was calm. The crossing from Dover to Calais lasted only an hour and at that of the six I was meeting myself in Paris. As I only thought to be outside of home fifteen days, I had not registered baggage, but only a suit-case, which I passed by the window of the coach to a porter. He called to a taxi, the which drove me to the station of Quai d'Orsay. The train was not to leave until the eight, for so much I supped in the restaurant of the station.

The office of tourism had reserved me a seat of front to the locomotive and I was content to find, when the train left, only other passenger in the compartment : a Spanish gentleman who told me that he was returning to Barcelona after to have passed three weeks in France.

Holding in account that I was a stranger, he spoke to me slowly, and I was able to understand him much of that which he said to me. As I was wearied after the journey from London, very soon I went to bed in the seat, with the head resting in a pillow hired for 4 francs to an official of the company of railways. I did not sleep very well, but I did not feel it, and when I woke up I found myself with that the train was passing by the heart of the Pyrenees.

FREE VERSION. It was raining when I left London. But on arriving at Dover, I found that the weather had cleared. The sun was shining. It was hot, and I was glad to see that the sea was calm. The crossing from Dover to Calais lasted only an hour, and at about six o'clock I found myself in Paris. As I was only intending to be away (from home) a fortnight, I had no registered baggage, but only a suit-case, which I passed out of the window of the coach to a porter. He called a taxi, which took me to the Quai d'Orsay station. The train was not due to start until 8, so I had supper in the station restaurant.

The tourist office had reserved me a seat facing the engine, and I was glad to find, when the train started, only one other passenger in the compartment : a Spanish gentleman, who told me that he was returning to Barcelona after spending three weeks in France.

Bearing in mind that I was a foreigner, he spoke to me slowly, and I was able to understand much of what he said to me. As I was tired after the journey from London, I lay down on the seat very soon, with my head resting on a pillow, hired for 4 francs from an official of the Railway Company. I didn't sleep very well, but I didn't mind, and when I woke up I found that the train was passing through the heart of the Pyrenees.

NOTES. *Llovía.* Many verbs are used impersonally in Spanish to describe states of the weather. *Helar*, to hail; *tronar*, to thunder; *amanecer*, to dawn, grow light; *anochecer*, to grow dark, to get dusk; *nevar*, to snow. In other expressions the verb *hacer* is used coupled with a noun or adjective. *Hace frío (calor)* = it is cold (warm). *Hace mal (buen) tiempo* = it is bad (fine) weather. *Tiempo*

also, of course, means " time ". *Hace mucho tiempo que* =
it is a long time since ——.

En llegando. In the notes to the previous extract it was
stated that after all prepositions the infinitive, not the
gerund, was used in Spanish, where the English equivalent
is "-ing". The only exception is a particular use with
en. And here it is. *En* is used when something happens
AFTER the completion of the action expressed by the gerund.
The English equivalent is generally " on ". *En acabando
mi trabajo, me acosté* = on finishing my work, I went to bed.
Acabando (without *en*) would mean " while finishing ".
All other prepositions, including *en*, apart from this usage,
require the infinitive. *Insistir en trabajar* = to insist on
working.

Después de usually requires the perfect infinitive—
después de haber pasado = after spending (having spent).

Encontrar = lit. to meet, often to find; but to find that
something has happened requires *encontrar con que*.

El sol brillaba. In speaking of the weather, an impersonal
verb cannot be used when there is a noun subject.

Hace buen tiempo, but *el tiempo era claro.*

Eso de las seis. The whole question of times of day,
etc., is dealt with in the lessons on numerals.

Solo as an adjective means " alone ", " single ". As an
adverb (with distinctive accent mark) it is equivalent to
solamente (only) and, being shorter, often preferred to it.
Solo must not be confused with the adjective *único* (sole,
only)—*hijo único* = only son.

Casa used with a preposition and without an article means
one's home or place of business (French, *chez*).

Voy a casa = I'm going home. *Voy a casa de B* = I'm
going to B's (place, home, shop, firm, etc.). *Estar en casa* =
to be at home.

Por tanto is identical with *por lo tanto* used in the previous
extract and means " so " or " therefore ".

Otro referring to a particular person or thing requires
the definite article or a possessive. Used indefinitely it
does NOT take the indefinite article. *Quiero otro* = I want
another; *quiero el otro* = I want the other. *Otra cosa* =
something else: with a negative in the sentence it means
" nothing else ".

Volver = to return. *Volver a* with an infinitive implies repetition : *volveré a verle* = I shall see him again.

Alquilada. A past participle used with *ser, estar* or without either agrees with the word to which it refers. Used with *haber* it is invariable. There are certain words mostly connected with taking—*i.e.*, stealing, borrowing, buying, etc.—when the English "from" is rendered, as in French, by *a*, and not by *de*.

Exercise 17

1. Aquel caballero es el hijo único del Sr. Galdos, a quien encontró Vd. ayer. 2. En llegando a la estación vendré a verle a Vd. 3. Después de haber leído el periódico fuí a casa de mi amigo. 4. Nos dijo lo que quería hacer. 5. Dice que hará frío mañana, pero no lo creo. 6. El tren saldrá de la estación a las ocho. 7. No hablábamos de asuntos políticos, sino de otra cosa. 8. Compré este auto a un amigo mío, quien no sabía conducir. 9. No me trajo el libro que quería, sino otro. 10. Como iba sólo hasta la iglesia, no tomé mi sobretodo. 11. Ayer no quiso venir a hablarle : hoy está contento de hacerlo. 12. Me hizo el favor de prestarme cinco pesetas. 13. Debemos volver a verle (a Vd.). 14. No puedo hallar la maleta que me dió Vd. 15. ¿No puede Vd. reservarnos habitaciones que dan al jardín? 16. Me dijo todo lo que sabía del asunto. 17. Hábleme más despacio, por favor : me es imposible entenderle. 18. No me gustan autos alquilados. 19. ¿Quiere Vd. venir a buscar mis anteojos? No puedo ver bien sin ellos. 20. Me vió á mí, pero no le ví á él.

Translation III

LITERAL VERSION. The clerk of the office of tourism had told me that I had two routes for Barcelona. I could pass the frontier by Port-Bou or by Puigcerdá. I chose the ultimate and rejoiced myself of to have done it. The scenery was magnificent. At the two sides of the way the mountains bathed by the rays of the sun which it made little had left, raised themselves to great height. In the summits I had rests of snow and streamlets slipped themselves by its sides in order to unite their waters to the growing river, near the way of the train. The train passed

through the little republic of Andorra, which until it makes
little time had not almost no communication with Spain
and France.

Soon we arrived at La Tour de Carol, the ultimate town
of the French side.   Then the train passed the frontier and
stopped itself in the station of Puigcerdá.   All the passengers
we got out of the train and directed ourselves to the Customs
House.   An official looked to me the passport and reviewed
the baggage.   He asked me if I had something to declare.
I said to him that I had not more than the cigarettes which
I had in the case and he permitted me to return to the train.
After of half hour of wait the train left from the station and
little by little we went ourselves removing from the mountains.   I looked at the landscape and entertained myself
noting the names of the stations.   The train stopped
itself at many of them.   The compartment where I was
going, was now full and I was doing how much I could in
order to understand that which my companions of voyage
were saying.   It was not very easy, since many of them
were speaking the Catalán, which is very different from the
Spanish.   By end the train arrived, I entered in a taxi and
directed myself to the hotel where I had reserved a room.

FREE VERSION.   The tourist office clerk had told me that
there were two routes to Barcelona.   I could cross the
frontier at Port-Bou or Puigcerdá.   I chose the latter, and
congratulated myself on having done so.   The scenery was
magnificent.   On either side of the track, the mountains,
bathed in the rays of the sun which had risen shortly
before, rose to a great height.   On the summits there were
remains of snow and little streams glided down their sides
to mingle their waters with the growing river near the
railway line.   The train passed through the little republic
of Andorra, which until a short while ago had virtually
no communication with Spain and France.

We soon reached La Tour de Carol, the last town on the
French side.   Then the train crossed the frontier and stopped
in Puigcerdá station.   All of us passengers got out and
made our way to the Custom House.   An official looked at
my passport and examined my luggage.   He asked me if
I had anything to declare.   I told him that I had nothing
but the cigarettes in my case, and he allowed me to return

to the train. After a half-hour wait the train left the station, and gradually we drew farther and farther away from the mountains.

I looked at the landscape, and amused myself by noting the names of the stations. The train stopped at many of them. The compartment in which I was travelling was now full, and I did my best to understand what my travelling companions were saying. It was not very easy, since many of them were speaking Catalán, which is very different from Spanish. At last the train arrived. I got in a taxi and made my way to the hotel where I had reserved a room.

NOTES. *Había.* The ordinary third person singular present indicative form of *haber* is *ha*. This also means " ago ", though it is sometimes written with the accent sign. The form *hay* means " there is " or " there are ". Consequently *había* and *hubo* can mean " there was (were) ", *habrá* " there will be ", and *ha habido* " there has (have) been ". Sometimes we use " there is " with the idea of drawing attention, possibly pointing a finger—*e.g.*, " There he is ! " For this *he* is used, followed by *aquí* for " here is ", and by *allí* for " there is ". This *he* is really an obsolete part of *ver*, to see. Being a verb, it takes an object in the accusative, so that " there he is " is really " see him there "= *héle allí*, and " here I am "= *héme aquí* (see me here) (French *me voici*).

Hacía poco, shortly before. This point has been fully dealt with in the introduction to this lesson.

Se paró, stopped. Many verbs are intransitive in English, and transitive (*i.e.*, must have an object) in Spanish. So they take the reflexive pronoun, which is untranslated in English.

Salimos del tren. Remember that *salir* cannot take a direct object. *De* is required. Similarly *en* after *entrar*. On the other hand, there are certain verbs requiring a preposition in English before the object, but used without one in Spanish : e.g., *aguardar* (to wait for), *aprovechar* (to profit by), *presenciar* (to be present at), *escuchar* (to listen to), *mirar* (to look at), *incendiar* (to set fire to). These do, of course, require the usual *a* when their direct object is a person.

Nos dirigimos. The first person is used because the speaker is including himself among the passengers. When a Spanish verb has subjects of different persons, the verb is in the resulting person. " He and I are good friends " becomes " he and I (we) are good friends " = *él y yo somos buenos amigos.*

Nos fuimos alejando—lit. " we went removing ourselves ". This use of *ir* (or of *venir* or *andar*) indicates that the action expressed by the verb in the gerund goes on progressively increasing. *El peligro va creciendo* = the danger is growing ever greater.

Exercise 18

1. ¿Qué instrumento de música ha aprendido Vd. a tocar? 2. Hace dos horas que los aguardo. 3. Ella y yo hicimos cuanto podíamos para enseñarle a cantar. 4. Después de haber pasado seis horas sin comer, teníamos mucha hambre. 5. Me convidó a cenar en casa de sus padres. 6. Hace dos años que compré esta bolsa para tabaco (compré esta bolsa dos años ha). 7. Me gusta mucho la música : tenga Vd. la bondad de poner la radio. 8. Se puso el traje que había comprado a su primo. 9. " Vd. no tiene razón," dijo el juez, echándose a reir. 10. Hacía dos horas que aguardábamos cuando entró el alcalde en el cuarto. 11. Me gustaría mucho llevar calcetines con cierres de cremallera. 12. ¡ Hélos allí ! ¿No puede verlos? 13. Yo tenía un auto, pero lo vendí hace dos semanas. 14. Sírvase tomar asiento. No tardarán en venir. 15 ¿Cuánto tiempo hace que mira Vd. las montañas? 16. Había ladrones en esta vecindad, pero no los hay ahora. 17. Estábamos contentos de encontrarnos con que brillaba el sol. 18. Es inútil decirme que no tiene Vd. nada que declarar. 19. ¿Me permitirá Vd. volver a verle? 20. Prometí prestarle dinero, pero no tengo la intención de hacerlo.

Translation IV

LITERAL VERSION. The hotel where I lodged myself was situated in a great avenue known by the Ramblas, which directs itself since the port until a magnificent square, called Plaza de Cataluña. The proprietor was speaking French and also a little of English, then Barcelona is a cosmopolitan city, but I told him that he may speak to me Spanish, since I was decided to improve the knowledge of the language. Smiling he said to me that it was an excellent idea. Then I went up to my room, which was on the second floor : I washed myself, undid my suit-case and went down to the dining-room. I had taken a cup of coffee before to cross the frontier, but since then I had not eaten nothing, then I had much hunger. I had an excellent lunch, the which consisted in *hors d'œuvres*, fish, chicken cooked to the Spanish manner, salad, cheese and fruits. I of wine do not understand much, and I told to the waiter that he should bring me a bottle of white wine of recommendable make. And in effect it was admirable.

After to eat I rested a short space of time in my room and went out after in order to see something of the city. I entered first into a bookshop, where I bought a guide of Barcelona with a map. Studying the plan, it surprised to me at the to see that great part of the city is of modern type, the streets stretch themselves in straight lines like the of a city of the United States. The part in which I found myself was the quarter most antique of Barcelona and contained many picturesque buildings and churches. I directed myself first to the long of the Ramblas towards the port, dominated by a gigantic statue of Christopher Columbus. At little distance was a mail-boat which was to leave that night for Majorca (Balearic Islands). There were also other many boats, then Barcelona is one of the ports most important of Spain.

FREE VERSION. The hotel where I was putting up was situated in a spacious avenue known as the Ramblas, which runs from the harbour as far as a magnificent square, called the Plaza de Cataluña. The proprietor spoke French and also a little English, for Barcelona is a cosmopolitan city, but I told him to speak Spanish to me, since I was determined to improve my knowledge of the language. He told me with a smile that it was an excellent idea. Then I went up to my room, which was on the second floor, washed, un-packed my bag and went down to the dining-room. I had had a cup of coffee before crossing the frontier, but since then I had had nothing, so I was very hungry. I had an excellent lunch, consisting of *hors d'œuvres*, fish, chicken

cooked in the Spanish style, salad, cheese and dessert.
I do not know much about wine, and I told the waiter to
bring me a bottle of white wine of a brand he could recommend. And, indeed, it was excellent.

After the meal I rested for a while in my room, and then
went out to see something of the city. I went first of all
to a bookseller's, where I bought a guide to Barcelona with
a map. Studying the plan, I was surprised to see that
much of the city is of modern design, the streets stretching
in straight lines like those of a city in the United States.
The part in which I found myself was the oldest quarter of
Barcelona, and contained many picturesque buildings and
churches. I made my way first along the Ramblas towards
the harbour, which is dominated by a gigantic statue of
Christopher Columbus. A short distance off was a mail-
boat, which was due to start that night for Majorca in the
Balearic Islands. There were also many other vessels, for
Barcelona is one of the most important harbours in Spain.

NOTES. *Conocida por*, "known as". *Conocer* means
to know a person, or to be acquainted with somebody or
something.

Saber is not used of people, but of things.

Desde means " since " in point of time. But, particularly
when coupled with *hasta*, it means " since " in the sense of
" starting from ", where " from " alone would probably
be used in English : *de* would not convey this idea.

Poco as an adjective is the opposite of *mucho*. In the
singular it means " little ", in the plural " few ". As an
adverb it means " little ", " not very ", and is the opposite
of *muy*. As an adverb it is, of course, invariable in form.

Discursos poco interesantes = rather uninteresting
speeches.

Pocos amigos = few friends.

Poco may have the indefinite article in front of it with the
same difference in meaning as is implied in English by
" little " (few) and " a little " (a few). When " a little "
means " a small quantity of " and is followed by a noun, *de*
is required before the noun.

Un poco de queso = a little cheese. (When the " little "
means " small ", *pequeño* is used.) *Habla poco* = he speaks
little. *Pues* = then, in the sense of " for ", " since ", or

" therefore ". Then in the sense of time is *entonces*; then meaning " next " or " after that " is *después*.

Dije que me hablara. Verbs of commanding, ordering, etc., require the verb after the " that " to be in the subjunctive.

Subir = to go up. *Bajar* = to come down. Both can be used transitively to mean " to take up " and " to fetch down ", respectively (of luggage, etc.).

Antes de is the preposition " before ", *antes* the adverb. A preposition must always govern a noun, a pronoun or a verb in the infinitive. The function of an adverb is only to limit or render more exact the meaning of a verb, an adjective or another adverb. " I never saw him before " (adverb). " I saw him before you " (preposition). *Delante* (*de*) is " before ", " in front of ", of place, *antes* (*de*) of time.

Mucha hambre. We say " to be hungry ", the Spanish " to have hunger ". Hunger is a noun, therefore, as explained in the previous note, an adverb (*muy*) is inadmissible. The adjective *mucho* is needed. (The French have the same usage.)

Rato = a short while, a minute (though not of exactly 60 seconds, which is *minuto*).

Librería = a bookshop, not a library, which is *biblioteca*.

El ver. Infinitives are sometimes used as nouns with an article preceding. *Un ser humano* = a human being.

El beber y el comer = eating and drinking.

Guía (masc.) = the guide (man) : (fem.), the guide-book. Similarly *la guardia* = the guard (body of men), *el guardia* = a member of that body.

Otros muchos = many others. Adjectives of quantity (*muchos, pocos*, etc.) or numerals generally follow the plural of *otro*(*a*).

E iglesias. To avoid two similar sounds in succession, *y* (and) is changed to *e*, when the word next to it begins with *i* (or *hi*, since *h* is unpronounced).

Fathers and sons = *padres e hijos*. Similarly *o* (or) becomes *u* when the next word begins with *o* or *ho*. *vacas u ovejas*, cows or sheep.

Exercise 19

1. Diré a la criada que baje la maleta. 2. Salió del cuarto sin decir nada. 3. ¿Hay algo de nuevo en el periódico?

4. Cuando miré por la ventana había alguien en el jardín.
5. Ni ella ni su hermana saben nadar. 6. Le prestaré este
libro. Tengo en mi biblioteca otros muchos. 7. Si Vd.
quiere aguardar un rato, diré al Señor Gutierrez que está
aquí. 8. No tengo nada que decirle. 9. No supe lo que
quería hacer. Ni ella tampoco. 10. No tenemos ningunos
amigos en esta ciudad : lo que es lástima. 11. No volveré
nunca a hablarle (a Vd.). 12. No he encontrado nunca a
aquel caballero, ni quiero conocerle. 13. ¿Antes de salir
para Londres, no le dijo nada a Vd.? 14. ¿Hay allí
alguien? No puedo ver a nadie. 15. ¿Cuánto tiempo
hace que le busca Vd.? Desde las ocho. 16. Tendremos
que comprar un poco de café. 17. Pocos hombres hablan
más de dos lenguas. 18. ¿Ha encontrado Vd. a alguien?
Sí, (señor). A tres caballeros. 19. Mi hermano no escribe
nunca a nadie. 20. ¿No tenía ella miedo? De ningún
modo.

Translation V

LITERAL VERSION. Having consulted my plan, I made my
way to the Plaza de Toros. In this period of the year
there were not courses of bulls, and even if there might have
been, I am not sure if I would have gone to see one. But I
interested myself much to see the arena. A guardian to
whom I gave to him a peseta of tip allowed me to enter.
That which more surprised me was the little extension of
the place. The circle had not much more than 60 yards of
diameter. Portraits of famous bull-fighters adorned the
walls, and the programme of the last festival showed me that
had been run (killed) six bulls during the race of the afternoon. I think that it is a cruel amusement, but the same
are the hunting of foxes, and both distinguish themselves
by skill and bravery. Besides, nobody can judge a thing
without to have seen it. The exterior was very beautiful.
The edifice was of red brick with two towers, Moorish style.

The walk had fatigued me, and I sat myself in one of the
tables of the part of outside of a café. I asked a glass of
beer, and had not begun even when a boot-black approached
himself and began to clean to me the shoes. It fixed to him
in that one of my heels was used, and before that I had time
to protest he had taken it off and was preparing other in

order to put it to me. This he did in less of 5 minutes.
Amused me much all it, and I paid to him the 12 pesetas
which he asked to me. I bought also a tie to a vendor that
was running over the cafés. I thought to meet the streets
full of beggars, but there were none, and the streets were as
clean as the of any city in which I have been. I began to
think that many of the ideas which I had concerning Spain
were false. Nor so little I met in spite of the poor knowledge
which I had of the language, no one who left off to do
the possible in order to reply to the questions which I
made to them.

At last I looked at my wrist-watch, and thought that it
would be better to return to the hotel in order to sup.

FREE VERSION. Having consulted my plan, I made my
way to the bull-ring. At this season of the year there were
no bull-fights and, even if there had been, I am not sure
whether I should have gone to see one. But I was greatly
interested in seeing the arena. A guardian (doorkeeper)
to whom I gave a peseta as a tip allowed me to go in. What
surprised me most was the smallness of the place. The
circle was not much more than 60 yards in diameter.
Portraits of famous bull-fighters adorned the walls, and the
programme of the last performance showed me that six
bulls had been killed during the afternoon's fight. I think
it is a cruel sport, but so is fox-hunting, and both are distinguished by skill and courage. Besides, no one can judge
of a thing without having seen it. The outside was very
handsome. The building was of red brick with two towers
in Moorish style.

The walk had tired me, and I sat down at one of the outside tables of a café. I asked for a glass of beer, and had
not even begun it when a boot-black drew near and began
to clean my shoes. He noticed that one of my heels was
worn and, before I had time to protest, he had taken it off
and was getting another ready to put on. This he did in
less than 5 minutes. All this amused me considerably, and
I paid him the 30 pesetas which he asked. I also bought a
tie from a vendor who was making the round of the cafés.
I expected to find the streets full of beggars, but there were
none, and the streets were as clean as those of any city I have
been in. I began to think that many of my ideas about

— Pas un officier français, dis-je, n'aimerait passer la nuit seul dans une de ces tours avec deux factionnaires affolés par la peur. On a vu des patrouilles livrer leurs officiers. Il arrive que les Viets obtiennent plus de succès en se servant d'un mégaphone que d'un bazooka. Je ne leur en fais pas un reproche. Eux non plus ne croient à rien. Vous et vos semblables, vous essayez de faire une guerre avec l'aide de gens qui ne s'y intéressent pas du tout.

— Ils ne veulent pas du communisme.

— Ils veulent une ration de riz suffisante, dis-je. Ils ne veulent pas recevoir de coups de fusil. Ils veulent que chaque jour soit à peu près semblable aux précédents. Ils ne veulent pas que nos peaux blanches se mêlent de leur apprendre ce qu'ils veulent.

— Si l'Indochine est perdue...

— Je connais le disque : le Siam sera perdu, la Malaisie sera perdue, l'Indonésie sera perdue. Qu'est-ce que cela signifie : perdu ? Si je croyais à votre Dieu et à la vie future, je parierais ma harpe céleste contre votre couronne dorée que dans cinq cents ans New York et Londres n'existeront peut-être plus, mais qu'ici, dans ces champs, ces gens feront pousser le riz, coiffés de leurs chapeaux coniques ; ils porteront leurs produits au marché sur de longs balanciers. Les petits garçons chevaucheront les buffles. J'aime les buffles, ils n'aiment pas notre odeur, l'odeur des Européens. Et n'oubliez pas que, du point de vue du buffle, vous aussi vous êtes un Européen.

— Ils seront forcés de croire ce qu'on leur dira, ils n'auront pas la liberté de penser librement.

— La pensée est un luxe. Croyez-vous que le paysan s'installe pour penser à Dieu et à la Démocratie quand il rentre le soir dans sa hutte de pisé ?

— Vous parlez comme s'il n'y avait que des paysans dans ce pays. Et ceux qui ont été éduqués, seront-ils heureux ?

— Oh ! non, dis-je. Nous les avons élevés suivant nos idées à nous. Nous leur avons enseigné des jeux dangereux, et c'est pourquoi nous sommes ici à attendre, à attendre qu'on nous coupe la gorge. Nous méritons qu'on nous la coupe. Je regrette que votre ami York ne soit pas ici avec nous. Je me demande s'il apprécierait la situation.

— York Harding est un homme très courageux. Tenez, en Corée...

— Il n'était pas soldat, n'est-ce pas ? Il avait un billet de retour. Avec un billet de retour en poche, le courage devient un exercice intellectuel, comme la flagellation pour un moine. Jusqu'à quel point vais-je le supporter ? Ces pauvres diables, eux, ne peuvent pas sauter dans un avion et rentrer chez eux.

« Hi ! leur criai-je, comment vous appelez-vous ? »

Je pensais que connaître leurs noms était une façon de les faire pénétrer dans le cercle de notre conversation. Ils ne me répondirent pas : ils nous regardèrent seulement d'un air menaçant derrière leurs cigarettes presque consumées.

— Ils croient que nous sommes français, dis-je.

— Précisément, dit Pyle. Vous ne devriez pas en vouloir à York, vous devriez en vouloir aux Français et à leur colonialisme.

— Assez d'ismes et de craties. Je veux des faits. Un planteur de caoutchouc bat son ouvrier, bon, je suis contre lui. Il n'a pas reçu pour le faire un ordre de son ministre des Colonies. En France, je suppose qu'il battrait sa femme. J'ai vu un prêtre, si pauvre que le pantalon qu'il porte est le seul qu'il possède, travailler quinze heures par jour, allant de hutte en hutte pendant une épidémie de choléra, ne mangeant que du riz et du poisson salé, disant sa messe dans une vieille tasse, une écuelle de bois. Je ne crois pas en Dieu et pourtant je suis pour ce prêtre. Pourquoi n'appelez-vous pas cela du colonialisme ?

— Mais c'est aussi du colonialisme. York dit que ce sont souvent les bons administrateurs qui rendent difficile de réformer un mauvais système.

— Quoi qu'il en soit, des Français meurent tous les jours : cela n'est pas une conception de l'esprit. Ils ne mènent pas ces gens en bateau à l'aide de demi-mensonges, à la manière de vos politiciens... ou des nôtres. J'ai été aux Indes, Pyle, et je connais le mal que font les libéraux. Nous n'avons plus de parti libéral : le libéralisme a infecté tous les autres partis. Nous sommes soit des conservateurs libéraux, soit des socialistes libéraux ; nous avons tous la conscience nette. J'aimerais mieux être un exploiteur qui se bat pour ce qu'il exploite, et meurt avec. Voyez ce qui s'est passé en Birmanie. Nous sommes allés envahir le pays ; les tribus locales nous ont soutenus ; nous avons remporté la victoire ; mais de même que vous, Américains, nous nous défendions d'être des colonialistes à cette époque. Ah ! mais ! Nous fîmes la paix avec le roi et nous lui rendîmes la province, en abandonnant nos alliés qui furent crucifiés ou sciés en deux. Ils étaient innocents. Ils croyaient que nous allions rester. Mais nous étions des libéraux, et nous ne voulions pas avoir une mauvaise conscience.

— C'est une très vieille histoire.

— Nous allons faire la même chose ici. Les encourager et puis les laisser avec quelques machines et des fabriques de jouets.

— De jouets ?

— Votre plastic.

— Oh ! oui, je vois.

— Je ne sais pas pourquoi je parle politique. Ça ne m'intéresse pas. Je suis reporter. Je ne suis pas *engagé*.

— Vraiment pas ? demanda Pyle.

— Rien que pour entretenir la conversation, pour faire passer cette saloperie de nuit, c'est tout. Je ne prends pas parti. Je continuerai à faire des reportages quel que soit le vainqueur.

— Si les autres sont vainqueurs, vos reportages seront des mensonges.

— Il y a généralement une façon de s'en tirer. D'ailleurs, je n'ai jamais eu l'impression dans vos journaux non plus d'un grand respect de la vérité.

Je crois que le fait que nous fussions assis là à bavarder encouragea les deux soldats : peut-être pensaient-ils que le son de nos voix blanches (car les voix ont, elles aussi, une couleur : les voix jaunes chantent et les voix noires glougloutent, tandis que les nôtres parlent, tout simplement), en produisant un effet de nombre, empêcherait les Viets d'approcher. Ils ramassèrent leurs gamelles et se remirent à manger, en grattant avec leurs baguettes, sans nous quitter des yeux, Pyle et moi, par-dessus le bord du récipient.

— Ainsi vous pensez que nous avons perdu ?

— Là n'est pas la question, répondis-je. Je n'ai aucun désir particulier de vous voir gagner. J'aimerais que ces deux pauvres bougres qui sont là soient heureux... c'est tout. Je voudrais qu'ils ne soient pas obligés de passer la nuit dans le noir, à trembler de peur.

— Il faut se battre pour la liberté.

— Je n'ai pas vu un seul Américain se battre ici. Et quant à la liberté, je ne sais pas ce que cela signifie. Demandez-leur.

Je leur criai en français d'un bout de la pièce à l'autre :

— La liberté... qu'est-ce que c'est, la liberté ?

Ils aspiraient leur riz avec un bruit de succion. Ils nous regardèrent fixement, sans dire un mot.

— Voudriez-vous que tous les gens soient coulés dans le même moule ? demanda Pyle. Vous discutez pour le plaisir de discuter. Vous êtes un intellectuel. Vous croyez à l'importance de l'individu autant que moi-même... ou que York.

— Pourquoi l'avons-nous découverte si récemment ? demandai-je. Il y a quarante ans, personne n'en parlait de cette manière.

130

Spain were wrong.   Nor, in spite of the meagreness of my
knowledge of the language, did I come across anyone who
did not do his utmost to answer the questions I put.   At
length I looked at my wrist-watch, and thought it would
be best to go back to the hotel for supper.

NOTES.   *Hubiera habido*.   The indicative is the mood of
certainty or fact, the subjunctive of doubt or supposition.
Thus the subjunctive is used after *aunque* (even if), since it
introduces a possibility not a fact.   NOTE here, too, that as
no estoy is negative, the negative pronoun *ninguna* is
needed instead of *una* or *alguna*.

Más que.   In an earlier lesson it was stated that " more
than ", followed by a numeral, is *más de*.   But if the
sentence is negative, *más que* can be used and is generally
considered preferable.

Lidiar is a special term limited to the killing of a bull in
a bull-fight.

Muerto, past participle of *morir*, to die, is generally used
instead of *matado*, the past participle of *matar*, to kill.
Matado generally refers to suicide or the slaughtering of
animals.   To be dead is *estar* (not *ser*) *muerto*.

Mismo.   *El mismo hombre* = the same man.

El hombre mismo = the man himself, or, even the man.

Lo mismo = the same thing.

Ambos = both.   It may be replaced by *los dos*.

Cada dos días[1] = every two days.

Haberla visto.   Note that the pronoun object is attached
to the infinitive of the auxiliary, and not to the past participle of the other verb.

Pedir means to ask, in the sense of to beg or to demand.
Preguntar is to ask, in questions.   To put a question to
someone = *hacer una pregunta a alguien*.

Heel = *talón* (of the foot), *tacón* (of the shoe).

Antes que is the conjunction introducing a clause, the
" that " being omitted in English.   *Antes de* is the preposition governing a noun, pronoun, or infinitive; *antes* is
the adverb.

Creí encontrar.   When the subject of *creer* is the same

[1] *Cada*, each, every, is invariable and used before singular nouns.
But it can be used with plural nouns, when these are preceded by a
numeral.

person as that of the following verb, the second verb is merely put in the infinitive, where we in English say: " I thought (that) I should ". But if the subjects are different then a *que* clause is required. " I thought that you —— " = *Creí que Vd.*, etc.

Cualquier = not " some " or " any ", but " any " in the sense of " anyone you like to mention ".

Mirar = to look at. When the *a* is inserted before an inanimate object it emphasises that the looking is purposeful and not just a casual glance.

Exercise 20

1. No entendemos nunca las preguntas que nos hace el profesor. 2. Habiendo acabado su trabajo, se acostó poco después de las diez. 3. Este caballero es estimado de todos los que le conocen (cuantos le conocen). 4. Cada tres días me convidaba a venir a verle. 5. No estoy seguro si tendré la ocasión de hablarles. 6. Yo me paseaba por el barrio antiguo de la ciudad, buscando una librería. 7. Creí tener razon, pero es evidente que yo me engañaba. 8. Antes de sentarse se quitó el sombrero. 9. Se venden aquí libros y periódicos. 10. Se sabe bien que soy yo quien he incendiado la casa. 11. Se arrojó a este pobre niño por la ventana. 12. Se ocultaron porque tenían miedo. 13. Se les ocultó en la parte más oscura del bosque. 14. Estábamos cansados cuando llegamos. 15. Creo que el tren va a pararse. 16. Llame Vd., por favor, a los guardias: me han robado. 17. Sentémonos un rato; tengo mucho calor. Y yo también. 18. Hace mucho calor en esta época del año. 19. ¿Han visto al juez? No sabe nadie dónde está. 20. Me dijo que no han escrito las cartas.

Translation VI

[From this point onwards only one English version of the Spanish passages will be given. Where the English equivalent differs considerably from the Spanish original, a literal translation will be appended in brackets.]

In many places in Spain it is often very hot. For this reason, during the middle of the day the shops are shut and people stay indoors for two hours or so (a little more or less). In order to make up for (to remake oneself of) this loss of time, they continue work until later than is the custom in England, and dine at eight o'clock or later, instead of at seven. Consequently, the performances in the theatres do not begin until nine, and many people go to bed after midnight.

Barcelona is a commercial city, and its inhabitants are industrious workers. It is never very hot there. Nevertheless, I found that dinner was rarely served in the restaurants before 8 o'clock. I therefore had plenty of time before supper, and I sat down at a café to drink a glass of sherry.

The Ramblas form a large avenue, on the two sides of which the trams run. On the long promenade stretching out in the middle there are kiosks where newspapers, flowers and tobacco can be bought. I was much amused to see (the seeing that ... amused me much) that parrots were also on sale. I watched all this with the greatest interest, while the inhabitants, their work done, walked up and down, laughing and talking.

My room in the hotel looked on to this street, which was still full of people when I went to bed. But the noise did not trouble me, and I slept well. The following morning the crowing of cocks awoke me : apparently (to the seeing) many people keep them on the roofs and balconies of their houses.

I dressed quickly and had breakfast. I read the papers for some minutes and, thinking how I was going to spend the day, decided to go by train to Sitges, a small town on the coast, not far from Barcelona. After Sitges I intended to visit Tarragona, one of the oldest cities in Spain.

NOTES. *Casa*. The following phrases are worth remembering :—

Casa de huéspedes = boarding-house ; *ser muy mujer de su casa* = to be a good housewife; *poner casa* = to set up house ; *ir a casa* = to go home.

Ir en auto (vapor, bicicleta) = to go by car (steamer, bicycle). Generally, *ir por tren*. To go on horseback, on foot = *ir a caballo, a pie*.

Hacerse = to become. *¿ Qué se ha hecho de él ?* = What has become of him ? *Se hizo actor* = he became an actor.

Exercise 21

1. ¡No toque Vd. eso! Lo romperá y tendrá que pagarlo. 2. Llegué a casa sin ver a nadie. 3. No pegue Vd. al pobre muchacho. Ha trabajado a más no poder. 4. Entréguele Vd. la carta cuanto antes. 5. Vd. debería conducir con más cuidado. 6. Hace sólo seis meses que aprende el español, pero lo escribe clara y correctamente. 7. De vez en cuando miré por la ventana para asegurarme que estaba todavía allí. 8. No hable Vd. tan aprisa (tan rápidamente). Nadie puede entenderle. 9. Los tranvías pasaban a los dos lados de la avenida que se extendía desde el río hasta la estación. 10. Algunas veces hace mucho calor en esta ciudad y se debe permanecer en casa. 11. El criado aguardaba con paciencia a su amo. 12. Mucha gente miraba de un modo admirador (con ojos admiradores) las obras del célebre pintor. 13. En llegando a Madrid expliqué a mis padres que no me había sido posible volver más temprano. 14. Sin embargo encontré que no era fácil rehacerme de esta perdida de tiempo. 15. El ha perdido la mayor parte de su dinero. 16. De todos estos libros el que más me gusta es aquél. 17. Tendrá (Vd.) que vestirse rápidamente para no perder el tren. 18. Andando a lo largo de la avenida, yo pensaba cómo iba a pasar la mañana. 19. Me acerqué silenciosamente a la casa (en) donde los ladrones se habían ocultado. 20. Después de haber pasado dos años en una casa de huéspedes decidimos poner casa en Burgos. 21. Se debe trabajar con diligencia para ganar su vida.

Translation VII

Sitges is not a large town. It is (it finds itself) only 40 kilometres from Barcelona—that is to say, about 25 miles—and the train journey does not last more than three-quarters of an hour.

When I got there, I made my way through a narrow street lined with picturesque houses (along which picturesque houses aligned themselves) to a parade adorned with palm trees. Small fishing-boats painted red were lying on the sand, which stretched in a magnificent curve for a distance of two miles. The sea was of a deep blue, and many people were bathing.

It was very pleasant, but I was not there long, for this little town was one of the many which one can see on the Mediterranean coast, and I was anxious to see as much as I could of the historic cities of Spain. So I went back to the station and took the next train for Tarragona, which is about 60 miles from Barcelona.

There were various merchant-vessels in the harbour. I had a look at them, and then made my way to the street leading to the oldest portion of the city, coming, a short way off, upon a small park with orange trees and little walls of coloured tiles. On one side I saw a great line of mountains. On the other stretched enormous walls, which date from the time of the Romans, who made of this city their first possession in Spain.

It was evident (it saw itself) that the inhabitants were not accustomed to the visits of tourists, because they looked at me wonderingly when I passed along the streets. But I did not pay any attention to that, for my interest in all I saw was very great. At last I saw with great regret that it was time to go down the hill leading to the station and return to Barcelona (that the hour of going down, etc., had arrived).

NOTES. *Encontrarse* (to find oneself) is frequently used with the meaning of " to be ", particularly in relation to position.

Kilómetro. This form of measurement is in use everywhere on the Continent. It is worth noting that a kilometre is five-eighths of a mile. In other words, 8 kms. = 5 miles.

Yacer (to lie). *I* and *y* are identical in sound. But it is important to note that *i* is NEVER used as the first letter of a word, if the next letter is a vowel. It is replaced by a *y*, or takes an *h* (which is an unpronounced letter) before it. For this reason *ir*, " to go ", has a present participle *yendo*, not *iendo*.

El mar. *Mar* is generally masculine. But when talking of the state of the sea—tide, calmness, etc.—it is often feminine. It is used figuratively in the feminine in various phrases : *la mar de trabajo* = heaps of work.

Hablar de la mar = to be a sheer impossibility. To put to sea in the ordinary nautical sense is : *salir a la mar*.

Encontrándome. It has been shown that object pronouns follow an infinitive and an imperative, provided that this is not negative. The object pronoun is also joined on to the gerund (present participle). In such phrases as " I am writing to him ", where, to denote that the action is proceeding at the time of speaking, *estar* + gerund is used, the object pronoun may either be joined on to the gerund or come before the part of *estar* :—

Le estoy escribiendo or *estoy escribiéndole.*

Naranja (orange), *naranjo* (orange tree).

Exercise 22

1. Hace mucho tiempo que conozco a este caballero. 2. Aranjuez se halla (encuentra) solamente a cuarenta kilometros aproximadamente de Madrid. 3. No obedezco siempre al amo : lo que le enfada mucho. 4. No apague Vd. esa lámpara. No podré ver nada. 5. Mientras yo leía (estaba leyendo) la luz se apagó. 6. ¿ Le gusta a Vd. esta alfombra ? Acabo de comprarla. 7. ¿ Dónde la ha comprado Vd. ? En casa de Fernández. 8. Todos los pasajeros se habían acostado cuando el vapor salió a la mar. 9. Creyó que nos habíamos ido para enfadarle. 10. Acababa de volver de Bilbao cuando Vd. vino a verme. 11. Encontrándose cerca del puerto se dirigió a lo largo del muelle. 12. Le pediré que me escoja un libro interesante. 13. ¿ No le ve Vd. a él ? Se está dirigiendo a lo largo de la calle. 14. La criada me condujo a una habitación en el segundo piso. 15. ¿ De quién se estaba Vd. riendo ? Del hermano de Juan. 16. Los dos ladrones se mataron el uno al otro. 17. Todos nos mirábamos extrañados los unos a los otros. 18. Yendo por tren al norte de España cojo siempre un resfriado. 19. Me quedaré aquí hasta eso de las seis. 20. No, yo no he visto a Carlos. Creo que está levantándose (se está levantando).

Translation VIII

Some people love writing letters. (To some people it " enthuses " them to write letters.) I detest it, especially when I am on holiday. But, nevertheless (in spite of all), I had to let my parents know how I was getting on. So, before leaving Tarragona, I bought some postcards. When one wants stamps (when stamps need themselves), it is very rarely that one has to go to the post office. They can be bought in the cafés and hotels.

On my return to Barcelona I asked the proprietor of the hotel what it cost to send a card to England.

" Three pesetas fifty centimos," he answered.

I bought a dozen stamps of the required value and rapidly wrote some cards.

Then I lit a cigarette and began to make plans. Being in Barcelona was very pleasant, but at the end of a week I had to return to England. I knew that Barcelona was not typical (a city like those of the rest) of Spain and, as I wished to see as many aspects of the country as I could, I resolved to go to Madrid.

The next morning I went to the tourist office in the Paseo de Gracia and heard the clerk recommending an old lady to go to Madrid by 'plane.

" I am very much afraid," she said.

" There is no reason to be, madam," he answered. " Our pilots are very skilful. The seats are very comfortable and the machines are of the most modern type."

I had not thought of going by air (flying), but after listening to this conversation, the temptation seemed to me irresistible.

" Can you reserve me a seat in the Madrid 'plane for to-morrow ? " I asked, when the good lady had declared that nothing would induce her to leave the ground.

" There is just one seat left," he said. " It costs 2500 pesetas, including the transport from the office to the airport."

" That suits me," I said. " Can you tell me where I can change some money ? "

" At the counter (lit. grill or little window) over there, sir."

" The rate of exchange to-day is 167 pesetas," said the clerk when I asked him to change £15 into Spanish money for me. " We take a commission of 1 peseta, which leaves 166 (by that which are 166). Here you have

2490 pesetas. Two 1000-peseta notes, four 100-peseta notes and nine 10-peseta pieces.

NOTES. *Todo* normally means " all ". *Todo el día* = all day. *Todos sus amigos* = all his friends. *Todos* (*todas*) with a definite article followed by an expression of time means " every ". *Todos los martes* = every Tuesday. *Todos los meses* = every month. *Todo* (*toda*), singular, followed by a noun, without a connecting article, generally means " every ". *Todo hombre valiente* = every brave man. *Todo*, invariable, means " all " or " everything ". *Dispuesto a todo* = prepared for anything (everything). *A pesar de todo* = in spite of everything. *Sobre todo* = above all. *Todos*, unaccompanied by a noun, may mean every one. *Todos prometieron ayudarle* = everyone promised to help him. As the object of a verb referring to people, it requires *a*. *Los mató a todos* = he killed them all. *Todos los que* = all those who. *Todo lo que sé* = all that (that which) I know. In " all of us " the " of " is not translated : *Nosotros todos*. All three = *todos tres*. A whole day = *todo un día* (note the order in Spanish).

" Each ", " every ", is *cada*, which can only be used in the singular : *cada día* = each day. " Each of " is *cada uno* (*una*). *Cada una de sus hermanas* = each (one) of his sisters.

Se tenga. Many impersonal verbs in Spanish require the subjunctive.

Me respondió. Note the tendency in Spanish to supply the pronoun object, where we should simply say : " he replied ".

Unos cuantos is stronger than *unos*, and is equivalent to *algunos* (some, a few).

País means a country as a whole or politically.

Región = a district or part of a country. *Campo* (also a field)—the country as opposed to the town. *Patria* is one's own country.

Hubo declarado. " I had declared " is *había declarado*. But after *cuando* and one or two other conjunctions of time, the PAST DEFINITE, not the IMPERFECT, of the auxiliary is required, provided that the action is not repeated or habitual, in which case the ordinary *había* construction is used. *Después que* (after), *apenas* (hardly), *en cuanto* (as soon as) are, in addition to *cuando*, the commonest expressions requiring this tense.

Exercise 23

1. Como (puesto que) no había recibido la carta, fuí a la oficina de Correos. 2. En cuanto se hubo recibido la noticia todos los habitantes se aparejaron a defender la ciudad. 3. Cervantes nació el veintinueve de septiembre de mil quinientos cuarenta y siete. 4. Las compañías de ferrocarriles de este país emplean unas cien mil personas. 5. Más de siete millones de personas viven dentro de cinco millas de la Plaza de Trafalgar. 6. Doscientos cincuenta y siete pasajeros se ahogaron cuando se fué al fondo el barco-correo, no muy lejos de la costa española. 7. Cuatrocientos noventa caballos se vendieron esta semana. 8. Me han robado quinientas cuarenta pesetas. 9. Los sábados no voy nunca a la escuela. 10. ¿ A cuántos estaremos mañana ? Estaremos a veinte. 11. Hoy vamos a Toledo, no volveremos antes de pasado mañana. 12. Fuimos anoche al puerto, de donde debía salir el barco-correo para Mallorca. 13. Me han dicho que, todos los días, bebe una botella entera de Jerez (vino de Jerez). 14. No se puede entrar en el palacio los martes. 15. No me queda nada de todo lo que me dió Vd. anteayer. 16. Esta calle se llama la " Avenida del dos de mayo ". 17. Me parece a mí que la primavera es la estación más deliciosa del año. 18. No he leído nunca las " Mil y una Noches ". 19. No perdí cien libras esterlinas sino ciento una. 20. Estaremos en Madrid hasta el diez de octubre.

Translation IX

I spent the rest of the morning exploring the old quarter of Barcelona. I went to the Cathedral. The outside was magnificent, but the interior was too dark to allow me to appreciate its beauty. Afterwards I went to see the old palaces, of which the most interesting is the Generalidad, the headquarters of the Government.

Formerly it was a royal palace, but Spain is now a Republic, and Catalonia is, up to a certain point, an independent state. The guards outside wear a very peculiar uniform which dates more or less from the 14th century. In an inner courtyard fountains and orange trees are to be seen. Near the Generalidad is the Palace of Justice, with a tortoise carved on the wall, an ironical symbol of the slowness of justice, which might also refer to other countries besides Spain.

In the afternoon I went up by funicular to the summit of Montjuich, which dominates the city, and looked at the buildings and gardens, remains of the great Exhibition which was held (had place) there some years ago.

There is there an aerial railway which goes direct from Montjuich to the harbour, and I made my way there, taking a return ticket.

From the height of the railway the boats looked tiny, and presently (at the little space of time) I thought that I should find myself the next day at a much greater height above the ground. I had been amused when the old lady had refused to travel (the travelling) by aeroplane, but at that moment I myself could not help thinking (could no less than think) that I had never travelled by air. Perhaps, after all, I had been a little hasty.

For this reason I was depressed when I arrived at the hotel; but a good supper and a glass of claret revived my spirits, and I found myself thinking calmly of my journey. But in spite of this I did not sleep as well as usual (as I am accustomed), and I was already awake when the cocks, discharging their office of " knockers up " (awakeners) began to sing.

NOTES. *Explorando*. This might be translated " in exploring ". But remember once more that the insertion of *en* in the Spanish would give the meaning " having explored ".

Cuartel general. Both the definite article (" the ") and the indefinite article (" a ") are generally omitted in Spanish when used before a noun in apposition: *i.e.*, when the second noun is merely explanatory of the one before it and could be omitted without making the sentence any the less grammatical. In English, on the other hand, the article is nearly always supplied in these circumstances. There is another instance of the same omission later in the extract (*restos de la Gran Exposición*). Remember, incidentally, that the Spanish do not use the indefinite article before a noun used after " to be ", as though it were an adjective, to express some quality or characteristic.

Soy español (adjective). *Soy profesor* (noun).

The second, in indicating something about the nature or occupation of the person, is just as fully an adjective as the first and, therefore, the article is omitted. But if there is an additional qualifying adjective, then the article must be inserted. *Es un profesor muy conocido* = he is a well-known professor.

Patio. Here a large courtyard. But the small *patio* is a characteristic feature of many houses, particularly in South Spain or Latin America.

Además = besides (adverb). *Además de* (prep.).

Fué un palacio. Note the tense. One might expect the imperfect, with the meaning of " used to be ", but the Spanish view is that the whole thing is over and done with, and belongs wholly to the past, so that the past definite is required.

Exercise 24

1. El palacio ocupa un área de más de quinientos pies cuadrados. 2. Mi hija tiene solamente diez años pero es la primera de su clase. 3. La distancia de Barcelona a la frontera es de más de cien kilometros. 4. Este cuento se encuentra en el capítulo diez y siete del libro. 5. De mañana en ocho días partiremos para Salamanca, capital de la provincia. 6. El río es ancho de treinta metros y profundo de cinco (El río tiene 30 metros de anchura y 5 de profundidad). 7. Aquella señora no es española sino francesa. 8. Deberemos volver a Madrid dentro de cinco días. 9. El tren debe salir a las tres menos cuarto.[1] 10. La biblioteca de mi tío contiene centenares de libros. 11. Se mató (asesinó) a Enrique cuarto de Francia en mil seiscientos diez. 12. No puedo menos de pensar lo que le ha sucedido. 13. Acababan de dar las siete cuando llegué al puerto. 14. Más de dos docenas de personas se dirigían hacia la iglesia. 15. No me gusta este libro. He leído

---

[1] In printed time-tables the 24-hour system is in use as elsewhere on the Continent. To avoid confusion between a.m. and p.m. 2.45 p.m. would be 14.45 (by the addition of 12), but this usage is mostly confined to writing, not speaking.

desde el primer capítulo hasta la página noventa y dos sin
encontrar nada interesante.   16. Carlos cuarto sucedió a
Carlos tercero el doce de agosto de mil setecientos ochenta
y ocho.   17. Cada uno sabe que un día es la séptima parte
de una semana y que diez es la mitad de veinte.   18. Luis
catorce tenía setenta y siete años cuando murió en mil
setecientos quince.   19. Me quedaré aquí hasta poco antes
de las seis.   20. Durante el verano del año pasado fuí por
segunda vez a San Sebastián, ciudad muy agradable.

Translation X

I dressed hurriedly, packed my bag (did the suit-case)
and had breakfast.   Afterwards I paid the bill.   The service was included, an extra charge of 10 per cent. had been
added to the account (to the expenses), but I gave the
waiter fifteen pesetas, with which he was (remained) very
pleased.

I told the proprietor to have my bag brought down (that
they should bring down the bag), and the porter called
a taxi.   I got in, and the porter told the driver to take
me (that he should take me) to the offices of the L.P.A.E.
(*Líneas Postales Aéreas Españolas*).

I was glad to see that there was no wind, but nevertheless
I was a trifle nervous.   They had told me that passengers
could take with them 15 kilograms (about 32 lbs.) of
luggage, but as my bag weighed a little more, I had to pay
5 pesetas excess (of difference).   They looked at my passport
and ticket.   Afterwards they weighed me.   When the
officer was sure (assured himself) that my camera was in
my bag and not in my pocket, I got into the bus, where
already a dozen other passengers were waiting.

We left shortly after, and arrived at the airport.   We got
into an aeroplane, whose wings were painted yellow and red,
the national colours of Spain.   The pilot and wireless
operator (telegraphist) took their seats, the motors began
to turn and the machine began to move over the field at
increasing speed (increasing its speed).   I held my breath
for a moment when a slight lurch warned me that we had
left the ground.

I am not one of those people who can stand on the point
of a steep rock and look down(wards), but very soon I got

used to the sensation. In five minutes I was enjoying myself, in spite of the fact that once or twice, when the machine
got into one of those air pockets, it seemed that it was
going to fall rapidly.

We went up very high, and flew over a carpet of clouds
with a brilliant sun. Shortly after the clouds disappeared,
and I looked downwards to where a wide expanse of ground
was visible. It looked flat, although there are considerable
chains of mountains between Barcelona and Madrid. At
last the plane began to come down, and for a moment I
had the sensation which one feels on going down in a lift.
We landed with a perceptible bump. The plane stopped,
and I got out with a dull humming in my ears caused by
the noise of the engines, to remind me (make me remember)
that I had just had my first experience of flying (of the air).

Notes. *Desayuno* (breakfast), *almuerzo* (lunch), and
comida (dinner) or *cena* (supper) are the nouns for the
various meals corresponding to the verbs *desayunar, almorzar, comer* and *cenar* respectively.

Pintadas de amarillo, note the *de* untranslated in English.

Hacerme recordar = to make me remember. *Hacer* is
used in various phrases followed by an infinitive :—

Hacer saber = to let know, to send word.
Hacer entrar = to show (someone) in.

Another common expression is " to have something
done ", *i.e.*, when you do not actually do it yourself, but
" get " it done. For instance, " he had a house built ".
Here " built " is rendered by the infinitive in Spanish, NOT
by the past participle, and the object (house, in this case)
follows the infinitive = *hizo construir una casa*, or, better,
se hizo construir una casa = he had a house built for himself.

Similarly, *el capitan hizo fusilar a los prisioneros* = the
captain had the prisoners shot.

To order is generally *mandar*.

Mandó a su criado traer el vino = he ordered his servant
to bring the wine.

Exercise 25

1. Cuando hubo matado al guardia civil, huyó el ladrón
para ocultarse en los bosques. 2. El rey hizo matar a
sus enemigos. 3. Le tengo por un pintor del mayor

talento. 4. Se dice que una batalla está para tener lugar entre las tropas de los dos partidos. 5. Eso está por ver. Me parece a mí que ninguno de los dos tiene bastante dinero para pagar a los soldados. 6. Mi hermana está mala (enferma), por tanto he venido por ella. 7. Mandamos a mi hermano por el médico, quien dice que no hay por qué asustarse. 8. He dicho a mi librero que me envíe todos los libros escritos por Palacio Valdés. 9. La casa, cuya puerta está pintada de rojo pertenece a un amigo nuestro que tiene noventa años. 10. Necesito dinero para comprar una casa. Mi primo ha prometido prestármelo a tres por ciento. 11. Me es imposible pagarle a Vd. una suma tan considerable, puesto que gano solamente tres libras esterlinas por semana. 12. Cuando yo estudiaba para médico, vivía en París. 13. En cuanto hubo empezado a moverse el aeroplano, cerré los ojos. 14. Para un niño de ocho años, escribe muy bien. 15. Estaba para salir, cuando vino Vd. a verme. 16. Pasó por uno de los hombres más inteligentes de la aldea. 17. Por falta de tiempo no he leído esta mañana el periódico. ¿Quiere Vd. decirme lo que ha sucedido? 18. Lo haré por Vd. con mucho gusto. 19. A pesar del calor que hacía decidimos ir a pie. 20. Tendrá Vd. que vestirse precipitadamente para no llegar tarde á la estación.

Translation XI

After leaving the bus which took me from the aerodrome to the Air Company's office in Madrid, I asked the official to recommend me a hotel where the prices were (might be) not very high. He mentioned (indicated) several: I called a taxi to go to the first, which was not very far from the Prado—the Prado is one of the most famous picture-galleries in the world.

The taxi stopped at the door of the hotel. I got down, and told the driver to wait a moment. I went in and asked the manager if he had a single room vacant.

" Are you thinking of staying (being) long? " he asked.

" No. I only require a room for three nights."

" In that case we can give you a room on the second floor. If you want full pension, it costs 500 pesetas."

" That suits me " (that is very well), I said.

I paid the taxi-driver, and the hotel porter picked up my bag. We went up in the lift and arrived at my room.

It was too late for dinner, and I was not hungry, so I asked for a cup of coffee and read a paper which someone had left on one of the tables in the lounge. Soon I fixed my attention on the entertainments guide (notice of shows), and saw that in one of the theatres they were performing " Women's Town " (English title—" The Women have their Way ").

It is always interesting to be present at a theatre in a foreign country, but it is also very difficult for a stranger to understand what it is about (of what it is a question, of what it treats). But I had read this work translated into English, and consequently thought that I should be able to follow the plot of the comedy without difficulty.

So I got up from the sofa and asked the manager if he would telephone to the theatre in order that they could reserve me a seat.

" Certainly, sir. When do you want to go ? "

" I should like a seat for this evening's performance. But I don't want a stall—something that is (may be) cheaper."

The manager unhooked the receiver.

" Central, give me (put me with) 47,98."

He waited a moment.

" Have you any seats for to-night ? " He went on. " What seats do I want ? Only one. Have you something in the pit stalls ? Good. How much is it ? A hundred pesetas ? Very well. Thank you."

He replaced (hung up) the receiver (the instrument) and turned to me.

" The performance begins at nine, sir."

NOTES. *Conductor*. This means a leader or guide, or the conductor of an orchestra. But since *conducir* means to drive, the noun means the driver, not, for instance, the " conductor " of a tram. *Chófer* is the more usual word for a car-driver.

Asistir may mean to aid, though *ayudar* is more common. *Asistir a* means " to be present at ".

Tratarse = to be a question of, to be about.

Si podría. Remember that the future and conditional

can be used after *si* meaning " whether ", but not after *si* meaning " if ".

Exercise 26

1. Mi padre se acuesta siempre antes de las once de la noche, pero no duerme bien. 2. Dése Vd. prisa. El tren está empezando a moverse. 3. Pienso alquilar un auto por seis semanas. ¿Cuánto cuesta hacerlo? 4. No cuelgue Vd. el receptor. Quiero convidar a su amigo a acompañarnos al teatro. 5. No se encuentra a nadie en esta calle. 6. Se sabe bien que el prisionero hirió a tres guardias, de los cuales murió uno antes del anochecer. 7. ¿A qué hora se cierran las tiendas los jueves? A las seis y media. 8. El almuerzo se sirvió ayer a mediodía en vez de a la una. 9. Se vistieron rápidamente para no llegar tarde a la estación. 10. Me pidió que le recomendase un hotel cerca del centro de la ciudad. 11. Hace seis semanas que aprendo a tocar el piano. 12. Hasta hace poco tiempo no había casi ningún extranjero en este país. 13. Le pregunté si podría venir con nosotros pero se fué sin decir nada. 14. ¿Le ha visto Vd. como pasaba por las calles? No, señor. No le he visto. 15. Advertí que (me fijé en que) la puerta estaba abierta, lo que me sorprendió. 16 Mis dos hermanas se encuentran cada cuatro días en casa de la Señora Martinez. 17. No tengo ahora el dinero de Vd., pero se lo daré el martes próximo. 18. Hasta luego. Estaremos muy contentos de verle a las cuatro y cuarto. 19. Más de cien personas murieron de hambre en esta ciudad durante el último año de la guerra. 20 Mañana por la mañana tendremos que desayunar(nos) antes de las ocho.

Translation XII

I arrived very early at the theatre, and an attendant showed me my seat. I was glad to find that I could see the stage well (glad of the well that I saw the stage). I had to wait half an hour for the performance to begin (until the performance might begin), but I was not bored. I was very much entertained by watching the spectators come in. Soon after a gentleman sat down beside me, and recognising, evidently by my clothes, that I was a foreigner, he asked

me if it was my first visit to Madrid (if it was the first time
I was visiting Madrid). I replied that it was (that yes),
and that it was also the first time I had been to a Spanish
theatre (that I was present at).

" The authors of this work, the Quintero brothers, have
written many good plays, haven't they ? " (is it not true ?),
I asked.

" Yes, more than fifty. Spanish dramatists are very
prolific. But modern authors cannot compare in this
respect with Lope de Vega, who, by the way (let it be said
in passing), was born in Madrid.

" His life was eventful (full of events). He was the son
of a poor tradesman, but a noble interested himself in the
boy and sent him to study at the University of Alcalá. When
he was still a young man he was banished from Madrid for
five years. Then he sailed in the 'Invincible Armada'
sent by King Philip II. He returned safe and sound,
and even wrote a poem against Drake. Afterwards he
began to write comedies. By the end of his life he had
written more than 1800, of which 450 have survived.
Moreover, his works were written in verse, not in prose.
Many of them were 'cloak-and-sword' comedies, dealing
with honour and the customs of the nobility in those days.
Playwrights of all countries have found a model from his
plots : the works of Calderón were also very popular.

" But the dramas of both belong to a past age. The
writers of to-day are observers of real life, and the Quintero
brothers are excellent dramatists : nevertheless, some prefer
the works of Benavente and Sierra. If you go to Seville
you will find a fountain surrounded with stone benches with
shelves containing the works of the Quintero brothers.
There are not many people who find themselves honoured
with a monument during their lifetime."

The gentleman had no time to tell me anything more,
for the theatre was already full, there was not a vacant seat,
and the curtain rose.

NOTES. *Extranjero* (adj.) = foreign ; (noun) foreigner.
Al extranjero = abroad. *Extraño* = strange, odd.

Contestar que sí (*que no*). This phrase is used when the
words " yes " and " no " are not in inverted commas.
But *Sí, le contesté* = Yes, I answered (him).

¿No es verdad? This phrase is equivalent to " Isn't it? ", " didn't you? ", etc., added to a sentence in English to make it interrogative. As the literal meaning is " isn't that so? ", it can be used for any of the various English phrases "wasn't it?", "won't they?", etc. In conversation it is frequently abbreviated simply to *¿verdad?* or sometimes to an enquiring *¿no?* But the full phrase is the safest to use.

Enviar a. Note the preposition. *A* is the preposition used before infinitives after many verbs of motion. Also after verbs of readiness or determination for action (*prepararse a*). Also after reflexive verbs of continuance or habit, *acostumbrarse a, dedicarse a* (to apply oneself to, give oneself up to). It is worth noting, too, that many verbs beginning with the prefixes *a, ab, ac, ante, ad, ar, as,* or *at,* are followed by *a* (*atenerse a lo seguro* = to keep on the safe side).

Hoy = to-day. *Hoy día* or *hoy en día,* nowadays.
Sea = let it be (present subjunctive of *ser*).

Exercise 27

1. El Vesuvio, uno de los volcanes más famosos del mundo está situado (se halla) en el centro de Italia, cerca de Nápoles. 2. Washington es la capital o ciudad principal de los Estados Unidos, pero Nueva York es la ciudad más grande del Nuevo Mundo. 3. Muchos de los edificios en varios barrios de Nueva York son extremadamente altos. 4. Reconocí tanto por el color de su tez como por su traje que era extranjero. 5. Cuando tenía solamente ocho años empezó a estudiar la música, pero despues se hizo actor. 6. El viejo Carlos fué muchas veces al Canadá, no es verdad? 7. El clima de la América del Norte es mucho más riguroso que el de España. 8. La Habana, capital de la isla de Cuba, es conocida por todo el mundo por los cigarros, a los cuales ha dado su nombre. 9. Las máquinas de escribir son muy útiles, sobre todo hoy día cuando mucha gente escribe de una manera casi ilegible. 10. El cafeto es una planta, el color de cuyos frutos se cambia de verde en colorado. 11. Cuando los granos se tuestan toman un color castaño oscuro. 12. El rey Jorge sexto acaba de volver de Francia, habiendo pasado cuatro días

en la capital francesa. 13. El general mandó construir murallas de piedra. 14. Tenderos, labradores, comerciantes—todos hacen cuanto pueden (a más no poder) para ganar su vida. 15. Los dos autores son excelentes dramáticos, pero ni el uno ni el otro puede ser comparado con Benavente quien, dicho sea de paso, vive ahora en Valencia. 16. Los libros que tratan de la ciencia de la economía política son muy numerosos—el leerlos me aburre muchísimo. 17. Es fácil acostumbrarse (or *hacerse*) al ruido y bullicio de la vida moderna. 18. El nombre " Pacífico " es impropio : la última vez que fuí a Hong Kong yo me mareé mucho. 19. Alejandro el Grande murió a la edad de treinta años, habiendo conquistado la mayor parte del mundo conocido. 20. Los cables de acero son más fuertes que las cuerdas de cáñamo.

Translation XIII

" The Women have their Way " is a very amusing comedy. It deals with a young lawyer from Madrid who comes to work in a small Andalusian town. While he is walking through the streets he sees a girl who is passing on the other side, and it happens (coincidence gives) that he notices that she is pretty. This is enough for the talkative women of the place. They are convinced that the lawyer has fallen in love with this girl, and, despite his denials, they insist on asserting that he wants to marry her. They talk to him so frequently of his supposed love affair that he ends by thinking that perhaps it would be pleasant enough to be married to her, and the play ends with their engagement.

This comedy is an entertaining and excellent satire of provincial life. Thanks to my knowing the work beforehand (to that I knew), I had no difficulty in appreciating its points and its charm. Besides, the actors who played the principal parts were so good that their gestures and the expression of their faces were almost sufficient to reveal the sense of the play.

It was after midnight when I left the theatre, but I didn't feel inclined to go to bed. It was a perfect night. The streets were well lighted, and I walked for a while, looking at the passers-by and trying to remember what I knew of the history of this city, which contains round about a million inhabitants.

It was Philip II who established his Court at Madrid in 1561 and made the city the capital of his kingdom. It was the same king who constructed the monastery of the Escurial, that great building which I decided to visit the next day. The successors of Philip II embellished (beautified) the city, especially Charles III. From his time date the Academy of Fine Arts and the Prado Museum, in which are to be found some of the early works of Velázquez and Goya, and, above all, many pictures of El Greco, Murillo and Ribera. I should have to find a moment to visit the Prado. Before leaving England they told me that I must not fail to see the National Palace, situated in the Plaza de Oriente, which contains, amongst other things, the finest collection of arms and armour in the world.

Meanwhile I had no idea in what part of the city I was, for I (had) walked a long while after leaving the theatre. At length I asked a gentleman to show me the best way to get back to the hotel. He pointed out (told me of) a tram which passed quite close to it. I waited at a stopping-place, and had the luck to find a seat in a crowded tram (in which there were a great many people).

NOTES. *Se fija en que.* Some verbs require a preposition to connect them with their object. When they have a dependent clause instead of a simple noun object the preposition is retained in Spanish, and connected with the dependent clause by *que.* For instance : *alegrarse de,* to be glad of.

Me alegro de que Vd. haya llegado = I am glad you have come (subjunctive used after a verb expressing an emotion).

Casar with an object means either to perform the marriage service or to give someone away in marriage. *Casarse* is to get married. *Casarse con* is to marry someone : *i.e.,* to be either the bride or bridegroom.

Termina por creer. Por is used before an infinitive with the meaning of " by ", with verbs of beginning and ending.

Desarrollar (or *desempeñar*) *un papel* = to play a part.

E hizo—note the change from *y* to *e* before a word beginning with *i* or *hi* (*h* being unpronounced).

Dejar = to leave, in the sense of to leave something

behind. It also means to let, in the sense of to allow. *Dejar de* means to leave off (*i.e.*, to stop doing something). *No dejar de* means to go on doing a thing, or not to fail to do it.

Exercise 28

1. La vieja María está muy inquieta. Teme que su hija se case con el Sr. González. 2. Siento que Vd. haya olvidado lo que le dije la semana pasada. 3. Aguardo (a) alguien que pueda conducirme a la estación. 4. Aguardo a mi primo que ha prometido encontrarme aquí. 5. No quiero hablar a aquel hombre. Me pide siempre que le preste dinero. 6. El diputado propondrá que todas las tiendas se cierren los sábados. 7. Es cierto que el obispo los casará. 8. Es preciso que lleguemos a la frontera antes del anochecer. 9. Tendremos que hallarle dondequiera se haya ocultado. 10. Es dudoso que este actor sea capaz de desempeñar un papel tan importante. 11. Terminaré por creer que Vd. no quiere ayudarnos. 12. ¿Cree Vd. que podremos convencerle? 13. Diré a mi empleado que vaya luego a la oficina de la Compañía de Aviación. 14. ¿Niega Vd. que el acusado haya injuriado al demandante de la manera más imperdonable? 15. Sentimos que le sea imposible a Vd. asistir a (presenciar) la representación. 16. Estaba contento de fijarme en que el teatro estaba lleno de gente. 17. Haré todo lo posible para volver a verle a Vd. 18. Me asombro de lo que ha sucedido. 19. Me asombro de que Vd. no se haya acostumbrado a trabajar aquí. 20. Les dije (a ellos) que no tenía hambre.

Translation XIV

The Escurial is an amazing building. It stands some distance from Madrid, and is surrounded by huge mountains. Before going there I did what I could to learn something of its history. This is how it came to be built (It came to be built as follows).

In the 16th century a battle was fought near the French town of St. Quentin. During the contest the Spanish artillery destroyed a church dedicated to St. Lawrence, and Philip II made a vow to build a monastery in honour of this saint. He ordered his architects to construct the building in the form of a gridiron, in order to commemorate the manner in which (how) St. Lawrence was martyred. A building on the east front, which served as a royal residence, represents the handle of the gridiron, and the bars of the same are represented by buildings which stretch in straight lines in the interior of the frame formed by the walls. The outer part contains no fewer than 1100 windows and 15 doors. Over the main door stands (is erected) a statue of St. Lawrence. This entry gives access to the Court of the Kings, and farther on stands a granite church, crowned by an enormous dome.

In this church there are 48 altars, and in the main chapel are the statues of Philip II and other Spanish monarchs.

Below the high altar is the mausoleum where many of the Spanish kings rest (are buried). I saw the royal apartments, including the simple gloomy room in which Philip II died in 1598. I looked at innumerable pictures and works of art of all kinds. Nevertheless, and in spite of the splendour of the building, the whole atmosphere of the place is indescribably sad and seems to reflect the cold, tormented spirit of the man who constructed it. It cost an immense sum and took 22 years to complete (they delayed 22 years in completing it).

It was an imposing building, but it did not satisfy me so much as other things which I saw in Madrid. The Manzanares, on the banks of which Madrid is situated, is not an important river. Especially in summer it is reduced to a diminutive stream, but there are one or two beautiful bridges over it, and in the neighbourhood some fine churches which date from the 17th century.

But what most attracted my attention was the *Retiro*, a park like that of the Bois de Boulogne in Paris, with lakes, fountains and a Zoological Garden besides spacious avenues. In winter it is often very cold in Madrid, for the city stands 635 metres (2000 ft.) above sea level. But in spring and autumn it is delightful, and I decided to return there as soon as I had (should have) an opportunity.

NOTES. *San*. This, the abbreviation of *Santo*, takes the short form before the name of a saint, provided that the name does not begin with *To* or *Do*. The feminine form is always *Santa*. *San Pedro* (St. Peter), but *Santo Tomás* (St. Thomas).

Servir de = to serve as a. Note that the indefinite article is not used in the Spanish equivalent.

Sencillo y lugubre. When two adjectives qualify the same noun, their position is not invariable. We know that short conventional adjectives come before the noun, so that both may precede. On the other hand, if one is an adjective of colour or nationality, the noun will be sandwiched between the two. Thirdly, both adjectives may follow the noun. Whether preceding or following the noun, the adjectives are liable to be connected by *y*. This is so if each is equally independent of the noun. But if the noun and one of the adjectives form a closely connected whole, the second adjective is joined on without *y* as a connecting link : e.g., *cuestiones económicas importantes*.

This is in contrast with *el frío y atormentado espíritu* and with *la sencilla y lúgubre habitación*, which occurs in this extract.

A orillas = on the banks. Note the omission of the article in certain prepositional phrases. *En casa*, etc. On the other hand, *a la escuela* = to school.

Riachuelo. A diminutive of *río*. Spanish has many diminutives, some affectionate, others depreciatory, formed by additions to the normal form of a word, though sometimes with a slight alteration needed to make the word easy to pronounce. There is no great need for the student to be able to use them himself, but he is liable to meet them fairly often in reading.

For instance : *pobre* = *pobrecillo*, *madre* = *madrecita*. These are affectionate, meaning something like " nice little ", " dear little ", or " poor little ".

Casita = a nice little house. But *casucha*, and still more *casucho*, are decidedly uncomplimentary to the building. Similarly *riachuelo* means, rather contemptuously, " a wretched little stream ". *Aldehuela* is a nasty little village —what in the United States might be tersely termed a " dump ". This is one of the ways in which Spanish is a language capable of infinitely fine shades of meaning. Somerset Maugham, by the way, stated in " Don Fernando ", an interesting book on Spain, that the Spanish language is finer than its literature.

Exercise 29

1. Ordenó a su criado que le despertara de madrugada para que tuviese tiempo de acabar su trabajo. 2. ¿Cree Vd. que va a llover? 3. Vamos al teatro a menos que (a no ser que) Vd. prefiera quedarse en casa. 4. Estaba contento de que ellos no hubieran olvidado lo que les había dicho. 5. Me pidió que me diera prisa, pues quería que llegásemos antes del anochecer. 6. Me dijo que importaba que nos diésemos prisa en caso de que lloviese. 7. Que todo esté listo para cuando él vuelva. 8. Le prestaré a Vd. mis zapatos a condición de que Vd. me los restituya (or restituyera) mañana. 9. Prometió enviarme el libro luego que lo hubiera leído. 10. Cuando hubo leído (or después de haber leído) el periódico, me lo dió. 11. Hasta que hubiere recibido del amo una carta, me quedaré aquí. 12. Nos asombramos de que no nos hubiese escrito. 13. Temíamos que ella estuviese mala. 14. Haga Vd. todo lo que le diga. 15. Andaré por las calles hasta que le encuentre (or encontrare). 16. ¿Supone Vd. que ella se haya enamorado de él? 17. Es posible que yo compre una casa en Burgos. 18. Es posible que él viviese en los Estados Unidos. 19. Luego que él se muera, supongo que su casa sirva de museo. 20. Trabajó con celo para que sus niños no muriesen de hambre.

Translation XV

The day of my departure arrived. In the morning I went out to take a final stroll (to give a walk) through the city, and bought several small presents for my parents. Afterwards I had my hair cut. I returned to the hotel, did my packing and had (took) lunch. I had taken my ticket the day before, and early in the afternoon I paid my bill, and with great regret hailed a taxi to take me to the North station.

This time I did not get a carriage to myself (for me alone). Two men were already seated, and one of them was talking incessantly to his companion about motor-cars. Not long before he had bought a second-hand car, and had been on a journey from Madrid to the South of Spain. As far as I could (for that which I could) understand, the journey had not been a success. The brakes did not work well. He had had an accident, the tyres burst, and at last he drove (put himself) into a roadside ditch. The other man began, in his turn, to talk about business. Apparently he was a stock-broker, and spoke of dividends and shares and the economic depression. He ended by reading aloud a letter from the director of a joint-stock company. His companion en-deavoured to listen attentively while (he was) reading a newspaper, and I looked out of the window. The other was still talking when I came back after dinner from the restaurant car, but fortunately they got out at Irún, the frontier town. I slept fairly well, and awoke when we were near Paris. When we arrived I had just time to pick up a taxi and go to the Gare du Nord to take the boat-train, and we arrived at Dover soon after five. It seemed strange to be back in England. A man who was travelling in the same carriage to London as myself, seeing the labels on my case, spoke to me about Spain. I told him that I had had a most enjoyable time there (had passed it admirably) and wanted to return, as there were many interesting things I wanted to see.

" For one thing," I said, " because I have not seen the Alhambra."

A workman who was in the corner seat opposite grinned.

" You won't be able to see it now. It's very difficult to recognise Leicester Square nowadays. They've pulled down the Alhambra. There's a cinema there instead ! "

NOTES. *Padres*. Remember that this, besides being the plural of father, means parents. *Parientes* = relations.

El pelo. Remember, also, that before clothes or parts of the body the definite article is used in Spanish instead of the possessive, the ownership being made clear by insertion of the appropriate personal pronoun before the verb.

La víspera = the day before; not to be confused with *ayer*, which merely means yesterday.

Coche. Originally a coach or carriage, but now used as one of the words for a car. *Coche de carrera* = a touring car; *coche de salón* = a saloon car : " to go by car " is generally, however, *ir en auto*.

Bolsa, with a capital letter, means the Stock Exchange

(French—La Bourse) ; *bolsillo*, the usual name for a purse, is really a diminutive of *bolsa*.

Una carta. This was a business letter. It probably began : *Muy estimado Señor X.* (Dear Mr. X.) Dear Sir = *Muy señor mío.* To a friend one might write *Querido González* (Dear Smith), or, a little more warmly, *Mi querido amigo.* *Querer* sometimes means " to love ", not only " to wish " or " want ", hence its use in this connection, but it is fairly formal, and does not necessarily denote any degree of intimacy. At the end of a business letter, addressed to a man, the letters *Q.B.S.M.* or *Q.S.M.B.* are likely to be found immediately before the signature. They stand for *que besa sus manos* (who kisses your hands). If the recipient is a lady, she may well find *Q.B.S.P.* (who kisses your feet). This sounds most poetic and chivalrous, but it is a mere formula of conventional politeness. It would be pleasant to try it on one's employer in England, but the experiment should be deferred until one is already under notice to leave. The letters *S.S.S.* found likewise in Spanish letters are short for *su seguro servidor* (your obedient servant). " I remain yours truly " would probably be : *queda de Vd. Af^{mo}. atento y S.S. Carlos Fulano.* *Af^{mo}.* is short for *afectísimo* (very devoted). *Fulano*, by the way, is the Spanish equivalent of " so and so ", " what's his name ", etc.

Exercise 30

1. Quisiera hacerme cortar el pelo, pero debemos darnos prisa (*or*, es preciso que nos demos prisa). 2. Si Vd. fuera agente de bolsa tendríamos mucho dinero. 3. Si Vd. no hubiera comprado un coche de segunda mano, habríamos llegado ya a Barcelona. 4. Temía que tuviésemos que partir antes del desayuno. 5. Estoy contento de estar de vuelta en Inglaterra, pero iré el año proximo a España si tengo bastante dinero. 6. Si no me hubiera cortado el pie, le habría acompañado. 7. Tendremos justamente tiempo para ir a verlos. 8. Acaba de volver de los Estados Unidos después de haber pasado tres años en Nueva York. 9. ¿Qué haría Vd. si fuera gobernador de la provincia? 10. Si Vd. me hubiese pedido mi sobretodo se le hubiera dado.

TABLE OF COMMON IRREGULAR VERBS

All tenses are not given. But by remembering the following simple rules the student can easily determine any tense from the parts of the verb that are shown.

1. The Imperfect, Past and Future Subjunctive tenses can be formed by adding the endings shown in Lesson XXIX to the first person of the Past Definite with the terminal vowel removed.

2. The Conditional is identical with the Future Indicative, save that the termination is *ia* not *é*.

3. With the exception of *saber* (*sepa*), *haber* (*haya*), *dar* (*dé*), *ser* (*sea*), *ir* (*vaya*), the stem of the Present Subjunctive is the same as that of the First Person Singular of the Present Indicative.

4. The stem of the Imperfect Indicative is regular, except in the case of *ir* (*ib-*), *ver* (*ve-*), and *ser* (*er-*).

Verbs whose irregularities depend only on orthographic or radical-changing peculiarities, explained elsewhere, are, for the most part, omitted. So also are compounds. For *convenir*, *proponer*, etc., see the simple verbs *venir*, *poner* and so on.

Infinitive.	Pres. Ind.	Past Def.	Future.	Participles.
adquirir = to acquire	adquiero adquirimos adquieren	adquirí — —	adquiriré — —	adquiriendo adquirido
andar = to go, walk	ando —	anduve —	andaré —	andando andado
asir = to seize	asgo ase asimos asen	así — — —	asiré — — —	asiendo asido
caber = to be contained in	quepo cabe cabemos caben	cupe — — —	cabré — — —	cabiendo cabido
caer = to fall	caigo cae caen —	caí cayó caimos cayeron	caeré — — —	cayendo caído
ceñir = to gird, surround	ciño ciñe ceñimos ciñen	ceñí ciñó ceñimos ciñeron	ceñiré — — —	ciñendo ceñido
concluir = to conclude	concluyo concluye concluimos concluyen	concluí concluyó concluimos concluyeron	concluiré — — —	concluyendo concluido

Infinitive	Present	Preterite	Future	Gerund / Participle
conducir = to lead	conduzco conduce	conduje condujo condujeron	conduciré	conduciendo conducido
crecer = to grow	crezco crece	crecí —	creceré	creciendo crecido
dar = to give	doy da	di dió	daré	dando dado
decir = to say, tell	digo dice decimos dicen	dije dijo dijimos dijeron	diré	diciendo dicho
estar = to be	estoy está están	estuve —	estaré	estando estado
haber = to have	he ha hemos han	hube hubo hubimos hubieron	habré	habiendo habido
hacer = to do, make	hago hace hacen	hice hizo hicimos	haré	haciendo hecho
ir = to go	voy va — van	fui fué fuimos fueron	iré	yendo ido

Infinitive.	Pres. Ind.	Past Def.	Future.	Participles.
oir = to hear	oigo	oí	oiré	oyendo
	oye	oyó	—	oído
	oímos	oímos	—	—
	oyen	oyeron	—	—
poder = to be able	puedo	pude	podré	pudiendo
	podemos	pudimos	—	podido
	pueden	pudieron	—	—
poner = to put	pongo	puse	pondré	poniendo
	pone	pusimos	—	puesto
	ponen	pusieron	—	—
querer = to wish	quiero	quise	querré	queriendo
	queremos	quisimos	—	querido
	quieren	quisieron	—	—
reir = to laugh	río	reí	reiré	riendo
	reímos	rió	—	reído
	ríen	reímos	—	—
	—	rieron	—	—
saber = to know	sé	supe	sabré	sabiendo
	sabe	supimos	—	sabido
	saben	supieron	—	—
salir = to go out	salgo	salí	saldré	saliendo
	sale	salió	—	salido
	salimos	salieron	—	—

	Present	Preterite	Future	Gerund / Past Participle
satisfacer = to satisfy	satisfago, satisface	satisfice, satisfizo, satisficimos	satisfaré	satisfaciendo, satisfecho
ser = to be	soy, —, es, somos, son	fuí, fué, fueron	seré	siendo, sido
tener = to have	tengo, tiene, tenemos, tienen	tuve, tuvo, tuvimos, tuvieron	tendré	teniendo, tenido
traer = to bring	traigo, trae, traemos	traje, trajo, trajeron	traeré	trayendo, traído
valer = to be worth	valgo, vale, valemos	valí, valió, valieron	valdré	valiendo, valido
venir = to come	vengo, viene, venimos, vienen	vine, vino, vinimos, vinieron	vendré	viniendo, venido
ver = to see	veo, ve, vemos	ví, vió, vimos	veré	viendo, visto

VOCABULARY

This Vocabulary does not include numerals, months, etc., complete lists of which are given elsewhere in the book. Nor does it include certain words which occur so frequently that the student cannot fail to know them after doing the first lesson or two. A few words, almost identical with their English equivalents, are likewise omitted. The present indicative of each radical-changing verb (otherwise regular) is shown in brackets after the infinitive. If no indicative is shown, it is safe to assume that the verb is quite straightforward and normal. Exceptions to this are the genuinely irregular verbs, in dealing with which the student should refer to the table of irregular verbs, printed immediately before this vocabulary. He should bear in mind that the tenses of such verbs as *convenir* or *sostener* may be found from the simple forms *venir* and *tener*.

A.

abogado, *m.*	lawyer.
abrir	to open.
abuela(o)	grandmother (grandfather).
aburrirse	to be bored.
acabar	to finish : acabar de, to have just.
acceso, *m.*	access.
acción, *f.*	share (stock market).
acomodador, *m.*	attendant, usher.
acerca	near, about.
acercarse	to draw near, approach.
aclarar	to clear up.
acontecimiento, *m.*	event, vicissitude.
acordarse (acuerdo)	to remember.
acostarse (acuesto)	to go to bed.
acostumbrarse	to get used to, to accustom oneself to.
además	besides.

aduana, *f.*	Custom House.
advertir (advierto)	to notice, observe.
aeroplano, *m.*	aeroplane.
agente de Bolsa	stockbroker.
agradable	pleasant, agreeable.
agua, *f.*	water.
aguardar	to wait (for), expect.
agudeza, *f.*	point, repartee.
ahogarse	to be drowned.
ahora	now.
ala, *f.*	wing.
alargarse	to stretch out.
alcalde, *m.*	mayor.
alcanzar	to reach, attain.
aldea, *f.*	village.
alegrarse	to be glad, rejoice.
alejarse	to withdraw, draw further off.
alemán	German.
alfombra, *f.*	carpet.
algo	something, somewhat (adv.).
alguien	someone.
alinearse	to be aligned, be ranged, extend.
allí	there.
almohada, *f.*	pillow.
almorzar (almuerzo)	to lunch.
almuerzo, *m.*	lunch.
alquilar	to hire.
alrededor	around, about.
los alrededores	the surroundings.
alto	high, loud.
altura, *f.*	height, altitude.
alumno, *m.*	pupil.
amarillo	yellow.
ambos	both.
a menudo	repeatedly.
amigo, *m.*	friend.
amo, *m.*	" boss ".
añadir	to add.
ancho	broad, wide.
anchura, *f.*	breadth.
andar	to walk, go.
año, *m.*	year.
anochecer, *m.*	dusk.
anotar	to note, take note of.
ansiar	to be anxious, eager.
antemano (de)	beforehand.
anteojos, *m. pl.*	spectacles.

anteriormente	previously.
antes (adv.)	before, beforehand.
apagar	to extinguish, put out.
aparato, *m.*	apparatus, instrument.
aparejarse	to get ready.
aplicado	hard working.
aprender	to learn.
aquí	here.
arena, *f.*	arena, sand.
arriba y abajo	up and down, to and fro.
armadura, *f.*	armour.
arrojar	to throw.
arroyuelo, *m.*	small river, stream, watercourse.
asa, *f.*	handle.
ascensor, *m.*	lift.
asegurarse	to make sure, ascertain.
asesinar	to murder.
así	so, thus.
asiento, *m.*	seat.
asistir(a)	to be present at.
asombrar	to astonish, surprise.
asunto, *m.*	affair, matter, business.
asustarse	to be alarmed.
atento	attentive.
aterrizar	to land.
atormentar	to torment, torture.
aumentar	to increase.
aún	yet, even.
aunque	although.
auto(móvil), *m.*	car, motor-car.
autor, *m.*	author.
avenida, *f.*	avenue.
avión, *m.*	aeroplane.
ayer	yesterday.
azul	blue.

B.

bajar	to bring down, go down.
balcón, *m.*	balcony.
bamboleo, *m.*	lurch, swaying.
bañar	to bathe.
banco	bench.
barato	cheap.
barco, *m.*	boat : barco-tren, boat-train.
barra, *f.*	bar.

barrio, *m.* . . . quarter.
bastante . . . enough, sufficient.
batalla, *f.* . . . battle.
baúl, *m.* . . . trunk (luggage).
beber . . . . to drink.
belleza, *f.* . . . beauty.
blanco . . . white.
bolsillo, *m.* . . . pocket.
bondad, *f.* . . . goodness, kindness.
bonito . . . pretty.
bosque, *m.* . . . wood.
botella, *f.* . . . bottle.
bóveda, *f.* . . . vault, dome.
brazo, *m.* . . . arm.
brillar . . . to shine.
bueno . . . good, well.
bullicio, *m.* . . . bustle.
buscar . . . to look for, seek.
butaca, *f.* . . . stall.

C.

caballero, *m.* . . gentleman.
caballo, *m.* . . horse.
cabeza, *f.* . . . head.
cacería, *f.* . . . chase, hunting.
cadena, *f.* . . . chain.
caer . . . . to fall.
café, *m.* . . . café, coffee.
calcetín, *m.* . . sock.
caliente . . . warm.
calle, *f.* . . . street.
calor, *m.* . . . heat, warmth.
cama, *f.* . . . bed.
camarero, *m.* . . waiter.
cambiar . . . to change.
cambio, *m.* . . . change, exchange.
camino, *m.* . . . way, road.
campo, *m.* . . . field.
cansado . . . tired, weary.
cantar . . . to sing.
canto, *m.* . . . song.
capa, *f.* . . . cloak.
capilla, *f.* . . . chapel.
capítulo, *m.* . . chapter.
cara, *f.* . . . face.
caro . . . . dear.

carretera, *f.*	road, roadway.
carta, *f.*	letter.
cartelera (de espectáculos), *f.*	list (of plays), theatre guide.
casado	married.
casi	almost.
caso, *m.*	case.
célebre	famous.
cenar	to sup, dine.
centenar, *m.*	hundred.
centro, *m.*	centre.
cerca (de)	near.
cero, *m.*	zero.
cerrar (cierro)	to close, shut.
cerveza, *f.*	beer.
cesta, *f.*	basket.
cierto	certain, sure.
cigarillo, *m.*	cigarette.
cine, *m.*	cinema.
cirujano, *m.*	surgeon.
claro	clear.
clima, *m.*	climate.
cocer (cuezo)	to cook.
coche, *m.*	carriage, car.
cocinera, *f.*	cook.
colgar (cuelgo)	hang, hang up.
color de tez, *m.*	complexion.
colorado	red, coloured.
comedor, *m.*	dining-room.
comer	to eat.
comerciante, *m.*	merchant, tradesman.
comercio, *m.*	commerce.
comida, *f.*	dinner.
compañero, *m.*	companion.
compañia, *f.*	company.
compartimiento, *m.*	compartment.
comprar	to buy.
comprender	to understand.
conducir (-uzco)	to lead, drive.
conocer (-ozco)	to know.
conocimiento, *m.*	acquaintance, knowledge.
conseguir (-sigo)	to obtain, procure.
construir (-struyo)	to construct, build.
contar (cuento)	to relate, recount.
contestar	to answer.
contienda, *f.*	contest.
convencer (-enzo)	to convince.

convenir . . . to suit, be convenient.
convidar . . . to invite.
copa, *f.* . . . cup, glass.
corazón, *m.* . . . heart.
corbata, *f.* . . . tie.
coronar . . . to crown.
correo, *m.* . . . post, mail.
correr . . . to run.
corrida de toros, *f.* . bull-fight.
cortar . . . to cut.
corte, *m.* . . . court.
cortés . . . polite.
cosa, *f.* . . . thing.
costa, *f.* . . . coast, cost.
costar (cuesto) . . to cost.
costumbre, *f.* . . custom.
creer . . . to believe.
criado, *m.* . . . servant.
cuadra, *f.* . . . stable.
cuadrado . . . square.
cuadro, *m.* . . picture, square, frame.
cuartel (general), *m.* (head)quarters.
cuarto, *m.* . . . room.
cuchillo, *m.*. . . knife.
cuenta, *f.* . . . account : tener en cuenta, to take
                    into account, bear in mind.
cuento, *m.* . . . story.
cuesta, *f.* . . . hill.
cuidado, *m.*. . . care.
cumbre, *f.* . . . summit.
cumpleaños, *m.* . anniversary, birthday.
cuneta, *f.* . . . ditch.
curva, *f.* . . . curve.

D.

dar . . . to give.
datar . . . to date.
debajo (de) . . . under, underneath.
deber . . . to owe, to have to.
decir . . . to say, to tell.
dedo, *m.* . . . finger.
defender (defiendo) . to defend.
dejar . . . to leave, let.
delante (de) . in front of, before.
demasiado . . . too, too much.
demostrar (demuestro) . to prove, demonstrate.

dentro (de)	within.
departamento, *m.*	compartment, apartment.
dependiente, *m.*	clerk.
deporte, *m.*	sport.
deprimido	depressed.
derrumbar	to pull down.
desaparecer (-ezco)	to disappear.
desayunar	to have breakfast.
desayuno, *m.*	breakfast.
desarrollar	to play (a part).
descansar	to rest, repose.
descolgar (-cuelgo)	to unhook, take down.
desde	since, from.
desear	to desire, wish.
desempeñar	to play (a part).
desgracia, *f.*	misfortune.
deshacer	to undo.
deslizarse	to slip, glide down.
despacio	slowly.
despedirse (-pido)	to take leave of.
despertador, *m.*	awakener, knocker up.
despertar (despierto)	to awake, wake up.
después (de)	after.
desterrar (-tierro)	to banish.
destruir (destruyo)	to destroy.
detrás (de)	behind.
dicha	said.
dirigir (dirijo)	to direct: (reflex.) to make one's way.
discípulo, *m.*	pupil.
disponer	to dispose.
divertir (divierto)	to divert, amuse.
docto	learned.
dormir (duermo)	to sleep.
duda, *f.*	doubt.
durante	during.
durar	to last, continue.

E.

edificar	to build.
edificio, *m.*	building.
efecto, *m.*	effect: en efecto, indeed.
ejercicio, *m.*	exercise.
elegir (elijo)	to elect.
elevarse	to rise.
embargo, *m.*	seizing: sin embargo, nevertheless.

embellecir (-ezco) . .	to beautify.
empezar (empiezo) .	to begin.
empleado, *m.* . .	employee, clerk.
enamorarse . . .	to fall in love.
encanto, *m.* . .	charm.
encender (enciendo) .	to light.
encima . . .	above, over.
encontrar (encuentro) .	to meet : (reflex.) to be, find one-self.
enemigo, *m.* . .	enemy.
enfadar . . .	to annoy, irritate.
engañar . . .	to deceive.
enojarse . . .	to get annoyed.
ensalada, *f.* . .	salad.
enseñar . . .	to teach.
entender (entiendo) .	to hear, understand.
entonces . . .	then.
entrada, *f.* . .	entrance.
entre . . .	between, among.
entregar . . .	to hand over, deliver.
entretener . .	to entertain.
entusiasmar . .	to delight, enrapture.
enviar . . .	to send.
época, *f.* . .	age, epoch.
equipaje, *m.* . .	luggage.
erigir (erijo) .	to erect.
escarpado . . .	steep.
escenario, *m.* .	scenery, stage.
escoger (escojo) .	to choose.
escribir . . .	to write.
escritor, *m.* .	writer, author.
escuchar . . .	to listen, listen to.
espacioso . . .	spacious.
espada, *f.* . .	sword.
espectador, *m.* .	spectator.
esperar . . .	to wait.
espeso . . .	thick.
espíritu, *m.* . .	spirit.
esquina, *f.* . .	corner.
establecer (-ezco) .	to establish.
estación, *f.* . .	station, season.
estado, *m.* . .	state.
estallar . . .	to burst.
estante, *m.* . .	book-case.
estatua, *f.* . .	statue.
este . . .	east.
estilo, *m.* . .	style.

estrecho	. . .	narrow.
estudiar	. . .	to study.
estupendo	. . .	wonderful, splendid.
etiqueta, *f.* .	. .	label.
éxito, *m.*	. .	success.
experimentar	. .	experience.
explicar	. . .	to explain.
exposición, *f.*	. .	exhibition.
expreso, *m.*	. .	express.
extensión, *f.*	. .	length, extent.
extrañado	. . .	surprised.
extraño	. . .	strange, odd.
extranjero .	. .	foreign, (noun) foreigner.

F.

facción, *f.* .	. .	feature.
fachada, *f.* .	. .	façade, front.
factura, *f.* .	. . .	bill.
facturar	. .	to register.
falta, *f.*	. . .	mistake, fault.
fecha, *f.*	. . .	date.
felicitar	. . .	to congratulate.
feo	. . .	ugly.
ferrocarril, *m.*	. .	railway.
fiesta, *f.*	. . .	feast, fête, festival.
fijarse .	. . .	to notice.
fin, *m.*	. . .	end, conclusion.
flor, *f.*	. . .	flower.
fósforo, *m.*	. . .	match.
freno, *m.*	. . .	brake.
frente, *f.*	. . .	front, outside : de frente, facing.
frío	. . .	cold.
frontera, *f.* .	. .	frontier.
fuente, *f.*	. . .	fountain.
fuera .	. . .	away : de fuera, outside.
fuerte .	. . .	strong.
fumar .	. .	to smoke.

G.

gallo, *m.*	. .	cock.
ganar .	. . .	to gain, earn.
gastar	. . .	to spend, waste.
gastos, *m. pl.*	. .	expenses.
género, *m.*	. .	kind, sort.
gente, *f.*	. . .	people.
gerente, *m.* .	. .	manager.

gobernador, *m.*	. . .	governor.
golpe, *m.*	. . .	blow, thud.
gozar .	. . .	to relish, enjoy.
gracias, *f. pl.*	. .	thanks.
guerra, *f.*	. . .	war.
guía, *f.*	. . .	guide (book).
gustar	. . .	to please, like.
gusto, *m.*	. . .	pleasure.

H.

habilidad, *f.*	. .	skill.
habitación, *f.*	. .	room.
habitante, *m.*	. .	inhabitant.
hablador	. .	talkative.
hacer .	. . .	to do, make.
hacia .	. . .	towards.
hallar .	. . .	to find.
hambre, *f.*	. .	hunger.
hasta .	. . .	until, up to, as far as.
herir (hiero)	. .	to wound.
hermoso	. .	beautiful, fine.
hora, *f.*	. . .	hour.
hospedarse .	. .	to put up (at).
hoy .	. . .	to-day.

I.

imponente .	. .	imposing.
incluir (incluyo)	. .	to include.
inmenso	. .	immense.
invierno, *m.*	. .	winter.
ir .	. . .	to go.

J.

jardín, *m.*	. .	garden.
jamás .	. . .	ever.
joven .	. . .	young.
juez, *m.*	. . .	judge.
jugar (juego)	. .	to play (of games).
juzgar	. .	to judge.

L.

labrador, *m.*	. .	farmer.
lado, *m.*	. . .	side.
ladrillo, *m.*	. .	brick.
ladrón, *m.*	. .	thief, robber.

lago, *m.*	lake.
lámpara, *f.*	lamp.
largo	long : a lo largo, along.
lástima, *f.*	pity.
lastimar	to hurt.
lavar	to wash.
leer	to read.
lejos	far.
lengua, *f.*	tongue, language.
lentitud, *f.*	slowness.
levantarse	to get up.
libra, *f.*	pound.
librería, *f.*	bookshop.
librero, *m.*	bookseller.
lidiar	to run (of bulls).
ligero	light, slight.
limpia-botas, *m.*	boot-black.
línea, *f.*	line.
localidad, *f.*	seat, place.
locomotora, *f.*	locomotive, engine.
loro, *m.*	parrot.
lucir (luzco)	to shine.
lúgubre	gloomy.
luz, *f.*	light.

LL.

llamar	to call.
llegada, *f.*	arrival.
llegar	to arrive.
lleno	full.
llevar	to bear, carry.
llover (llueve)	to rain.

M.

madre, *f.*	mother.
madrugada, *f.*	dawn.
maleta, *f.*	suit-case.
malo	bad, ill.
mañana	to-morrow, morning (*f.*).
mandadero, *m.*	errand boy.
mandar	to send, order.
manera, *f.*	manner, way.
mano, *f.*	hand.
máquina de escribir, *f.*	typewriter.
mar (*m.* or *f.*)	sea.
marca, *f.*	brand, make.

marcha, *f.* . . . departure.
marearse . . . to be sea-sick.
marido, *m.* . . . husband.
más . . . . more.
matar . . . . to kill.
mayor . . . elder, main.
medio . . . . half, mid.
mejorar . . . to improve.
melodioso . . . tuneful.
mendigo, *m.* . . beggar.
menor . . . minor.
menos . . . less.
mentir (miento) . . to lie.
mentira, *f.* . . . lie.
mercante . . . merchant, mercantile.
mes, *m.* . . . month.
miedo, *m.* . . . fear : tener miedo, to be afraid.
mientras . . . while.
milla, *f.* . . . mile.
mirar . . . . to look at.
mismo . . . self, same.
mitad, *f.* . . . half, middle.
modo, *m.* . . . way, manner.
molestar . . . to annoy.
moneda, *f.* . . . coin, piece (of money).
montaña, *f.* . . mountain.
morder (muerdo) . . to bite.
morir (muero) . . to die.
morisco . . . Moorish.
mozo, *m.* . . . porter.
muchacha(o) . . girl, (boy).
mucho . . . much : muchos, many.
muelle, *m.* . . . quay, wharf.
mujer, *f.* . . . woman, wife.
mundo, *m.* . . . world.
muralla, *f.* . . . wall.
museo, *m.* . . . museum.

N.

nacer (nazco) . . to be born.
naciente . . . growing.
nada . . . . nothing.
naranja, *f.* . . . orange.
naranjo, *m.* . . orange tree.
necesitar . . . to need.
negar (niego) . . to deny.

negocios, *m. pl.*	business.
negro	black.
neumático, *m.*	tyre.
nieve, *f.*	snow.
niño, *m.*	child.
nivel, *m.*	level.
nobleza, *f.*	nobility.
noche, *f.*	night.
nombre, *m.*	name.
norte, *m.*	north.
noticia, *f.*	news.
novela, *f.*	novel, tale.
noviazgo, *m.*	betrothal, engagement.
nube, *f.*	cloud.
número, *m.*	number.

O.

obedecer (-ezco)	to obey.
obispo, *m.*	bishop.
obra, *f.*	work (of art).
obrero, *m.*	workman.
ocultar	to hide.
oficial, *m.*	officer, official.
oficina, *f.*	office.
oir (oigo)	to hear.
olvidar	to forget.
ordenar	to order.
ordinario	ordinary.
orilla, *f.*	bank.
oscuro	dark.
otoño, *m.*	autumn.
otro	other.

P.

padre, *m.*	father.
pagar	to pay.
página, *f.*	page.
país, *m.*	country.
paisaje, *m.*	landscape.
pájaro, *m.*	bird.
palabra, *f.*	word.
palacio, *m.*	palace.
palco, *m.*	box.
palmera, *f.*	palm tree.
pan, *m.*	bread.
panadero	baker.

panteón, m. . . pantheon, mausoleum.
pañuelo, m. . . . handkerchief.
papel, m. . . . paper, rôle.
par, m. . . . pair.
para . . . . for, in order to.
parada, f. . . . stopping place.
parar(se) . . . to stop.
parecer (parezco) . . to seem, appear : se parecer a, to resemble, take after.
pared, f. . . . wall.
pariente, m. . . relation.
parque, m. . . . park.
parrilla, f. . . . grid-iron.
parte, f. . . . part.
pasajero, m. . . passenger.
pasar . . . . to pass.
pasear(se) . . . to walk.
paseo, m. . . . a walk.
patio, m. . . . court, courtyard.
pedir (pido) . . . to ask, beg.
pegar . . . . to beat, thrash.
pelo, m. . . . hair.
pena, f. . . . regret.
pensar (pienso) . . to think, intend.
peor . . . . worse.
perder (pierdo) . . to lose.
pérdida, f. . . . loss.
permanecer (-ezco) . to remain.
permitir . . . to permit.
pero . . . . but.
perro, m. . . . dog.
pertenecer (-ezco) . to belong.
pesar . . . . to weigh : a pesar de, in spite of.
pescado, m. . . . fish : barco de pesca, fishing boat.
pie, m. . . . foot.
piedra, f. . . . stone.
pierna, f. . . . leg.
pintar . . . . to paint.
pintoresco . . . picturesque.
piso, m. . . . floor, story.
pitillera, f. . . . cigarette case.
plan, m. . . . plan, scheme.
plano, m. . . . plan, drawing.
plaza, f. . . . square : plaza de toros, bull-ring.
poder . . . . to be able.
pollo, m. . . . chicken.
poner . . . . to put, put on.

por	by, for : porque, because : por (lo) tanto, consequently.
posada, *f.* . .	inn.
postal (adj.) . .	post(al) : (noun, fem.), postcard.
precio, *m.* . .	price.
precipitado . .	hasty.
preciso . .	necessary.
preferir (prefiero) .	to prefer.
preguntar . .	to ask.
presentar . .	to present, introduce.
prestar . .	to lend.
prima(o) . .	cousin.
primavera, *f.* .	spring.
principio, *m.* .	beginning.
profundo . .	deep.
prometer . .	to promise.
pronto . .	quick, prompt.
pronunciar . .	to pronounce, deliver.
propina, *f.* . .	tip, gratuity.
proprietario, *m.* .	owner, landlord.
pueblecito, *m.* .	small town.
pueblo, *m.* . .	town.
puente, *m.* . .	bridge.
puerta, *f.* . .	door, gate.
puerto, *m.* . .	harbour.
puesto que . .	seeing that, since.
punta, *f.* . .	point, tip.
punto, *m.* . .	point, dot.

Q.

quedar . .	to remain.
querer (quiero) .	to wish, want, love.
queso, *m.* . .	cheese.
quienquiera . .	whoever.
quitar . .	to take away, take off.
quizá(s) . .	perhaps.

R.

radio, *f.* . .	wireless.
rato, *m.* . .	moment, while.
rayo, *m.* . .	ray.
razón, *f.* . .	reason : tener razón, to be right.
real . . .	royal.
recibir . .	to receive.
reconocer (-ozco) .	to recognise.
recordar (recuerdo)	to remember.

recorrer	. . .	to traverse, make the round of.
recto	. . .	straight.
referirse (refiero)	. .	to refer.
reflejar	. . .	to reflect.
regalo, *m.*	. . .	present.
regreso, *m.*	. .	return.
rehacer	. . .	to do again, remake.
rehusar	. . .	to refuse.
reino, *m.*	. . .	kingdom.
reir (río)	. . .	to laugh.
reloj, *m.*	. . .	watch : reloj de pulsera, wrist-watch.
replicar	. . .	to reply.
representación, *f.*	. .	performance.
requerido	. . .	required.
resfriado, *m.*	. .	cold, chill.
resto, *m.*	. . .	remains, rest.
retrato, *m.*	. . .	portrait.
revisar	. . .	to examine.
rey, *m.*	. . .	king.
rezar	. . .	to pray.
riachuelo, *m.*	. .	small river, stream.
rico	. . .	rich.
río, *m.*	. . .	river.
robar	. . .	to rob.
roca, *f.*	. . .	rock, cliff.
rodear	. . .	to surround.
rojo	. . .	red.
romper	. . .	to break.
ropa, *f.*	. . .	clothes.
ruido, *m.*	. . .	noise.
ruso	. . .	Russian.
ruta, *f.*	. . .	route.

S.

saber	. . .	to know.
salir	. . .	to go out, leave.
sano y salvo	. .	safe and sound.
sastre, *m.*	. . .	tailor.
satisfecho	. . .	satisfied.
sed, *f.*	. . .	thirst.
seguir (sigo)	. .	to follow.
según	. . .	according to.
segundo	. . .	second.
seguro	. . .	sure, certain.
sello, *m.*	. . .	stamp.

señalar	to point out, indicate.
sencillo	simple.
sentarse (siento)	to sit down.
sentido, *m.*	sense, respect.
sentir (siento)	to feel, regret.
servir (sirvo)	to serve.
siempre	always.
siglo, *m.*	century.
siguiente	following.
silla, *f.*	chair.
sino	but.
soberbio	proud, haughty.
sobre	on, over, above.
sobrecargo, *m.*	extra charge.
sobretodo, *m.*	overcoat.
sobrevivir	to survive.
sociedad anónima agregada, *f.*	joint stock company.
sol, *m.*	sun.
solo	only, alone.
sombrero, *m.*	hat.
sonreir (sonrío)	to smile.
sorprender	to surprise.
sostener	to hold, sustain.
subir	to go up, bring up.
suceder	to happen, succeed.
sucesor, *m.*	successor.
suelo, *m.*	ground.
sueño, *m.*	sleep.
suerte, *f.*	chance, fate.
suma, *f.*	sum.
superior	superior, upper.
suponer	to suppose.
sur	south.

T.

tacón, *m.*	heel (of shoe).
tallar	to fashion, carve.
también	also.
tampoco	neither, not either.
tardar	to delay, take long.
tarde, *f.*	afternoon.
tarde, adv.	late.
tarjeta, *f.*	card.
taza, *f.*	cup.
teatro, *m.*	theatre.

teja, *f.*	. . .	tile.
tejado, *m.*	. . .	roof.
telón, *m.*	. . .	curtain.
temer	. . .	to fear.
temprano	. . .	early.
tendero, *m.*	. . .	shop-keeper.
tener	. . .	to have, hold : tener que, to have to.
tentación, *f.*	. .	temptation.
terminar	. . .	to end, finish.
tía(o)	. . .	aunt, uncle.
tiempo, *m.*	. . .	time, weather.
tienda, *f.*	. . .	shop.
tinta, *f.*	. . .	ink.
tipo, *m.*	. . .	type.
tocar	. . .	to touch, play (of instruments).
tomar	. . .	to take.
torero, *m.*	. . .	bull-fighter.
toro, *m.*	. . .	bull.
torre, *f.*	. . .	tower.
tortuga, *f.*	. . .	tortoise, turtle.
tostar (tuesto)	. .	to toast, roast.
trabajador, *m.*	. .	worker.
trabajar	. . .	to work.
trabajo, *m.*	. .	work.
traducir (-uzco)	. .	to translate.
traer	. . .	to bring, bear.
traje, *m.*	. . .	costume, suit.
trama, *f.*	. . .	plot.
tranvía, *m.*	. .	tramway, tram-car.
tratar	. . .	to treat : tratarse, to be about, concern.
travesía, *f.*	. .	crossing.
tren, *m.*	. . .	train.
tropa, *f.*	. . .	troops, soldiery, crowd.
turismo, *m.*	. .	touring.

U.

| último | . . . | last. |
| unir | . . . | to unite. |

V.

vaca, *f.*	. . .	cow.
vacación, *f.*	. .	holiday.
vacío, *m.*	. . .	vacuum, void : vacío de aire, air-pocket.

vacío, adj.	empty.
vagón-restaurant, *m.*	restaurant-car.
valentía, *f.*	courage.
valer	to be worth.
valiente	brave.
vaso, *m.*	glass, vase.
vecindad, *f.*	neighbourhood.
vecino, *m.*	neighbour : (adj.) neighbouring.
vencer (venzo)	to conquer.
vendedor, *m.*	seller, vendor.
vender	to sell.
venir	to come.
ventana, *f.*	window.
ventanilla, *f.*	grill, small window.
ver	to see.
verano, *m.*	summer.
verdad, *f.*	truth.
vestirse	to dress, get dressed.
vez, *f.*	time.
vía, *f.*	way, track.
viajar	to travel.
viaje, *m.*	trip, journey.
vida, *f.*	life.
viejo	old.
vino, *m.*	wine : vino de Jerez, sherry.
visitar	to visit.
víspera, *f.*	eve, day before.
vivir	to live.
volar (vuelo)	to fly.
volver (vuelvo)	to return.
voz, *f.*	voice.

Y.

ya	already, indeed, now.
yacer	to lie.

Z.

zapatero, *m.*	shoemaker.
zapato, *m.*	shoe.
zorro, *m.*	fox.
zumbido, *m.*	humming, buzzing.